"Tad Daley makes a compelling case for eliminating nuclear weapons now, before they are used intentionally by a terrorist group or accidentally by a nuclear-armed nation. The weight of the evidence supplied in *Apocalypse Never* leads to an inescapable conclusion: the fewer nuclear weapons there are, the safer we all will be. And it makes it clear that our ultimate security depends on getting rid of these terrible weapons once and for all."

—William D. Hartung, New America Foundation,
and coeditor of *Lessons from Iraq: Preventing the Next War*

"The late U.S. Senator Alan Cranston (D-CAL, 1969–1993) served as a mentor both to me and to Tad Daley. Senator Cranston's single greatest passion was to rid the world of the scourge of nuclear weapons. *Apocalypse Never* identifies and counters every one of the daunting challenges inherent in this task. This book is a compelling call to action."

—Congressman Mel Levine (D-CAL, 1983–1993)

"In a fresh, lively, accessible style, *Apocalypse Never* goes to the essence of complex issues of why and how to leave the age of nuclear weapons behind. Read, act, and survive!"

—John Burroughs, executive director, Lawyers Committee
on Nuclear Policy, and coeditor, *Nuclear Disorder
or Cooperative Security?*

"*Apocalypse Never* describes why the abolition of nuclear weapons is both imperative and possible. In clear, everyday prose, Tad Daley breathes new life into the anti-nuclear movement with a strong sense of hope and an inspiring call to action."

—Eric Garcetti, president, Los Angeles City Council

"Tad Daley not only provides a scholarly review of reasons for ridding the world of nuclear weapons, he uses the essential but underused gift of imagination to design a plausible pathway to a new world."

—David Krieger, founder and president, Nuclear Age Peace
Foundation and author of *Nuclear Weapons and the World Court*

"*Apocalypse Never* is a compelling book whose time has come. Tad Daley's prose, like his charismatic oratory, is forceful and exciting. His blueprint for abolition is a wonderful stew of history, humor, and strategic thinking—and it will motivate readers to make it a reality."

—Don Kraus, chief executive officer, Citizens for Global Solutions

"In real terms, not just in theory, Tad Daley answers all the hard questions. Buy it, read it, and take action with the millions of citizens joining this growing movement."

—Tim Carpenter, executive director,
Progressive Democrats of America

"*Apocalypse Never* is a roadmap for a world free of nuclear weapons. If ordinary people get to decide—and not just those who believe in nuclear brinksmanship—this book will be our guide to a safer, saner world."

—Michael J. Wilson, national director,
Americans for Democratic Action

"This book is a timely discussion of the difficult choices our country must make as we move towards a world free of nuclear weapons."

—Ambassador Robert T. Grey, Jr., former U.S. Representative
to the U.N. Conference on Disarmament; director,
Bipartisan Security Group

"Tad Daley joins the ranks of Henry Kissinger, George Schultz, Sam Nunn and other statesmen calling for abolition. He alerts us to the challenges we face in a netherworld of psychological disarmament, and reveals that, thanks to Bush and Cheney's fabulous misadventure, 'Axis of Evil' dictators have learned that it is better to have WMDs than be wrongly accused of having them."

—Ian Masters, *Background Briefing*, KPFK/Pacifica Public Radio

"Read this book as though your life and the lives of your children depend on it . . . because they do."

—John Loretz, International Physicians for the Prevention of
Nuclear War, Nobel Peace Laureate organization

"It's been said that a wise man knows what's watt and Tad Daley's book is what one might call a power generator."

—Edward Asner, Emmy Award–winning actor

Apocalypse Never

Apocalypse Never

FORGING THE PATH TO A NUCLEAR WEAPON–FREE WORLD

TAD DALEY

RUTGERS UNIVERSITY PRESS
New Brunswick, New Jersey, and London

LIBRARY OF CONGRESS CATALOGING-IN-PUBLICATION DATA

Daley, Tad.
    Apocalypse never : forging the path to a nuclear weapon–free world /
Tad Daley.
        p.   cm.
    Includes bibliographical references and index.
    ISBN 978-0-8135-4661-2 (hardcover : alk. paper)
    1. Nuclear disarmament.   2. Nuclear arms control   3. Nuclear
nonproliferation.   I. Title.
    JZ5665.D35   2010
    327.1'747—dc22   2009018769

A British Cataloging-in-Publication record for this book is available
from the British Library.

Visit our Web site: http://rutgerspress.rutgers.edu

Manufactured in the United States of America

For my late parents,
Diana Jankey Daley and Claude Daley, Jr.,
who planted the seeds of what I hope blossoms in here,
and who live on in many elsewheres.

And for H. G. Wells, George F. Kennan, Robert A. Heinlein,
and Professor Philip S. Haring of Knox College,
who taught me to ponder not only what we are,
but what we might become.

And, most of all, for my beloved wife, Kitty Felde,
who never, for a single moment, did not believe
that I could, and should, and would.

CONTENTS

Apocalypse Never

CHAPTER 1

Apocalypse Soon?

A NUCLEAR WAR broke out in the northwest suburbs of Chicago when I was a child there at the end of the 1960s.

The area was growing rapidly: every year thousands of acres of venerable Illinois farmland, some tilled by young Lincoln's contemporaries a century and a half earlier, simply disappeared. In its stead arose sprawling new housing developments. The new houses were soon filled with new children, who needed new schools. And the new schools needed new names. Many of these schools received banal and predictable designations, such as Olive School on Olive Street, Forest View High School on the edge of a forest preserve, Ivy Hill School in the massive new Ivy Hill subdivision. Two, however, acquired names that, in the politically supercharged atmosphere of the day, were like lightning in a bottle.

Most of the children's parents were politically quite conservative—electing a rising young Republican star named Donald Rumsfeld to Congress in the mid-1960s, and later dispatching paleoconservative Phil Crane to represent them throughout the last third of the twentieth century. Consequently, during the sixties, one faction on the school board chose to engage in a bit of political mischief at a moment when slogans such as "I ain't got no beef with no Viet Cong," "Ban the Bomb," and "Hey, hey, LBJ, how many kids did you kill today?" were stirring up the nation. So they decided to launch a nuclear strike. How? By arranging to name a high school after James B. Conant, the Harvard president whom President Roosevelt had asked to chair a new National Defense Research Committee to oversee all atomic research, the same committee that later advised President Truman to drop the new atomic bomb on a "vital war plant employing a large number of workers and closely surrounded by workers' homes."[1]

But there was another school board faction that included, apparently, some of the few people in the area who did not make a habit of voting for Don Rumsfeld or Phil Crane every two years. These members, it seems, took umbrage at naming a high school after a man who had played a key role in creating what Conant's own granddaughter, writer Jennet Conant, later called "the most diabolical weapon in the history of mankind."[2] So they decided to launch a nuclear counterstrike. How? By arranging to name another area high school, just a dozen or so old alfalfa fields away, after the first great antinuclear writer: John Hersey, the Pulitzer Prize–winning *New Yorker* correspondent who reported on life, death, and misery in Hiroshima just weeks after America's incineration of the city on August 6, 1945. (New York University later named his reporting there as the top work of journalism in the twentieth century.)[3] Some years later, I myself graduated from this very high school.

James B. Conant High School in Hoffman Estates and John Hersey High School in Arlington Heights are still in business today, possibly competing against each other in girls' gymnastics or boys' wrestling or girls' cross-country at this very moment. Whether the larger nuclear truth of James B. Conant or John Hersey will ultimately prevail beyond Chicago's northwest suburbs is a question that has not yet been resolved. It is hardly hyperbole, however, to suggest that the fate of the human race may depend upon the answer.

Apocalypse Never reveals why we must abolish nuclear weapons, how we can, and what the world will look like after we do. I insist that if humanity hangs on to nuclear weapons indefinitely, some kind of nuclear catastrophe will ensue almost certainly. I illuminate the towering hypocrisy behind the nuclear double standard (according to which our nation possesses thousands of nuclear weapons but insists that others cannot aspire even to one) and contend that such a standard is not only morally indefensible, but also politically unsustainable. I confront humanity's fundamental long-term choice, bleak but inescapable: zero nuclear weapon states and zero nuclear weapons, or dozens of nuclear weapon states, thousands more nuclear weapons, and nuclear cataclysm only a matter of time.[4]

Apocalypse Never also demonstrates that the United States and other nuclear weapon states absolutely committed themselves, both politically and legally, to eliminating their entire nuclear arsenals when they entered into the Nuclear Nonproliferation Treaty (NPT) more than four long decades ago. I argue that, for the United States today, nuclear weapons are militarily both unnecessary and useless—but that other, less powerful states can rationally draw different conclusions. I suggest foreign policy strategies that could alter the national security calculations of those less powerful states. I maintain that a comprehensive nuclear weapons policy agenda from President Barack Obama, one that fully integrates nonproliferation with disarmament, can both dramatically reduce immediate nuclear dangers and set us irrevocably on the road to abolition. I describe possible verification measures, enforcement mechanisms, and political architectures of a post-abolition world. I decisively repudiate the most frequent objection to abolition, "the breakout scenario"—the possibility that after abolition some state might whip back the curtain, reveal a dozen or so nuclear warheads (newly constructed or previously squirreled away), and proceed to rule the world.

Most importantly, *Apocalypse Never* asserts that the abolition of nuclear weapons is not only essential for the human race, but also achievable by the human race. I detail what both governments and social movements can do to get us from here to there. I sketch plausible future scenarios for eliminating nuclear weapons perhaps even as soon as the seventy-fifth anniversary of Hiroshima's bombing—August 6, 2020. And I insist we can transform the abolition of nuclear weapons from a utopian fantasy into a concrete political goal.

In 1947, President Truman's secretary of state, George Marshall, asked George F. Kennan to set up and lead the State Department's first Policy Planning Staff, with the goal of thinking long-range about American national interests beyond the foreign policy issues of the hour. Kennan recalled, "The only advice [Marshall] had to give me was expressed in two deeply serious and unforgettable words: avoid trivia."[5] Similarly, in this book, my aspiration is to think beyond the nuclear policy issues of the hour and the nuclear headlines of the day. I grapple instead with the nuclear big picture, evaluating our alternative nuclear futures and exposing the magnitude of the challenge that the Bomb ultimately poses to the human race.

Nevertheless, in doing so, I unapologetically envision an eventual answer to the nuclear question. I make the case that nuclear weapons abolition can indeed come to pass, and that the nuclear peril can be put behind us for good. I aspire to persuade the reader that the threat of nuclear apocalypse can become a remote part of the human past, rather than remaining, as President Kennedy put it in his first address before the United Nations in 1961, "a nuclear sword of Damocles, hanging by the slenderest of threads," hovering over us for all eternity.[6] (John F. Kennedy, it turns out, first came to the attention of the wider public in the summer of 1944, when an article about his exploits in the South Pacific aboard the U.S. Navy motor torpedo boat PT-109 appeared in the *New Yorker*—written by John Hersey.)

ATOMIC ORIGINS

The first man to envision the vast potential of nuclear energy, for both good and ill, was arguably the historian, futurist, socialist, feminist, speculative fiction pioneer, and united world visionary H. G. Wells. Wells was responsible for the germ of the idea of what might be the three most transformative military inventions of the twentieth century. First, in 1903, he published an essay called "The Land Ironclads" in the *Strand* magazine. He anticipated therein the tank warfare that began experimentally toward the end of the First World War and reached its apex two decades later with the Nazi German blitzkreig that unleashed the Second World War, followed five years after that by the vast Soviet, American, British, and Canadian tank counteroffensives that brought about the final defeat of the German armies. Then, in 1908, only five years after the Wright brothers' flight, Wells published a little book called *The War in the Air*, which not only anticipated military aircraft, but foresaw that air warfare would soon make obsolete the traditional wartime distinction between combatant and civilian. Finally, in 1914, before the First World War had commenced, he published a big book called *The World Set Free*. Drawing upon the work of British physicists Ernest Rutherford and Frederick Soddy (who had speculated that the atoms of certain elements might be split, thereby producing almost limitless quantities of energy), Wells described a future in which the human race enjoys the benefits of abundant atomic energy that is virtually infinite and free, but is then devastated by a vast conflagration waged primarily with atomic weapons. It was the first appearance, in literature, of the idea of nuclear war.[7]

Even Wells, however, probably did not anticipate that such a war would ensue scarcely three decades down the road. (He died, deeply despondent about the human prospect, on August 13, 1946.) The world's first atom bomb was detonated near Alamogordo, New Mexico on July 16, 1945. It was a plutonium implosion device, and yielded an explosion equivalent to the detonation of approximately 18,600 tons of dynamite (or "18.6 kilotons," a term coined to help people describe, if not comprehend, the new destructive powers of the nuclear age). J. Robert Oppenheimer, the chief scientist of the Manhattan Project that had built the bomb, referred to it simply as "the gadget."

The world's second atom bomb was dropped from the American B-29 superfortress *Enola Gay* and detonated over the Japanese city of Hiroshima on August 6, 1945. This bomb, nicknamed "Little Boy," was a uranium gunlike device, and it yielded an explosion of approximately thirteen kilotons. It had a much simpler design than the first bomb, and the atomic scientists were so certain that it would work that they did not even feel the need to test a prototype before using it in combat.

The world's third atom bomb was dropped from the American B-29 superfortress *Bockscar*, and detonated over the Japanese city of Nagasaki on August 9, 1945. This bomb, nicknamed "Fat Man," was a plutonium-implosion device like the first, and yielded an explosion of approximately twenty-two kilotons.

As a rule, the number of human beings who perish from the radioactive fallout of nuclear detonations is comparable to the number of those who die during the immediate blast and consequent mass fires. For example, the best estimates (and they are certainly only gross estimates) of the consequences of our bombings of Hiroshima and Nagasaki indicate that about 80,000 people died immediately at Hiroshima and about 40,000 at Nagasaki, with perhaps 200,000 more dying in subsequent weeks, months, and years.[8] (The casualties were reduced at Nagasaki, despite Fat Man's greater explosive force, because haze over the city forced *Bockscar*'s bombardier to deliver the payload by radar instead of by visual reckoning, and because the hills around the city served to contain the blast.) Similarly, a 1984 study forecasting the effects of a massive 3,000-weapon atomic attack on the United States predicted that 50 to 100 million Americans would die immediately, with another 50 to 70 million perishing down the road.[9]

Many of the bombs constructed after Alamogordo, Hiroshima, and Nagasaki were much more powerful still, especially after the 1952 invention of the hydrogen bomb, sometimes called a thermonuclear device, which uses the nuclear fission reaction of an atom bomb to trigger a significantly larger nuclear fusion reaction. (The term *nuclear weapon* generally encompasses both atom and hydrogen bombs.) It is almost impossible to comprehend the power unleashed by one of these devices. Perhaps, as a way to at least take a stab, we can recall the bare facts of the detonation of the world's first thermonuclear device—the so-called "MIKE" test in the middle of the Pacific Ocean on November 1, 1952 (just three days before the election of Dwight D. Eisenhower as president).[10]

MIKE could not really be called a deliverable bomb or weapon. The device looked more like a factory—six stories high and as wide as an aircraft hangar. The chosen land was the Eniwetok atoll, a collection of about forty coral reefs in the Marshall Island chain, roughly 3,000 miles west of Hawaii. More than 10,000 U.S. Army, Navy, Air Force, and civilian personnel gathered at Eniwetok for the test. They bulldozed the entire island of Elugelab and constructed more than five hundred scientific monitoring stations on thirty different surrounding islands.

At 7:15 A.M., a team on a nearby ship sent off a precise sequence of radio signals—and MIKE exploded. It registered at 10.4 megatons, almost 1,000 times as large as the detonation of Little Boy at Hiroshima. Within seconds, it created a blinding white fireball more than three miles across. It hurled some 80 million tons of dirt and debris high into the air—radioactive material that, in the ensuing weeks, rained down on virtually every point on our planet, like a very fine atomic fairy dust, sprinkled upon us all. And it generated a hot mushroom cloud that rose vertically to an altitude of twenty-seven miles and spread horizontally for a distance of one hundred miles.

It's astounding that human beings can create such a thing. Imagine a mushroom cloud rising twenty-seven miles over the Eiffel Tower, or Buckingham Palace, or Red Square, or Tiananmen Square, or the Empire State Building, with pure devastation below, millions upon millions of incinerated corpses, not just humans but all living things, a perfectly sterilized landscape. All, in a single instant, from the detonation of a single bomb. One cannot help but marvel at this testament to humanity's scientific and technological prowess. And more than a half century since the MIKE test, and a good ten or fifteen millennia since our ancestors emerged from the caves, at our persistent political, social, and ethical adolescence.

THE MAGNITUDE OF THE NUCLEAR PERIL

A curious transition took place during the course of the twentieth century, a transition that few seem to have noticed. For it has only been in the past hundred years or so that humanity has become the greatest enemy of humanity. Before the twentieth century, the greatest cataclysms were those inflicted by natural forces—earthquakes, tsunamis, hurricanes, volcanoes, pandemic. The deadliest earthquake known to history probably took place in 1556 in Shaanxi, China, killing an estimated 830,000 people. The bubonic plague killed 6 million in India in the 1890s, perhaps 43 million all around the world in the 1300s, and, in what must be the greatest natural mass death in all of history, about 100 million in the sixth and early seventh centuries, about half of all the humans on the planet. Fearsome as were the depredations inflicted by the Sargons, Alexanders, Caesars, Attilas, and Tamerlanes of the world, none of these could accumulate slaughters to compete with nature's tallies.

According to one estimate, however, in the first half of the twentieth-century alone, the cataclysms wrought by humans in the two world wars and their aftermath—through war, massacre, or human-induced famine—killed no less than 187 million people.[11] None of the trepidations inflicted by nature during this time, not even the great influenza pandemic of 1918–19, which may have killed as many as 50 million (and which probably was intensified by the devastation recently wrought by the Great War), could accumulate slaughters to compete with that tally.

Of course, a vigorous global thermonuclear exchange could outdo that 187 million on any Thursday morning. Among all the other great challenges we face at the dawn of the twenty-first century, nuclear weapons still hold the greatest potential to inflict the greatest harm on the family of humankind. Global thermonuclear war is still the worst-case scenario for the human race.

The post–cold war world has brought us a great paradox. The good news is that the apocalyptic threat that haunted humanity after 1945— thousands of intercontinental nuclear missiles simultaneously in flight, passing each other as they streak in opposite directions over the North Pole, a climactic east-west showdown ending in a tie—has dramatically decreased (though this book may surprise readers by revealing that it has not entirely disappeared). But the bad news is that the prospect that an individual city, without warning, will suddenly be vaporized by an atomic warhead is probably now far more likely than before.

Speaking before a National Academy of Sciences conference in 2004, former secretary of defense William Perry said starkly, "I have never been as worried as I am now that a nuclear bomb will be detonated in an American city."[12] The worldwide consequences of such an event—political, economic, psychological—are scarcely imaginable. While a single detonation would not bring about nuclear winter, mass extinctions, or the end of the world—the scenarios we feared would follow a massive Soviet-American nuclear exchange during the cold war—it would certainly kill thousands, perhaps hundreds of thousands, perhaps even more than a million. It would profoundly disrupt the world economy for years. It would likely leave hundreds or thousands of square miles of virgin earth uninhabitable for decades. As the late U.S. senator Alan Cranston, a Democrat from California who served from 1969 to 1993, liked to say, if a single nuclear weapon goes off a single time in a single city in the world, all other issues will instantly become trivial by comparison.

From the moment of his retirement from the Senate in 1993 until his death on the last day of the twentieth century, December 31, 2000, Senator Cranston devoted himself almost exclusively to the cause of nuclear weapons abolition—at a time when few from the mainstream foreign policy establishment were willing to join him. "I don't miss the Senate," he told the *San Francisco Examiner* just weeks before he died. "I had 24 years there, and that was great. . . . [But these days], I get more done on this issue because I can concentrate."[13] In 1998, Jonathan Schell wrote, "Alan Cranston . . . has, in all likelihood, quietly done more than any other American to marshal public opinion behind the abolitionist cause."[14] I served as Senator Cranston's research director, grass-roots organizer, and brainstorm partner during the last three years of his life, when he served as head of the Gorbachev Foundation USA, the State of the World Forum, and the Global Security Institute. He was, to me, a great mentor, a great role model, and a great friend.

It is difficult to dispute that global climate change poses the single greatest long-term peril to human civilization, at least as such things can be perceived from our present vantage point. But it is equally difficult to dispute that the nuclear peril, in its many incarnations, poses the single greatest immediate peril. Although climate change is undoubtedly already having profound effects in certain areas, its most worrisome impacts probably still lie some two, three, or five decades down the road. But tomorrow morning, a major world city, without any warning, could suddenly disappear into a vaporized radioactive cloud. All in the blink of an eye, the snap of a finger, the single beat of a human heart.

Moreover, no matter how badly we screw up the earth's climate in the next century or so, it is difficult to conceive of any scenario by which such changes could wipe out the entire human race, let alone our planet's entire vast circle of life. Not so with nuclear weapons. The worst-case scenario in the nuclear realm—one that we survived so precariously for nearly half a century and one that we may well have to confront again—is extinction. Of not only our own species but perhaps even all species. The eradication of all life on our planet . . . brought about by our own hands.

"There's something so extreme about these weapons and their capacity to destroy much of the world's population that has a dimension of absurdity," says psychiatrist and writer Robert Jay Lifton. "In my view, the only relatively accurate kind of perception of nuclear weapons is to see them in their apocalyptic dimension, in their world-destroying dimension. . . . One has to draw upon the apocalyptic dimension of what they do, and one also has to draw on the absurdity of us destroying our species by our own technology."[15] To say that forever until the end of time we must base our national security on the threat to incinerate millions of innocents, and the possibility of exterminating us all, must be the most profoundly cynical doctrine imaginable. As Daniel Ellsberg (who, among other roles in American history, was intimately involved in the Cuban missile crisis as a consultant to the Kennedy White House) asks, "Is it really true that the only way to avert the ultimate evil is to threaten the ultimate evil?"[16] What could be more immoral than that? What possible national security justification could there be for that? What kind of people are we to just complacently accept that? Even the barest possibility that we could conduct such an act, in one quick orgy of miscalculation or misunderstanding, must be beyond our toleration. At bottom, the continued deployment of the nuclear weapon in national military arsenals represents a profound failure of our political and moral ingenuity. Surely, the human imagination has the capacity to devise some other, better ideas for maintaining peace on earth.

THE ASPIRATION OF *APOCALYPSE NEVER*

When I set out to write this book, I did not intend to create an academic work for scholars, nuclear experts, and policy wonks. Nor did I want simply to preach to the antinuclear choir. My hope, instead, was to write a book for ordinary folks about our larger nuclear destiny. I actually gave serious thought to calling the book *Avoiding Thermonuclear War for Dummies*.

Apocalypse Never is not about some remote international political issue, and it does not engage in arcane and mysterious policy analysis. It is directly relevant to the lives of ordinary Americans and other citizens around the world. This book is about saving Chicago, and Los Angeles, and New York. It is about saving Manchester, and Lyon, and Haifa, and Mumbai, and Hyderabad, and Shanghai, and Seoul, and Hiroshima. For in 2013, or 2023, or tomorrow morning, one of these cities—and all the history, all the potential, all the lives therein—might simply disappear from the face of the earth.

In addition, my hope for this book is not just that many readers will buy it, learn from it, and enjoy it. Rather, *Apocalypse Never* aims to invigorate, expand, and empower the nuclear disarmament movement in this country and around the world. My deepest ambition is not only to offer a message of hope on the nuclear question, but to convince people that they can make those hopes real. I aspire for *Apocalypse Never* to play a crucial role in reawakening the long-dormant antinuclear movement. I want my readers to come away believing there is a struggle to be waged, a glorious goal to be achieved, an epochal triumph that our hands alone can bring to fruition.

I hope that you, the reader, will come to three conclusions after finishing *Apocalypse Never*. First, nuclear weapons abolition is essential. Second, nuclear weapons abolition is achievable. Third, you can play a crucial role in helping to bring it about. Consequently, I hope that you will decide to devote your blood, toil, tears, and sweat—and perhaps even your treasure—to the cause. And I hope as well that you will recommend this book to your friends, colleagues, classmates, compatriots, and anyone you call a lover of peace. The more people who read this book and act upon its precepts, the more likely it will become that the human race can dodge the nuclear bullet forever, and eliminate nuclear weapons for good.

Books have certainly achieved such lofty goals in the past. *Common Sense*, a pamphlet by Thomas Paine, sold no less than half a million copies (fully 13 percent of the population of the thirteen colonies in 1776) and, by shaping public opinion, incalculably shaped the subsequent unfolding of the American Revolution. *Uncle Tom's Cabin*, by Harriet Beecher Stowe, did much the same for the slavery abolitionist movement in the middle of the nineteenth century. *The Jungle*, by Upton Sinclair, influenced change on such diverse fronts as food safety, labor protections, anu ˅imal rights at the beginning of the twentieth century. *Silent Spring*, by Racɪ˅ ˅˅son, helped to shape the environmental movement in the early 1960s. ˙he *Feminine Mystique*, by Betty Friedan, did the same for the second wave of the women's movement at about the same time. And *The Other America*, by Michael Harrington, almost singlehandedly instigated President Lyndon Johnson's War on Poverty.

Indeed, *The Fate of the Earth*, by Jonathan Schell, (along with *Protest and Survive*, a pamphlet by E. P. Thompson that offered a brilliant parody of a British civil defense pamphlet called *Protect and Survive*), played an enormous role in mobilizing the nuclear freeze movement, which reached its zenith on June 12, 1982, when perhaps as many as a million hardy souls gathered in New York's Central Park to demand that American and Soviet leaders freeze an arms race that was spiraling out of control. The slogan of the hour was "We've got to stop the train before we can put it in reverse."

"Playing small," said Nelson Mandela, quoting Marianne Williamson in his 1994 inauguration speech as president of South Africa, "does not serve the world."[17] Therefore, in this undertaking, I confess to harboring large goals. Like the aforementioned authors, I want *Apocalypse Never* to force the course of the river of history. I want it to serve as a key, crucial stimulus for putting that nuclear train in reverse and driving it all the way back into the station.

I take as a role model here one of my great literary heroes, Robert A. Heinlein, the futurist and science fiction genius. Heinlein did not make his reputation in the nuclear field. He was a fierce conservative or libertarian on many social and political issues, and his name does not often arise in the arena of nuclear disarmament. But after the atom bomb was revealed to the world in August 1945, Heinlein immediately grasped the historical stakes. So he decided to devote substantial efforts, in the wake of Hiroshima and Nagasaki, to alerting the public to the nature of the nuclear peril. Here is Heinlein, reflecting in 1980 on this period of his life:

> After World War II I resumed writing with two objectives: first, to explain the *meaning* of atomic weapons through popular articles; second, to break out from the limitations and low rates of pulp science-fiction magazines. . . . My second objective I achieved in every respect, but in my first and much more important objective I fell flat on my face. . . . Unless you were already adult in August 1945 it is almost impossible for me to convey emotionally to you how people felt about the A-bomb, how many different ways they felt about it, how nearly totally ignorant 99.9% of our citizens were on the subject, including almost all of our military leaders and governmental officials. . . . I wrote nine articles intended to shed light on the post-Hiroshima age, and I have never worked harder on any writing, researched the background more thoroughly, tried harder to make the (grim and horrid) message entertaining and readable. . . . Was I really so naif that I thought that I could change the course of history this way? No, not really. But, damn it, I had to try![18]

I, too, do not consider myself a naïf. But I, too, have to try. I cannot guarantee any more success at this task now than Heinlein managed to achieve then. But as the hockey legend Wayne Gretzky likes to say, "You always miss 100 percent of the shots that you don't take."

CHARTING THE COURSE AND
CARRYING THE TORCH

Dr. Martin Luther King liked to quote the nineteenth-century American preacher Theodore Parker, who said, "The arc of the moral universe is long, but it bends toward justice."[19] This book aspires to assess the whole of the nuclear challenge, our collective nuclear future, humanity's long-term nuclear destiny, and to reveal what we must do to see that it ultimately bends toward abolition rather than catastrophe. I will argue that we ought to set nuclear weapons abolition as a concrete, attainable, real world political goal. One way to move toward any goal is to describe it in its ideal form. That is why this book devotes a great deal of attention to describing what a world free of nuclear weapons might actually look like.

In the very first paper I wrote as a college undergraduate—for Political Science 101 at Knox College in Galesburg, Illinois—I pronounced my verdict that Plato's *Republic* was "too unrealistic" to hold any enduring philosophical merit. Professor Philip S. Haring awarded me a C+. When I stormed up to his office to demand an explanation, the professor, in fine Socratic form, immediately agreed with my assessment of Plato's direct applicability. But then he asked me to consider whether a writer whose works have endured for some twenty-five centuries might still have something to teach. And he urged me to contemplate whether Plato might have had some other, deeper motive for writing such a philosophical fantasy. I sat for many hours in Knox's Seymour Library contemplating our conversation. Eventually, I got it through my thick skull that, in writing about an ideal, Plato hoped he might cause readers to aspire to an ideal—and perhaps then endeavor to move the real world just a bit in that direction.

In January 2007 and again in January 2008, four lions of the American foreign policy establishment—former Republican secretary of state Henry Kissinger, former U.S. senator and chair of the Armed Services Committee Sam Nunn, former Democratic secretary of defense William Perry, and former Republican secretary of state George Shultz— authored a pair of landmark opinion pieces published in the *Wall Street Journal*. They called not only for greater attention to immediate nuclear dangers, but for the elimination of nuclear weapons everywhere.[20] In a stroke, the twin op-eds thrust the idea of abolition front and center into the nuclear policy debate. "The goal of a world free of nuclear weapons is like the top of a very tall mountain," said the authors. "From the vantage point of our troubled world today, we can't even see the top of the mountain, and it is tempting and easy to say we can't get there from here." The twin contributions I aspire to make with this book are to discern clearly what the top of that mountain might look like, and to envision clearly the path by which we might navigate our ascent.

In April 2009, the clarion of abolition was sounded by an even higher-profile figure. President Barack Obama, speaking before a huge outdoor rally in Prague, said, "Today, I state clearly and with conviction America's commitment to seek the peace and security of a world without nuclear weapons." In this, in other statements, and in his early nuclear initiatives, the new American president indicated that the goal of universal nuclear weapons elimination would serve as the ultimate objective of all U.S. nuclear weapons policy actions. Nearly six months later, on September 24, the United Nations Security Council unanimously resolved "to create the conditions for a world without nuclear weapons, in accordance with the goals of the Treaty on the Non-Proliferation of Nuclear Weapons (NPT)," stamping the formal imprimatur of the international community on the vision of Prague.

But in Prague, just seconds after Obama made the statement quoted above, before anyone had the chance to imagine that the dream might be transformed into reality anytime soon, the president declared that complete nuclear disarmament would not "be achieved quickly, perhaps not in my lifetime."[21] Then, in November, in Tokyo, he used the same formulation—only now "perhaps" had become "probably." Japan, of course, is the land of the *hibakusha*—the survivors of Hiroshima and Nagasaki—many of whom have devoted their lives to seeing the last nuclear weapon dismantled before the last survivor has gone to the grave. The American president might just as well have said to them, "probably not in my lifetime . . . and definitely not in yours."

These sentences doused the advocates of abolition with a sudden and jarring bucket of cold water. But they also arguably offered the abolitionist movement a new central organizing principle, for at least the outset of the age of Obama.

In Chapters 3, 4, 5, and 6, I present four scenarios—nuclear terror, accidental nuclear launches or detonations, nuclear crises spinning out of control, and conscious intentional use—by which the indefinite preservation of nuclear weapons will almost certainly lead eventually to the detonation of nuclear weapons. The first two could happen, without any warning whatsoever, tomorrow morning. The second two probably would offer just a little bit of lead time—before delivering the same result. Abolitionist advocates are often called naïve and idealistic, but what then should we call the notion that humanity can keep nuclear weapons around for another half century or so, yet manage to dodge all four of these nuclear bullets every time the trigger is cocked? Our message to President Obama must be that the time frame he presented in Prague and Tokyo fails utterly to appreciate the magnitude and immediacy of the nuclear peril. Can we wait until the second half of the twenty-first century before arriving at nuclear weapons abolition, President Obama? No, we can't.

In addition, in Chapters 9, 10, and 11, I present the outlines of the architecture we will need to invent to govern and perpetuate a nuclear weapon–free world, the likely consequences if someone tries to break out of that architecture and cheat, and plausible political processes that might be undertaken to enable us to achieve abolition by the seventy-fifth anniversary of Hiroshima's bombing. I do not presume these to be the last words on these subjects. But I do know that if we say today that we cannot achieve abolition before, say, August 4, 2061, Barack Obama's one hundredth birthday, then, undoubtedly, we will not. But if we set ourselves a far more urgent goal, we will begin to generate the political will and the political imagination that will be required to meet that deadline, and to get the job done. Can we achieve nuclear weapons elimination long before the end of your lifetime, President Obama? Yes, we can. Yes, we can.

In the end, the possibility of nuclear apocalypse risks not just the lives of our descendants, but also the legacies of our ancestors. Think about how they toiled to build the art, the science, and the civilization that all of us temporarily now enjoy, and use, and inhabit. Could anything degrade their memories more than to dance with this kind of disaster? Theodore Sturgeon calls upon us to honor "the main current which created you and in which you will create a greater thing still, reverencing those who bore you and the ones who bore them, back and back to the first wild creature who was different because his heart leaped when he saw a star."[22] Our imperative to keep ourselves from blowing up our world is our obligation to our vanished predecessors, those who invented writing, and before that language, and before that rational thought—the geniuses who took us slowly, step by step by step, from creatures not so very far from our animal origins, to something a little bit closer to our divine destiny.

We must abolish nuclear weapons, and keep them abolished forever, because that is the debt we owe to Jane Addams and Dorothy Day, to Simon Bolivar and Johan Sebastian Bach, to Johannes Gutenberg and Galileo Galilei, to Ferdinand Magellan and Michelangelo Buonarotti, to Asoka and Caesar Augustus. It is our debt to the slaves who sweated, toiled, and perished to build the Great Pyramids—the tallest structures on Planet Earth until the construction of the Eiffel Tower in 1889, considered by their builders to be "stairways to heaven," pointing toward the infinite sky. It is our debt to the unnamed Cro Magnon women and men, our grandparents, who painted those breathtaking landscapes in the Lascaux and Chauvet and Altamira caves some two hundred long centuries ago, and who held in their hearts the barest glimpse of a human destiny of infinite possibility.

It is up to us to carry on their work.

CHAPTER 2

The Essence of the Problem

AMERICA'S NUCLEAR HYPOCRISY

IN JUNE AND JULY OF 2006, an enormous tempest arose over the possibility that North Korea might test a long-range Taepodong 2 missile. Pyongyang's sin? Some believed that such a missile might someday be able to reach the west coast of the United States. In response to this perceived threat, the U.S. government issued repeated warnings to North Korea's leader, Kim Jong Il. The talking heads on *Fox News* could barely contain their outrage. Former U.S. secretary of defense William Perry and his former deputy Ashton Carter even advocated a preemptive strike to take out the missiles on their launch pads.[1] Not to prevent the North Koreans from attacking anyone with these missiles, mind you, but simply to prevent them from testing missiles.

But North Korea went ahead anyway, testing seven missiles on July 5. None traveled more than a few hundred miles. The one Taepodong failed after only forty seconds, and all splashed down harmlessly into the Sea of Japan. Nonetheless, U.S. national security advisor Stephen Hadley described the tests as "provocative behavior." Secretary of state Condoleezza Rice said Pyongyang was engaging in "brinksmanship." According to an official White House statement, "these missile launches . . . demonstrate North Korea's intent to intimidate other states." And President Bush, speaking with CNN's Larry King on July 6, said that he had a message for Mr. Kim: "We expect you to adhere to international norms."[2]

But what exactly are those norms? The question is not easy to answer, especially since, on June 14, the U.S. Air Force had test-launched a Minuteman III intercontinental ballistic missile from Vandenberg Air Force Base in California. Minutes after launch, thousands could see its contrails streaking across northern California's Pacific sky. Some thirty minutes later, its three warheads, with great precision, struck dummy targets at the Kwajalein test range in the western chain of the Marshall Islands, 4,800 miles away.[3] This was not an isolated incident: the United States had conducted five similar long-range missile launches during 2006 and 2007 alone.[4]

On June 29, a couple of weeks after the Minuteman III test, a Russian ballistic missile was test-launched from a submarine in the Barents Sea and came down directly upon its intended target on Russia's Kamchatka peninsula, 5,000 kilometers away.[5] A few days after the North Korean missile tests, India announced that it had for the first time tested its new Agni-III ballistic missile, firing it high and far into the Bay of Bengal. Reports claim that the Agni-III can pinpoint targets up to 3,500 kilometers away, which, according to Indian defense analyst Rahul Bendi, means that India "can now reach large parts of northern China, making our deterrence capacity stronger."[6]

Why, when some countries conduct missile tests, do we hear barely a whisper of comment, while, when others do exactly the same thing, those tests generate a torrent of righteous indignation? More fundamentally, why can some countries possess many dozens of nuclear warheads (for example, India) or even many thousands (the United States and Russia), while others cannot aspire to even one? What's the principle? What's the argument? It is never said, because it cannot be defended, and because the situation cannot last.

THE NUCLEAR DOUBLE STANDARD

Some use the phrase "America's nuclear hypocrisy," others the "nuclear double standard," and still others "nuclear narcissism." Iranian president Mahmoud Ahmadinejad, echoing the phrase used by Indian foreign minister Jaswant Singh at the time of India's 1998 nuclear tests, often calls the status quo "nuclear apartheid."[7] North Korea, which tested not only missiles in July 2006 but an actual nuclear warhead during the following October and then tested both again in the spring of 2009, said in its official newspaper, *Rodong Sinmun,* "We do not intend to possess nuclear weapons forever. . . . If the U.S. nuclear threat is removed . . . not a single nuclear weapon will be needed."[8] For decades, the United States has said to other countries, "We need them, but you don't. They're good for us, but not good for you. We can have them, but you can't."

How can America and other nuclear weapon states maintain that atomic arsenals are vital to their own national security, but assert that other nations' acquisition of atomic weapons will be harmful to their security? To much of the rest of the world, such double standards appear to be sanctimonious and self-righteous, based on a notion that some countries are responsible enough to be "trusted" with these weapons of the apocalypse, while others are not.

The chasm between the nuclear haves and have-nots came into particularly sharp relief on May 27, 2005, when the Nuclear Nonproliferation Treaty's five-year review conference at the United Nations collapsed in fiasco: no new protocols, no new antinuclear strategies, no international consensus about the road ahead. U.S. officials at the gathering had complained relentlessly about the nuclear aspirations of Iran and North Korea. But representatives from much of the rest of the world, in concert with numerous nongovernmental voices (including a large delegation of impassioned but aging *hibakusha*), directed their ire at the colossal and renascent nuclear firepower of the United States under the Bush administration. On that issue, the silence of American diplomats was deafening.

Three and a half months later, U.N. secretary general Kofi Annan said it was "a real disgrace" that nuclear weapons had not been addressed in the document produced by the General Assembly for the sixtieth-anniversary world summit in September, which was intended to bring about the most ambitious U.N. transformation since the organization's creation. While a number of issue areas in the document had been watered down on the altar of consensus, the section on nuclear dangers had been dropped from the joint statement entirely because of the breadth of the gulf on the issue. "The big item missing is nonproliferation and disarmament," said Annan. "We have failed twice this year: we failed at the [NPT] Conference, and we failed now."[9]

Many prominent American citizens have raised their voices against the persistent "do as we say, not as we do" message from the American government. Former president Jimmy Carter, with his usual clarity, says that the nuclear states "refuse to initiate or respect restraints on themselves, while . . . raising heresy charges against those who want to join the sect."[10] Ed Markey, a longtime congressman from Massachusetts and staunch opponent of the nuclear arms race, likes to say in his broad Boston accent, "America cannot credibly preach nuclear temperance from a nuclear barstool."[11] According to the late Senator Cranston, "The leaders responsible for America's defense warn that the only significant threat today to the security and survival of the U.S. is nuclear proliferation. Their Alice in Wonderland position seems to be that the danger lies in nations that do not possess nuclear weapons, not in those who do."[12] U.S. Air Force general Chuck Horner, commander of allied air operations during Operation Desert Storm, says, "It's kind of hard for us to say 'You are terrible for developing nuclear weapons' when the U.S. has thousands of them. Think of the high moral ground we [would] secure by having none."[13] And the Reverend William Sloane Coffin, one of the great peace activists of the twentieth century before his death in 2006, said, "A fat man cannot speak persuasively to a skinny man about the virtues of not overeating. . . . [E]ither the world becomes nuclear free or the whole planet becomes a nuclear porcupine."[14]

Non-Americans, as one might expect, have made the same assertions with even greater frequency and fervor. The time has come, says Mohamed El-Baradei, Nobel peace laureate and chief of the International Atomic Energy Agency (IAEA), the international body charged with encouraging the peaceful use of nuclear energy and discouraging its military use, to "abandon the unworkable notion that it is morally reprehensible for some countries to pursue nuclear weapons but morally acceptable for others to rely on them."[15] "The members of the nuclear club are not setting a good example for other countries," says former Soviet president Mikhail Gorbachev. "They insist that other countries cannot develop nuclear weapons, while at the same time they strive to perfect their own."[16] "There cannot be one law for the nuclear powers and another for the non-nuclear powers," says Judge C. G. Weeramantry of the International Court of Justice. "No policeman can enforce a law which the policeman himself openly violates."[17] "Countries that have the atomic bomb themselves are all telling us not to have peaceful nuclear energy," says President Ahmadinejad, in one of his frequent outbursts on the subject. "It is one of the biggest jokes of today."[18]

The 2006 report of the independent and influential Weapons of Mass Destruction Commission, convened by the government of Sweden and chaired by Hans Blix, declared boldly that it conclusively "rejects the suggestion that nuclear weapons in the hands of some pose no threat, while in the hands of others they place the world in mortal jeopardy."[19] Blix has served both as El-Baradei's predecessor as director general of the IAEA and as head of the U.N.'s Monitoring, Verification, and Inspection Commission (UNMOVIC), a body specially created to find and dismantle Iraqi weapons of mass destruction, a task at which it was superbly successful. "It is not a recipe for success," says Blix, "to preach to the rest of the world to stay away from the very weapons that nuclear states claim are indispensable to their own security."[20]

The U.N. General Assembly (UNGA), for all its inadequacies, is arguably the closest thing we have at the present hour to a world legislature, or at least to any body representing the collective voice of the peoples of the world. And since the vast majority of states are also non-nuclear weapon states, the UNGA is the closest thing we have to a body representing their collective voice. Every single year since 1996, it has adopted a resolution, always by wide margins, calling for not just nuclear weapons abolition but also the commencement of formal negotiations that would lead to the conclusion of a convention to eliminate nuclear weapons forever.[21] Few actions could more formally signal the world's vast dissatisfaction with the nuclear status quo, with the notion that the world can remain permanently divided between a few nuclear haves and a great many nuclear have-nots.

Even A. Q. Khan, a Pakistani nuclear scientist and trafficker who may be the individual most responsible for spreading nuclear know-how around the world, revealed one of his fundamental motives as early as 1979, when he said in a letter published in the German news magazine *Der Spiegel,* "I want to question the bloody holier-than-thou attitudes of the Americans and the British. Are these bastards God-appointed guardians of the world to stockpile hundreds of thousands of nuclear warheads, and have they God-given authority to carry out explosions every month? If we start a modest programme, we are the satans, the devils."[22]

Khan exaggerated the quantities slightly; in 1986, at the high point of the nuclear age, the total number of nuclear weapons on the planet was "only" about 65,000.[23] But the larger truth that he so passionately expressed is not diminished by the exaggeration. And how many others

around the world will feel the same kind of rage today that Mr. Khan
felt in 1979? If he could generate such anger only a third of a century
into the nuclear age, how much more might be generated in other hearts
now that we're nearly two-thirds of a century beyond 1945? More
importantly, how many others, as a direct consequence, will choose to
follow the path that Khan chose for himself?

THE DOUBLE STANDARD'S MANY ELEMENTS

It is easy to suppose that the resentment over the double standard is
limited to "Why can they have them when we can't?" But a close examination reveals multiple layers of hypocrisy. First is the reality that the
nuclear arsenals of some countries are tolerated without complaint,
while the prospect that others might acquire them is greeted with outrage and alarm. While some seem bent on retaining nuclear weapons
into perpetuity, others are threatened with, in President Bush's words,
"all options on the table" if they begin to develop the scientific and technological capacities that might enable them to develop such weapons.

Second is the implication that the international community consists
of good guys and bad guys, that some can be "trusted" with the nuclear
prize while others are too "unpredictable" or "irrational." Third is
the truth that the judges who designate the good guys and bad guys are
self-appointed. The nuclear weapon states choose to anoint themselves
with the right to possess nuclear weapons, and to appoint themselves to
the task of assessing whether others can be allowed to possess the same
rights. Fourth is the fact that the judges make those assessments on an
entirely subjective, ad hoc, case-by-case basis. There are no rules or
standards, formal or informal, for adjudicating who passes and who fails.
If the Bush administration, for example, decides that Iraq before 2003
doesn't make the cut but that India or Israel do, there are no grounds
for appeal.

ONE STANDARD FOR ISRAEL,
ANOTHER FOR IRAN

It is difficult to ascertain if the Israeli nuclear arsenal creates the same
kind of resentments throughout the rest of the Middle East as does the
American nuclear arsenal throughout the rest of the world. An observer's
first inclination might be to say that it should not. Although Israel has

possessed the bomb for four decades, it has not obviously attempted to use its nuclear capability to coerce a non-nuclear actor in the region to accede to its will. Israel's nuclear arsenal is perhaps the purest case of nuclear deterrence on the planet. Potential aggressors, which, the historical record suggests, are likely to be many, will probably be deterred by Israel's nuclear ability to inflict catastrophic retaliatory damage upon them.

Unfortunately, neither the citizens nor the leaders of neighboring states in the region take this view. Arab and Muslim government officials speak openly about their resentment of the Israeli nuclear arsenal and the Middle Eastern nuclear double standard. An Iranian diplomat made this point explicitly in 2003, not long after all hell broke loose regarding his own country's nuclear aspirations. "Stability cannot be achieved in a region where massive imbalances in military capabilities are maintained," said Ali Asghar Soltanieh, "particularly through the possession of nuclear weapons that allow one party to threaten its neighbors and the region."[24] Similarly, in late 2006, Saudi foreign minister Saud al-Faisal proclaimed, "We want no bombs. . . . Our policy is to have a region free of weapons of mass destruction. . . . This is why we call on Israel to renounce [nuclear weapons]." Theirs, he insisted, was the "original sin." A few weeks later, in an early 2007 interview with the Israeli newspaper *Haaretz,* Jordan's King Abdullah II maintained, "I personally believe that any country that has a nuclear program should conform to international regulations and should have international regulatory bodies that check to make sure that any nuclear program moves in the right direction."[25] Given that he was speaking to an Israeli newspaper, the reference could hardly have been clearer.

Indeed, even Israeli figures occasionally acknowledge the existence of a nuclear double standard in the Middle East—and recognize that it will be difficult to maintain forever. Former Israeli foreign minister Silvan Shalom told Israeli army radio in late 2006, "We are in the midst of a huge [diplomatic] onslaught against Iran's attempts to make a nuclear bomb . . . [while] we always face the same question which our enemies ask: 'Why is Israel allowed [to possess nuclear weapons], and not Iran?"[26]

Israeli prime minister Ehud Olmert offered a direct answer to that enduring question in an interview with the German television network SAT 1. His comments received a great deal of attention because Olmert essentially admitted what everyone already knows: that Israel does indeed possess a potent nuclear weapons arsenal. He said, "Israel is a democracy, Israel doesn't threaten any country with anything, never did. . . . The most that we tried to get for ourselves is to try to live without terror, but we never threaten another nation with annihilation. Iran openly, explicitly and publicly threatens to wipe Israel off the map. Can you say that this is the same level, when they are aspiring to have nuclear weapons, as America, France, Israel, Russia?"[27] Olmert does make a profound point that is difficult to dispute: Israel has never directly threatened the existence of Arab and Muslim states, in words or deeds, as many of these states, in words and deeds, have directly and repeatedly threatened the existence of Israel.

But what are we to do with this conclusion? Proclaim that it means that Israel can possess nuclear weapons forever while neither Iran nor any of Israel's Arab neighbors ever can? Rule that any country that doesn't choose a leader who engages in deplorable rhetoric, that doesn't "threaten another nation with annihilation," is permitted to acquire a nuclear weapons arsenal? What if Iran or another of Israel's neighbors dramatically changes its rhetoric, acknowledges Israel's right to exist, and explicitly disavows any intent to annihilate it? Will that nation then be offered membership in the nuclear club? What if a future Israeli leader, perhaps to bolster support on the Israeli street, engages in bombastic rhetoric about annihilating certain neighboring states? Will Israel's membership card consequently be revoked?

Neither Israeli national security, nor American national security, nor common human security will be well served if certain parties appoint themselves with the right to make perpetual subjective judgments about which countries can or cannot be permitted to possess nuclear weapons and which countries cannot. Does Israel intend, for the next ten or twenty-five or ninety-nine years, to retain a potent nuclear arsenal but insist that none of its regional neighbors may ever acquire the same? Will it ensure the perpetuation of that reality through the force of Israeli and/or American arms? It is difficult to imagine any posture more likely to ensure that several Middle Eastern states, and several million Middle Eastern citizens, will dedicate themselves to upending the region's nuclear apple cart, challenging the region's nuclear status quo, and getting their hands on some nuclear weapons of their own.

ISRAEL, IRAN, AND THE AMERICAN
PERFORMANCE REVIEW

During the waning days of 2007, two leading Bush administration officials, U.N. ambassador Zalmay Khalilzad and secretary of defense Robert Gates, made separate remarks that illuminated the nuclear double standard more starkly than ever. They did not focus, as usual, on the diverging rules of the game for countries such as Iran and for countries such as our own. No, this time it was the double standard separating American expectations for countries it likes, and those it doesn't.

On October 29, Khalilzad repeated the administration's oft-expressed formulation about Iran: "Given the record of this regime, the rhetoric of this regime, the policies of this regime, the connections of this regime, it cannot be acceptable for it to develop the capability to produce nuclear weapons."[28] The argument was wearily familiar. Our assessment of the character of the Iranian regime determines whether we will permit it to proceed down the nuclear road.

A few weeks later, and just days after Washington's release of a national intelligence estimate concluding that Iran had no active nuclear weapons development program, Secretary Gates traveled to Bahrain for a conference of Persian Gulf nations. At this meeting, several Arab delegates argued that the United States was "hypocritical" for challenging Iran's nuclear activities while tolerating Israel's nuclear weapons. "Not considering Israel a threat to security in the region is considered a biased policy that is based on a double standard," said Abdul-Rahman al-Attiyah, secretary general of the six-nation Gulf Cooperation Council, during his opening remarks. Then Gates spoke and, directly after his speech, was challenged by Bahraini minister of labor Majeed al-Alawi, who asked whether, in Washington's view, "the Zionist nuclear weapon is a threat to the region."

Gates hesitated and then answered: "No, I do not." When the minister asked if that viewpoint invoked a double standard, given Washington's incessant pressures on Iran, Gates replied, "I think Israel is not training terrorists to subvert its neighbors. It has not shipped weapons into a place like Iraq to kill thousands of innocent civilians covertly. . . . So I think that there are significant differences in terms of both the history and the behavior of the Iranian and Israeli governments."[29]

So it appears that the Bush administration, in its wisdom, chose to assess the record, rhetoric, policies, and connections of both Israel and Iran, and then pronounce that one state would be allowed to make the nuclear choice while the other would not. Admittedly, many would agree with the assessments that Khalilzad offered about Iranian words and deeds, and with the distinctions that Gates drew between Iranian and Israeli behavior in the international arena. Others might suggest examples of Israel's international irresponsibility to counterbalance those proffered by Gates and Khalilzad about Iran. But the underlying notion implicit in these twin Bush administration remarks is that nuclear security and stability can be achieved when one country—ours—stands as the self-appointed judge over other countries and renders a verdict, based on whatever criteria it invents, that some can be permitted to possess nuclear weapons while others cannot. Such an approach can only result in many more nuclear weapon states, many more nuclear weapons, and eventual and certain nuclear catastrophe.

A MORE SOPHISTICATED NUCLEAR RESENTMENT

On May 5, 2008, Iran's ambassador to the IAEA, Ali Asghar Soltanieh, spoke in Geneva to the preparatory committees that were meeting in advance of the forty-year NPT Review Conference coming up in 2010. He offered a complex elucidation of the range of grievances regarding the nuclear status quo in the Middle East, beginning with a complaint about nuclear apartheid. He was specifically referring this time, however, to the American imposition of harsh export controls on countries such as Iran while, he claimed, it secretly assisted Israel in the development of its sizable nuclear arsenal.

"Access of developing countries to peaceful nuclear materials and technologies has been continuously denied," Soltanieh said, "to the extent that they have had no choice [other] than to acquire their requirements for peaceful uses of nuclear energy . . . from open markets." Usually, he said, that means that countries such as his own must purchase items that are more expensive, of poorer quality, and less safe. Moreover, "Israel, with huge nuclear weapons activities, has not concluded" any kind of agreement with the IAEA to allow for inspections of its own nuclear facilities. Therefore, the ambassador insisted that Iran would not submit to more intrusive IAEA inspections as long as these discrepancies persisted. "The existing double standard shall not be tolerated anymore by non-nuclear-weapon states," he said. "No additional measure in strengthening [IAEA] safeguards can be accepted by non-nuclear-weapons parties unless these serious constraints and discrimination are removed."[30] In this rendering, Soltanieh conveyed a more sophisticated nuclear resentment: first, by alleging that Washington was assisting with Israel's nuclear technologies while hampering Iran's abilities to obtain the same; second, by highlighting Washington's demand that certain adversaries submit to rigorous IAEA inspections—profound intrusions on national sovereignty—while certain allies are under no such obligation.

Israel has never signed the NPT, so it is under no international legal obligation to conclude such an agreement with the IAEA. Still, the aspiration for the NPT has always been that it would eventually apply universally. Israel's failure to join the treaty can hardly be expected to diminish simmering antipathies (not just in Iran) arising from the perception that, in the nuclear realm, there are different rules for different actors.

Ironically, the American envoy to the same Geneva meeting, Christopher A. Ford, conveyed a much more traditional understanding of the nuclear double standard, not so much by what he said but by what he did not say: "This treaty regime faces today the most serious tests it has ever faced: the ongoing nuclear weapons proliferation challenges presented by Iran, by North Korea and now by Syria."[31] Now there is an unvarnished example of nuclear narcissism for you. A Bush administration official labels the alleged nuclear quests of certain non-nuclear weapon states as the "most serious" challenges confronting the NPT "ever." Yet he says not one single word about continued U.S. deployment of many thousands of nuclear weapons, nor about the Bush administration's explicit and detailed plans to build new generations of nuclear weapons and delivery systems during the next three or four decades, nor about the complete absence of any administration initiative to comply with our country's obligation under the NPT (see Chapter 7) to achieve universal nuclear disarmament.

One might venture to say that these American nuclear policies posed at least as much of a "serious test" to the fate of the NPT as the alleged nuclear activities of Iran, North Korea, and Syria. Indeed, Ford's brief remarks in Geneva might have been the Bush administration's most straightforward description, "ever," of America's nuclear hypocrisy.

CONVENTIONAL MILITARY SUPERIORITY AND PERPETUAL NUCLEAR POSSESSION

Toward the end of his 2007 book *The Atomic Bazaar,* William Langewiesche quotes "a smart man close to the military" in Pakistan:

> You cannot have a world order in which you have five or eight nuclear-weapons states on the one hand, and the rest of the international community on the other. There are many places like Pakistan, poor countries which have legitimate security concerns— every bit as legitimate as yours. And yet you ask them to address those concerns without nuclear weapons, while you have nuclear weapons *and* you have everything else? It is not a question of what is fair, or right or wrong. It is simply not going to work.[32]

The sentiment "and you have everything else" begs for elaboration. Few on this planet can be unaware of America's awesome military supremacy over any possible adversary or combination of adversaries. Most, too, are aware that this military dominance can be exercised through conventional means alone. Now consider the underlying credibility of the U.S. nuclear weapons claim. The nation possesses overwhelming conventional military power, yet insists that it cannot protect its own national security without also maintaining a vast nuclear arsenal. Moreover, it superciliously declares that other states, with laughably smaller conventional military establishments, should be fully able to protect their national security without nuclear assets. Not only is it impossible for such a claim to pass the chuckle test on Jay Leno or David Letterman or whatever their equivalents are in the Muslim world. As the "smart man close to the military" recognized, that strategy simply is not going to work.

When one includes Department of Energy allocations for nuclear weapons (which astonishingly are not part of America's official defense budget), veterans' benefits (which, more than a half century from now, our children and grandchildren will still be paying to those wounded in

Iraq and Afghanistan), and repeated supplemental allocations for the invasions and occupations of Iraq and Afghanistan, we can see that the United States probably spends more on its military prowess than do all the other countries in the world—combined.[33] This situation is probably unprecedented in world history. Yet according to the Bush administration's nuclear posture review of December 2001, nuclear weapons must continue indefinitely to "play a critical role in the defense capabilities of the United States, its allies and friends."[34] Other states, which by any measure possess conventional military capabilities only a tiny fraction of our own (Iran, for example, spends about 1 percent of what the United States does on its military), are told that they ought to be able fully to protect themselves from external threats with those forces alone.[35] But we, with vastly greater conventional capabilities (especially in relation to any of our most likely adversaries), maintain that we also must possess the nuclear hammer. What conclusion could any other state possibly draw? If nuclear weapons are necessary to protect the national security of the mightiest country in the world, then surely they must be necessary to protect the national security of other countries as well.

PERPETUAL POSSESSION MEANS
PERPETUAL PROLIFERATION

Isaac Newton's laws of action and reaction do not apply solely to billiard balls. The problem with America's nuclear hypocrisy is not just that it is unfair, illegitimate, and morally indefensible. The greater problem is that the nuclear double standard cannot persist indefinitely. Iran and North Korea are only the tip of the future proliferation iceberg. A decade, a quarter century, a half century down the road, can the world really still have only a handful of nuclear weapons states? When your now ten-year-old children are raising families in 2025, they may live in a world of twenty-five nuclear weapon states. When their children are raising families in 2050, they may live in a world of fifty nuclear weapon states.

The rest of the world will not forever forego nuclear weapons if some insist on forever retaining nuclear weapons. "If there is naked cynicism on the part of the nuclear weapon states and a total disregard of nuclear disarmament commitments," said U.N. undersecretary general for disarmament Jayantha Dhanapala at the 1995 NPT Review

Conference, "then we might see not just one or two countries for individual reasons wanting to opt out . . . but a major threat of an exodus from the treaty."[36] "As long as these weapons exist in the arsenals of some," said South Africa's deputy foreign minister Abdul Minty at the 2000 review conference, "others will aspire to possess them."[37] "The U.S. Administration demands from other states not to have any nuclear weapons, while it fills its own arsenals," said Mohamed El-Baradei in 2003. "If we do not give up such double standards, we will have even more nuclear powers."[38]

The Indian case is instructive on this point. India fully joined the nuclear club when it conducted a series of test nuclear detonations in the spring of 1998. Experts estimate that Delhi now possesses about seventy powerful nuclear warheads, with more in the pipeline.[39] Although the Indian decision was undoubtedly driven by multiple motivations— deterring aggression from China and Pakistan, international prestige, domestic politics—it is difficult to dispute that a leading factor was Indian resentment of the nuclear double standard. Elaborating on his repeated objections to nuclear apartheid, foreign minister Jaswant Singh thundered in the Indian parliament as the 2000 NPT Review Conference was taking place on the other side of the world that the nuclear weapons states have "arrogated a permanent special right to possess nuclear weapons for their exclusive security."[40] For years before the 1998 tests, the Indian government repeatedly indicated that its refusal to sign the NPT was due in large measure to its belief that the treaty would establish a permanent, two-tier structure. Indeed, as early as 1964, before the NPT was even signed, Indian prime minister Lal Bahadur Shastri said, "We cannot at present think in terms of making atomic bombs in India. We must try to eliminate the atomic bombs in the world rather than enter into a nuclear arms competition."[41] More than a third of a century later, when the prospect of that elimination seemed even more remote, India finally gave up on Shastri's choice, and joined the nuclear club for good.

"This Administration in Washington," said Richard Butler, an Australian who, as head of UNMOVIC's predecessor, the U.N. Special Commission on Monitoring (UNSCOM), led the extraordinarily successful inspections and dismantling of Iraqi weapons of mass destruction during the 1990s, "is honestly asking other human beings to believe that American security is so precious that it can have in its possession whatever weapons of mass destruction it might want, but others can't. . . . [When Delhi decided to go nuclear in 1998], the Indians were quite compelling, saying, 'We can't accept that somehow American security is more important than ours. . . . We can't accept the basic inequity that is involved in that position.'"[42] A decade later, it became clear that India had not budged from this position when Ambassador Nirupama Rao, speaking before the U.N. Conference on Disarmament in Geneva in May 2009, said that her country considered its nuclear arsenal "an integral part of our national security and will remain so pending the global elimination of all nuclear weapons on a universal, nondiscriminatory basis."[43]

Today the double standard does not operate only between the American nuclear leviathan and aspirants such as Iran and North Korea. Those states, like many other countries, were stung by the massive nuclear assistance deal that the Bush administration accorded to India in 2008. Under those terms, the United States will provide India with substantial quantities of fuel for its civilian nuclear reactors so that India can devote virtually all of its own nuclear fuel supplies to the construction of nuclear warheads. In other words, India has virtual carte blanche to continue to develop its nascent nuclear arsenal. What is Washington's goal in such a deal? It wants India to serve as a counterweight to China's growing power. What is the message to countries such as Iran? America's enemies are forbidden to acquire even a single nuclear warhead, but its friends are encouraged to acquire even more.

Solidarity among the nuclear have-not majority is likely to become more important down the road. Even now, many with no stake in the outcome must be cheering on Iran, hoping that it can somehow breach the castle wall and demonstrate that the disarmed, the powerless, the underdogs of the world can stand up straight under the long nuclear shadow of the hypocritical hyperpower. American citizens are aware of this reality. An August 2008 survey by Harris Interactive found that two-thirds of Americans believe that the possession of nuclear weapons by some countries inexorably encourages others to acquire them. Fully 68 percent of respondents said they believe that, if the nine nuclear weapon states retain their arsenals indefinitely, others will seek nuclear arsenals of their own. Twenty-two percent said retention will have no impact, while only 11 percent said that continued possession will discourage others from making the nuclear choice themselves.[44]

In 1995, just a few years after the end of the cold war, the Australian government assembled a distinguished group of diplomats, military officers, and nuclear experts and asked them to propose concrete steps that would set in motion an irreversible process leading to a world free of nuclear weapons. The August 1997 final report of the Canberra Commission on the Elimination of Nuclear Weapons remains one of the most eloquent and persuasive statements on why abolition is necessary to the fate of the human race, and how we might act to bring it about.[45] According to the commission, "the possession of nuclear weapons by any state is a constant stimulus to other states to acquire them." And if they do? "The proposition that nuclear weapons can be retained in perpetuity and never used—accidentally or by decision—defies credibility. . . . The only complete defence is the elimination of nuclear weapons and assurance that they will never be produced again."[46]

Even early in atomic history, the notion that nuclear weapons could serve as not only a deterrent, but also a proliferant, was quite evident. In November 2007, the Nixon Library released a series of recently declassified national security documents indicating that the Nixon administration was quite worried that a nuclear Israel would eventually lead to other nuclear weapon states in the region. In a July 1969 memorandum to the president, national security advisor Henry A. Kissinger argued that an Israeli nuclear program could motivate the Soviet Union to begin supplying nuclear technology to Tel Aviv's Arab adversaries. "Ideally," he said, the U.S. objective should be to "halt actual Israeli possession."[47]

Four decades later, nuclear technology and nuclear energy are spreading throughout the Middle East. Various nuclear programs are progressing in Morocco, Libya, Egypt, Saudi Arabia, Syria, Jordan, and the United Arab Emirates.[48] It's easy to envision scenarios in which an Iranian bomb is quickly followed by Syrian, Egyptian, and Saudi bombs. Saudi Arabia, in particular, might have an astonishingly rapid route into the nuclear weapons club. Riyadh wouldn't necessarily have to build its own indigenous uranium enrichment program and then build nuclear weapons from the resulting weapons-grade nuclear materials. It wouldn't even have to acquire those materials from elsewhere and then build nuclear weapons itself. No, the Saudi sheiks might simply invite their good friends in Islamabad, whose nuclear program Riyadh helped to finance, to station Pakistani nuclear weapons on Saudi soil. Pakistan could see this as a straight ticket to expanding its influence and projecting its power into the region. Saudi Arabia could see it as a straight ticket to acquiring a nuclear deterrent overnight. Of course, today no country in the world has nuclear weapons stationed outside its own territory—except for the United States. But Washington has established a precedent that someone else will inevitably follow.

On the sixtieth anniversary of the atomic obliteration of Hiroshima, U.N. secretary general Kofi Annan spoke of the increasing potential for a "cascade of nuclear proliferation."[49] He was referring not only to the worrisome situation in the Middle East, but also to challenges in Northeast Asia. Joseph Cirincione has written about how easy it would be for South Korea to decide to cross the nuclear threshold and then to carry out that decision. Since the uneasy 1953 truce that brought active hostilities in the Korean War to an end, the Republic of Korea (ROK) in the south has seen itself as threatened by the Democratic People's Republic of Korea (DPRK) in the north. Few Americans remember that that war has never been formally concluded, but most Koreans do. Several times in the ensuing half century, when American security guarantees have appeared to Seoul to waver, the ROK has contemplated acquiring a nuclear deterrent. When the Nixon administration, reeling from a decade-long quagmire in Vietnam, indicated in the early 1970s that America's Asian allies should make greater efforts to ensure their own security, South Korea actually commenced a nuclear weapons development program. In response, the United States pressured the ROK to halt this program and reaffirmed both its security assurances and its intent to maintain its forces on the Korean peninsula. Largely the same thing happened during the Carter administration. Years later, after the DPRK's nuclear ambitions were revealed in the 1990s, the IAEA discovered that South Korean scientists had undertaken secret nuclear experiments as recently as 2000 (which the government claims were unauthorized).[50]

Given that North Korea has already acquired a few nuclear weapons, any new uncertainties in Seoul about Washington's security guarantees might well push South Korea to rapidly develop a nuclear arsenal of its own. Similarly, if Taiwanese leaders conclude that the Chinese threat is greater than America's willingness to defend the Taiwan Straits, they might well come to the same conclusion. Both Taiwan and South Korea have minimal economic barriers to such a course, and their degree of technical advancement would make constructing a nuclear weapons deterrent relatively quick and easy. And should Tokyo ever conclude that the threat from China, or Russia, or North Korea requires more than American security can guarantee, Japanese civilian stockpiles of weapons-usable plutonium are so large that the nation could probably construct its own sizable nuclear weapons arsenal within a few months. This is why South Korea has long identified Japan as an "associate member of the nuclear club."[51]

At some point, nuclear proliferation will likely begin to feed on itself and proceed forward even faster still. Every new nuclear weapon state will increase the threat perception of some other non–nuclear weapon state. Every new nuclear weapon state will increase the availability of both nuclear technologies and nuclear scientists. And every new nuclear weapon state will diminish the taboo against obtaining nuclear weapons—and, eventually, against using them.

Try to imagine the world in forty years, still with only nine nuclear weapon states but with no nuclear weapon resentments, or challenges, or aspirations from any other states. The absurdity of that scenario is apparent to even the most casual observer. If anything seems certain about the future political landscape, it is that the nuclear status quo cannot last. We can seriously commit ourselves to move toward abolition, or we can resign ourselves to more and more nuclear weapon states, and more and more nuclear weapons stockpiled in hundreds of locations all around our fragile planet. "Under the conditions of a nuclear state of nature," said philosopher Conrad Brunk a quarter century ago, "our life as a species on this planet will indeed be [as Thomas Hobbes said about our remote ancestors in the primordial state of nature] 'poor, nasty, brutish, and short.'"[52] The notion that a handful of states can forever maintain a nuclear oligarchy, and forever frustrate the nuclear yearnings of others, is nothing but a forlorn fantasy. Humanity must eventually choose between a world of many dozen nuclear weapon states or a world of zero nuclear weapon states. As Abraham Lincoln said about a nation half slave and half free, a world with a few nuclear haves and a great many have-nots cannot forever endure.

So Why Hasn't It Happened Already?

As early as 1961, Robert A. Heinlein saw the inexorability of perpetual nuclear proliferation and discussed it in his typically unvarnished fashion: "Another change, just over the hill, is that the so-called nuclear bomb club, now consisting of us, the Soviets, France, and Britain, is . . . going to become about as exclusive as the Benevolent and Protective Order of Elks. All of the little nations are going to have them too. . . . Don't blame me for it—*I* don't know how to make A-bombs. It is just that this development is clearly in the cards."[53] In the same year, however, another observer made a similar forecast, a prediction that did not in fact specifically happen. "By 1970," said President Kennedy, "there may be ten nuclear powers instead of four, and by 1975, fifteen or twenty."[54] If perpetual proliferation is so inevitable, then why didn't JFK's forecast come to pass?

Since the dawn of the nuclear age, any individual state that has chosen to forego the nuclear option has undoubtedly considered a number of political, economic, environmental, and other variables in performing a cost-benefit analysis on the question. But for most of the states in the world during the past two-thirds of a century, two overriding factors were probably in operation. The first reason that many states did not go nuclear during the cold war was, in fact, the cold war. Many states probably concluded that they did not need a nuclear deterrent because they fell under the nuclear umbrella of either the United States or the Soviet Union. Germany, Italy, Japan, and South Korea, for example, might well have judged that a nuclear first strike by the Soviets (or even some kind of nuclear coercion or compulsion) was a real possibility without a nuclear deterrent, but believed they had such a deterrent in the United States. Cuba, Poland, Romania, and North Korea might well have harbored similar fears—but their deterrent came from the USSR. Although alternative history is inevitably speculative, it's plausible to suppose that, without the cold war, many more states would have sought the nuclear prize during the first forty-five years of the nuclear age.

The second reason that many states have not gone nuclear is that the world reacted to the geostrategic logic underlying President Kennedy's warning and, during the same decade, created the NPT. The treaty, in a stroke, dramatically increased the political and diplomatic costs of going nuclear by making it formally and legally unacceptable to do so. Indeed, since 1970, virtually every state that has flirted with choosing the nuclear course, and especially each state that has made the choice, has met widespread international political ostracization and opprobrium.

Unfortunately, these two historical dynamics provide few grounds for optimism today. The Berlin Wall fell on November 9, 1989. The cold war has been over for more than two decades now. Since then, the number of nuclear weapon states has increased by 50 percent, from six in 1989 to nine today—with Iran looking as if it may soon become the tenth. The dampening effect that the cold war exercised for the first half century of the nuclear age will not prevail for the second half century.

More importantly, the NPT regime is currently under siege. The motivations moving North Korea and Iran to pursue the nuclear course—explored below in the Chapter 8 on the military utility of nuclear weapons—are not likely to be limited to those countries. The resentments about the nuclear double standard explored in this chapter, both so widespread and so multifaceted, are not likely to diminish without serious progress on nuclear disarmament. They will instead only continue to grow. President Kennedy's forecast, while delayed, may ultimately not be denied.

HYPOCRISY AND ITS DISCONTENTS

Few have expressed the bitterness that the nuclear double standard generates more vividly than Mao Zedong, founder of the People's Republic of China. In 1963, before China had any nuclear weapons of its own, he declared, "It is absolutely impermissible for two or three countries to brandish their nuclear weapons at will, issue orders and commands, and lord it over the world as self-ordained nuclear overlords, while the overwhelming majority of countries are expected to kneel and obey orders meekly, as if they were nuclear slaves."[55] And, sure enough, China did not remain meek, and within a couple of years, had become a full-fledged nuclear weapon state. The leaders of many other nuclear have-not states may not possess the late chairman's gift for gripping expression. Nevertheless, nearly a half century later, it is difficult to believe that a number of them will not eventually follow his course.

Perhaps the most direct expressions of the realities of the nuclear double standard were revealed over the past decade by none other than

George W. Bush. The forty-third American president repeatedly claimed that the greatest danger facing America and the world today was the threat posed by nuclear weapons and other weapons of mass destruction . . . in the hands of others. "Men with no respect for life must never be allowed to control the ultimate instruments of death," he said in March 2002.[56] Five months later, he said, "I have constantly said that we owe it to our children to free the world from weapons of mass destruction in the hands of those who hate freedom."[57] "The gravest danger facing America and the world," he said in his 2003 State of the Union address, "is outlaw regimes that seek and possess nuclear, chemical, or biological weapons."[58] "You've often heard me worry about [weapons of mass destruction] winding up in the hands of the wrong people," he said in April 2004.[59] And at the end of 2005, he insisted, "We cannot allow the world's most dangerous men to get their hands on the world's most dangerous weapons."[60]

Here, surely, we have the baldest, most candid answer to the 64,000-dollar nuclear question. Some countries are rational and sober and righteous, and hence can be trusted with the nuclear prize. Others are simply too volatile, too unpredictable, or too freedom hating to be permitted to venture down the same road. And who will decide? Who will render subjective, ad hoc, case-by-case verdicts on whether certain leaders and certain peoples can be trusted with nuclear weapons? Who will serve as prosecutor, judge, jury, and enforcer?

Why the freedom lovers, of course—who already possess nuclear weapons of their own.

CHAPTER 3

The Nightmare of Nuclear Terror

WESTERN LEADERS would do well to recall that the
very first word in the very first work of western literature, Homer's
Iliad, is *menis*. Anger. Wrath. Rage.

I once asked a seasoned public radio reporter, who had been chained
inside the courtroom during every single day of the O. J. Simpson trial,
the obvious questions: "Did he do it? Or did the Los Angeles Police
Department plant a boatload full of fake evidence in an effort to frame
a famous defendant?"

"How do you know," she replied, "that it wasn't both?"

As a nuclear weapons policy analyst and disarmament advocate, I am
sometimes asked whether the danger of nuclear terror is real, or whether
certain modern-day Machiavellis are manipulating our deepest fears to
promote their own cynical political agendas. "How do you know," I am
inclined to reply, "that it isn't both?"

Nuclear terrorism is almost certainly the most likely nuclear threat
today, and it may well be the single greatest immediate peril facing
world civilization today. This chapter articulates the nuclear terror scenario, emphasizing how easy it could be to implement and how difficult
it will be to prevent. But that case has been amply made elsewhere. This
chapter makes a case that has rarely been made elsewhere. First, our
bloated nuclear armory does nothing to protect us from nuclear terror.
Second, our nuclear weapons, in fact, make it far more likely that we
will eventually suffer from nuclear terror. Third, the entire human race
could suffer catastrophic and enduring consequences from even a single
episode of nuclear terror. Fourth, a coherent combination of short-,
medium-, and long-term strategies offers our best hope for indefinitely
dodging the bullet of nuclear terror. Finally, and most importantly, the
only long-term solution for this—and all the other nuclear dangers this
book will illuminate—is the abolition of nuclear weapons.

JACQUES CHIRAC: JANUARY 19, 2006

The prospect that the *menis* simmering in the breasts of so many might result in cataclysms exceeding even those portrayed by Homer has never been presented so starkly as it was on January 19, 2006. Two public statements delivered on that day, almost simultaneously, show just how much western leaders seem to misunderstand the paramount security threat of the modern age.

During a visit to a nuclear submarine base in Brittany on January 19, French president Jacques Chirac issued a warning to "the leaders of states who would use terrorist means against us." He declared, "Those who would envisage using . . . weapons of mass destruction must understand that they would lay themselves open to a firm and fitting response on our part. This response could be a conventional one. It could also be of a different kind." Chirac emphasized the "flexibility" of France's nuclear arsenal, which consists of air-launched nuclear cruise missiles, air-dropped nuclear gravity bombs, and submarine-launched nuclear ballistic missiles. He indicated that France had developed nuclear warheads of a relatively small explosive yield, permitting Paris to deliver a precise nuclear strike "directly against the centers of power"—that is, the leaders of such states themselves. Because France consequently would not have to incinerate an entire metropolitan area in order to decapitate a regime, its deterrent threat arguably became more credible. "All our nuclear forces," said Chirac, "have been configured in this spirit."[1]

Disarmament advocates immediately condemned Chirac's remarks. "Far from ridding France of nuclear weapons," said the French peace group Sortir du Nucleaire, "the president is on the contrary considering the actual use of nuclear bombs."[2]

OSAMA BIN LADEN: JANUARY 19, 2006

On the same day, Al Jazeera aired the first audiotape released in more than a year by Osama bin Laden, a non-state actor who, since the ejection of the Taliban regime in Afghanistan in late 2001, does not appear to have much direct support from the leaders of any state. The Al Qaeda leader explicitly warned that new terror attacks inside the United States were imminent: "The operations are under preparation, and you will see them in your homes the minute they are [arranged], God willing."[3]

On this tape, Bin Laden positioned himself as a statesman, one equal in stature to the American head of state—and one who was open to negotiations. He suggested that if the west were to allow Muslims to "rebuild Iraq and Afghanistan" after American withdrawals, the warring parties might be able to strike "a long-term truce on fair conditions that we adhere to . . . so both sides can enjoy security and stability." He also appealed directly to the American people, emphasizing not just sanctuary from his terror but the benefits that would flow from following his advice: "An overwhelming majority of you want the withdrawal of American troops from Iraq. There is no shame in this solution, which prevents the wasting of billions of dollars that have gone to those with influence and merchants of war in America." But he also warned that, without such a truce, his holy warriors intended to persevere: "Don't let your strength and modern arms fool you. They win a few battles but lose the war. . . . We were patient in fighting the Soviet Union [in Afghanistan] . . . and now they are nothing. In that there is a lesson for you."

WHAT DO WE MEAN BY
NUCLEAR TERROR?

During the cold war, MAD, the abbreviation for "mutually assured destruction," was commonly considered the most appropriate acronym in human history. But one of its closest contenders must have been the label sometimes given to nuclear use theorists, whom one can hardly resist identifying as NUTS. (The term was apparently first coined by sociologist Paul Joseph of Tufts University.)[4] Today's NUTS usually identify four broad scenarios that we can loosely group under the phrase "nuclear terror."[5] In one scenario, perpetrators obtain, perhaps through theft, bribery, or a paramilitary operation, an intact nuclear warhead, find a way to transport it to a high-value target (for example, a large American city), then find a way to set it off. Such an act might kill hundreds of thousands of people instantly and, in the days and weeks to follow, would also condemn hundreds of thousands more to excruciating deaths from radiation poisoning.

In a second scenario, perpetrators obtain, through similar methods, highly enriched uranium (HEU) or weapons-grade plutonium. (HEU is more likely because it is easier to handle, procure, and use in a bomb design.) Then they assemble it into a crude nuclear device, transport it to the target (unless they had actually built the device in, say, a Staten Island garage), and set it off. If successfully constructed with a large enough yield, such an act could produce consequences identical to those in the first scenario.

In a third scenario, perpetrators attack or sabotage a nuclear power plant, causing a release of lethal radioactivity. Such an act could kill thousands of people and contaminate hundreds of square miles for many years to come. Finally, in a fourth scenario, perpetrators obtain some quantity of radioactive material, assemble a conventional bomb around it, transport it to the target (if it is not already there), and set it off, discharging radioactive material in all directions. This is a so-called "dirty bomb." While such a bomb could kill hundreds (from the conventional explosive alone), radioactively contaminate several square miles, and pose a widespread psychological shock, its consequences would be nowhere near as severe as those of an actual nuclear explosion.

This book is about abolishing nuclear weapons. Thus, worrisome as these last two scenarios may be, this chapter will address only the first two. Although they are probably less likely than the last two, they are enormously, inconceivably, more catastrophic.

NOT JUST TERROR—NUCLEAR TERROR

"Today, the United States rightly lives in fear of the Bomb it created, because the decision to use it—if and when it becomes available—has already been made," says Pakistani physicist Pervez Hoodbhoy. "But this time around, pious men with beards will decide when and where on American soil atomic weapons are to be used."[6]

In the tape released on January 19, 2006, Osama Bin Laden did not mention nuclear terror. But he didn't need to. Several books published in the past decade have carefully documented Al Qaeda's thirst for the atom bomb.[7] The group's interest dates back at least to 1992, when Bin Laden reportedly tried to purchase nuclear materials in South Africa. American troops in Afghanistan discovered drawings of rudimentary nuclear devices in captured Al Qaeda sanctuaries.[8] The 9/11 Commission concluded, "Al Qaeda has tried to acquire or make nuclear weapons for at least 10 years . . . and continues to pursue its strategic goal of obtaining a nuclear capability."[9] And former CIA director George Tenet provided details about several CIA operations undertaken to counter Al Qaeda's nuclear ambitions. Tenet writes, "I am convinced that this is where [Bin Laden] and his operatives desperately want to go. . . . If they manage to set off a mushroom cloud, they will make history."[10]

After his organization had murdered nearly 3,000 innocent people on 9/11, Al Qaeda spokesman Suleiman Abu Gheith alleged that, over the decades, American policies had killed many more Muslims than that, and drew what was for him a logical conclusion: "We have not yet reached parity with them. We have the right to kill 4 million Americans—2 million of them children."[11] Sheik Nasir bin Hamad al-Fahd, a radical Islamist Saudi intellectual not affiliated with Al Qaeda, has made almost an identical argument, albeit claiming greater numbers still. "Some Brothers," he writes, "have added up the number of Muslims killed directly or indirectly by [American] weapons and come up with a figure of nearly 10 million." This, he argues, would authorize the killing of 10 million Americans "with no need for further argument."[12] Moreover, Bin Laden himself has argued that mass attacks on American civilians are justified because "the American people are the ones who choose their government by their own free will . . . [and who] have the ability and choice to refuse the policies of their government."[13]

In the twenty-first century, we have seen the emergence of a new kind of terrorist—or, more precisely, new kinds of terrorist goals. In the final three or four decades of the twentieth century, most terrorists appeared to possess specific political aspirations, calculating that outrages beyond a certain level would diminish their likelihood of obtaining them. The venerable terror scholar Brian Michael Jenkins has neatly summarized the traditional approach: its objective was to have "a lot of people watching, but not a lot of people dead."[14] But many recent terror attacks—Madrid, London, Bali, the Aum Shimrikyo chemical attack in Tokyo, 9/11, the foiled London liquid bomber plot—appear to have been driven by a different strategic calculus. The political goal seemed to be to inflict the maximum amount of suffering, pain, and death upon the target society (and, in the case of 9/11, to strike a blow against symbolic centers of American economic and military power as well). In 2006, *Foreign Policy* magazine and the Center for American Progress conducted a survey of more than one hundred foreign policy gurus. The experts were asked,

"Would you say that the world is becoming safer or more dangerous for the U.S. and the American people?" In response, 10 percent said, "Much or somewhat safer," while 86 percent said, "Much or somewhat more dangerous." The experts were also asked, "What is the single greatest threat to U.S. national security?" The top two responses were "nuclear materials/weapons of mass destruction" at 47 percent and "Al Qaeda/ terrorism" at 32 percent.[15] *Foreign Policy* and the Center for American Progress conducted similar surveys in 2007 and 2008 and reported some diminishment in the expert perception of peril. For example, in May 2008 only 70 percent said that the world was becoming "more dangerous" for the United States.[16] Yet while 70 percent is certainly less than 86 percent, the finding that seven of ten experts still think our vulnerability is going to get worse before it gets better is hardly reassuring. Such results are disturbingly evocative of the famous manifesto against "war with nuclear bombs" that Bertrand Russell and Albert Einstein issued in July 1955: "We have not yet found that the views of experts on this question depend in any degree upon their politics or prejudices. They depend only . . . upon the extent of the particular expert's knowledge. We have found that the men who know most are the most gloomy."[17]

President Bush's first secretary of defense, Donald Rumsfeld, ruminated famously on the difference between "known unknowns" and "unknown unknowns." Possibly the greatest concern might be those groups, present and prospective, that have little or no connection to Al Qaeda but share its aspirations. For example, in 2008 intelligence officials began to focus on a shadowy Al Qaeda offshoot calling itself the Islamic Jihad Union (IJU). According to former CIA officer Marc Sageman, "it is a splinter organization trying to make its mark. The only way to do that, to make their mark, is to do an attack. . . . The IJU wants to claim to be the new Al Qaeda."[18] The as-yet-uncovered details about the IJU's operational preparations might fall into Rumsfeld's category of known unknowns. But how many unknown unknowns might be out there, perhaps not even Al Qaeda offshoots, perhaps simply terrorist wannabes who aspire to outdo Osama Bin Laden and his compatriots, terrorist aspirants that we don't even know we don't even know about?

Lest anyone think that all this antipathy and malevolent intent was directed solely at George Bush's America and would magically disappear after the ascension of President Barack Obama, recall that just a few weeks after Obama's election in November 2008 Al Qaeda's number 2 official, Ayman Al-Zawahiri, slammed Obama for not converting to the Islamic faith of his father, dismissed him as a "house negro" serving the white American ruling class, and said, in response to Mr. Obama's intent to escalate American force levels in Afghanistan, "The dogs of Afghanistan have found the flesh of your soldiers to be delicious, so send thousands after thousands of them."[19]

Al Qaeda itself, of course, has its share of internal dissensions and disagreements. Lawrence Wright, winner of the Pulitzer Prize for his masterful study *The Looming Tower: Al Qaeda and the Road to 9/11*, discussed some of them in the June 2, 2008, issue of the *New Yorker*. Wright described no less than an ideological and theological civil war inside the worldwide terrorist organization and pointed to the transformation of longtime Bin Laden colleague Sayyid Imam al-Sharif. This man, known widely as Dr. Fadl and writing from prison in Egypt, now conclusively rejects all Islamic justification for Al Qaeda's terror attacks and insists that 9/11 was, on balance, "a catastrophe for Muslims."[20]

Peter Bergen and Paul Cruickshank explored similar themes in the June 11, 2008, issue of the *New Republic*. They emphasized that several individuals with impeccable jihadist credentials now argue both that the innocent citizens of western states are blameless and should not be attacked, and that such attacks cause far more harm than good for the Muslim world as a whole and especially to Al Qaeda itself.[21] And Noah Feldman, writing in the October 2008 issue of *Esquire*, maintained that Al Qaeda began a long, steep slide toward its own oblivion when it started, in its attacks in the middle of the decade, to kill far more Muslims than infidels.[22]

Nevertheless, internal unity and ideological unanimity are hardly essential to pulling off a successful nuclear terror attack. Even if almost all Muslim clerics opposed direct attacks on the United States, that opinion would not necessarily stop those who were determined to launch them. As this chapter will elaborate, some experts believe that a very small group of focused and committed individuals could successfully carry out a nuclear terror attack. Few things could be more fatuous than to read the reports of these investigative journalists, and then conclude that, because some within the jihadist world have foresworn the terrorist road, no one else remains on the march.

THE IRRELEVANCE OF NUCLEAR
DETERRENCE TO NUCLEAR TERROR

But the United States has immense military capabilities, including many nuclear weapons of unimaginable destructive power. So does France, and so do several other potential targets of nuclear terror. So why won't Chirac's explicit nuclear threats, the vast American nuclear arsenal, and the potent nuclear weapons capabilities of other potential targets cause Bin Laden and his acolytes and imitators to pause, rethink their aspirations for nuclear mass murder, and step back from the atomic abyss?

The answer lies in the object of those threats. Chirac's comments on January 19, 2006, were all directed at the leaders of states. American nuclear doctrines are all directed at the power of states. But Al Qaeda is not a state. Osama Bin Laden does not control any territory. And our vast, bristling nuclear arsenal can do absolutely nothing to deter a non-state actor.

Many Americans have an intuitive, primal reaction to the threat of nuclear terror. They are vaguely aware, in the wake of 9/11, that there is such a threat and feel certain that we must defend ourselves against it with our own nuclear arsenal. But for a genuine non-state actor, traditional theories of nuclear deterrence become meaningless.[23] There are at least five fundamental reasons why this is so.

First, if the terrorist does not control a state or a territory, then we have no capital city, no place to threaten to retaliate against. (Recall the headline in the *Onion*, American's funniest newspaper, shortly after 9/11: "Bush Calls on Terrorists to Form Country, So He Can Bomb It.") This is the crucial difference between someone like Bin Laden and someone like Mahmoud Ahmadinejad, the president of Iran. For all the current turmoil about the possibility that Iran might someday acquire nuclear weapons, Ahmadinejad would commit both national and personal suicide if he ever actually used them. Bin Laden, however, does not face that constraint. There is nothing for us to deter because there is nothing for us to retaliate upon. In a major speech in Munich in February 2008, El-Baradei stated this truth as clearly as anyone: "This, to me, is the most danger we are facing today. Because any country, even if they have nuclear weapons, would continue to have a rational approach. They know if they use a nuclear weapon, they will be pulverized. For an extremist group, there is no concept of deterrence. If they have it, they will use it."[24]

Second, if the terrorists are not traditional "rational actors" who want to preserve their own lives, threatening them with nuclear obliteration is no discouragement at all. As we saw on 9/11 and as we have seen in many horrific terrorist episodes since, many radical Islamists are quite willing to commit suicide to serve their odious aims. Moreover, an aspiring nuclear terrorist would not necessarily have to commit suicide to be successful. The traditional utility of suicide bombing is that it enables one to get extremely close to the desired target. Detonating a conventional bomb by timer in one's own garage or apartment is not likely to wreak the desired damage unless one happens to live next door to, say, the New York Stock Exchange or the White House. But a nuclear bomb holds immensely greater destructive potential. Thus, detonating it by timer in one's own garage or apartment while tuning in to CNN a couple of cities away may be just the ticket.

Third, if the terrorist does want to preserve his own life and we seek to deter him by threatening to kill him, we can do that in any conceivable circumstance with conventional weaponry alone. Fourth, we may not know where the perpetrators can be found. After all, many years after the horror of 9/11, the United States has still not managed to locate the elusive Osama Bin Laden; and Israel has consistently failed to find Hezbollah leader Nasrallah even in the tightly confined spaces of Lebanon. Finally, we may not even know who the perpetrators are. Several recent terror attacks have been followed by no claims of responsibility. Imagine that it is the day after, the month after, or the year after the sudden disappearance of an American city, and we never get any idea at all about who did it.

What could a single nuclear warhead have done to stop Mohammed Atta? How can all our nuclear bombers and missiles and submarines prevent some loathsome creature from smuggling a nuclear warhead into an American city, slaughtering all its inhabitants, and erasing all the life and history and potential within? The U.S. Army didn't protect us on 9/11. The U.S. Air Force didn't protect us on 9/11. The U.S. Navy didn't protect us on 9/11. And the thing that protected us the least on 9/11 was our swollen atomic stockpile, our so-called nuclear deterrent, our arsenal of the apocalypse. More than 10,000 U.S. nuclear warheads, of incomprehensible destructive force, and they failed utterly to deter nineteen men armed with box cutters. Nor will they deter the nuclear terrorists. What are we going to do—threaten to fire a nuclear cruise missile through the balcony window of their 750-dollar-a-month bachelor apartment in Las Vegas?

How Difficult Will It Be to Pull Off Nuclear Terror?

The threat of nuclear terror is hardly new; it is inherent in the nature of the technology itself. "Clearly if such bombs are available, it is not necessary to bomb our cities from the air to destroy them," wrote Manhattan Project physicist Leo Szilard in a 1945 memorandum to President Roosevelt before the world's first nuclear weapon had even been tested at Alamogordo, New Mexico. "All that is necessary is to place a comparatively small number of such bombs in each of our ten major cities and to detonate them at some later time."[25]

In 1946, a U.S. Senate panel asked J. Robert Oppenheimer, the Manhattan Project's director, "whether 3 or 4 men couldn't smuggle units of a bomb into New York and blow up the whole city." Oppenheimer said, "Of course it could be done, and people could destroy New York." When an alarmed senator then asked what high-tech gadget the great scientist might use to detect a warhead hidden somewhere in New York, Oppenheimer replied dryly, "A screwdriver." To open every crate, every cabinet, every garage in the entire New York metropolitan area.[26] A few years later, the U.S. Atomic Energy Commission published a classified study of the problem titled "The Screwdriver Report."[27] And in 1947, Henry Stimson, who was President Truman's secretary of war and intimately involved in the decision to use the bomb against imperial Japan, wrote, "The future may see a time when such a weapon may be constructed in secret and used suddenly and effectively with devastating power by a willful nation or group. . . . With its aid even a very powerful and unsuspecting nation might be conquered within a very few days."[28]

An aspiring nuclear terror group would have to obtain an intact nuclear warhead or build one itself. The first course has probably become far easier as we have progressed through the nuclear age. Over many generations of development, nuclear weapons have become increasingly smaller, making them easier to move. The late Eugene Carroll, a U.S. Navy rear admiral, recited just how many different kinds of highly portable nuclear warheads have been constructed over the years: "Among the 70,000 U.S. nuclear weapons produced during the Cold War were suitcase bombs, neutron bombs, torpedoes, depth charges, artillery shells, air-to-air missiles and anti-tank rockets. The laboratories were like nuclear ice cream factories, churning out the flavor of the day to meet the latest craving of the customers."[29] The Soviet Union, of course, had ice cream factories of its own. And for his part, Osama Bin Laden wants only to procure a single Eskimo Pie.

It would of course be quite difficult to obtain a fully assembled nuclear warhead and then smuggle it into the United States. But even if terrorists did manage to pull off both of those formidable tasks, they would still have to figure out how to disable the complex security mechanisms contained in most nuclear weapons (known as permissive action links, or PALs) to prevent unauthorized detonations. So the more likely course of action would be for potential nuclear terrorists to assemble a crude device themselves. That would only be possible if they could obtain HEU or weapons-grade plutonium.

The global stockpile of those two materials currently amounts to about 2,300 tons, enough to construct some 200,000 nuclear warheads.[30] These materials are maintained in hundreds of locations in more than forty countries, with security operations ranging, according to the IAEA, "from excellent to appalling."[31] In his February 2008 Munich speech, El-Baradei said that his agency tackles on average about 150 cases of nuclear smuggling every year. Some of the material reported stolen has never been recovered, and "a lot of the material recovered has never been reported stolen."[32]

In an article titled "The Bomb in the Backyard," which appeared in the November–December 2006 issue of *Foreign Policy*, Peter D. Zimmerman and Jeffrey G. Lewis described how easy it would be for terrorists to build a crude nuclear weapon inside the United States. The authors constructed a frightening scenario involving, like 9/11, only nineteen terrorists: among them, a few nuclear physicists, a few expert machinists, an experienced metallurgist, a couple of ballistics specialists, and a couple of electrical engineers. Assuming they had managed to procure the necessary nuclear fuel, this team, in the space of a year, for a cost of less than 5.5 million dollars, perhaps on an isolated American farm purchased for the purpose, could, according to Zimmerman and

Lewis, easily construct the kind of simple gunlike device that was detonated over Hiroshima.[33] Such a bomb is set off by firing a projectile of HEU down a conventional artillery barrel into a properly shaped and similarly sized mass of HEU, causing the fissile material to reach critical mass. The concept is so simple that the original atomic scientists on the Manhattan Project did not even feel the need to test this device before releasing it over Hiroshima.

In the December 2006 issue of the *Atlantic Monthly* and again in his 2007 book *The Atomic Bazaar*, William Langewiesche examined, in chillingly plausible detail, the many sources and mechanisms by which aspiring nuclear terrorists might obtain and transport that crucial HEU or weapons-grade plutonium.[34] He suggests that the building of a primitive nuclear device might be best concealed in a warehouse or machine shop in any number of noisy and chaotic cities throughout the developing world. In his rendering, the team does not need to consist of more than "a nuclear physicist or engineer, a couple of skilled machinists, an explosives expert, and perhaps an electronics person, for the trigger."[35]

None of these tasks will be easy for prospective nuclear terrorists to pull off. Those who aspire to nuclear terror may try many times but fail repeatedly. But they are probably not in a hurry. Time is on their side. Everything we have learned since 9/11 about those in the inner circles of terrorism indicates that these individuals are tough, smart, patient, and implacably dedicated. Recall the enormous flap when television host Bill Maher, immediately after 9/11, asserted that men who chose to slam themselves into concrete buildings could hardly be identified as cowards. As members of the Irish Republican Army used to say, "You have to be lucky every single time. We have to be lucky just once."[36]

NUCLEAR TERROR: INFLATED?
EXAGGERATED? OVERBLOWN?

The September–October 2006 issue of the *Bulletin of the Atomic Scientists* featured an exchange between Graham Allison and William Arkin, with Allison sounding the alarm about nuclear terror dangers and Arkin arguing that those dangers have been cynically exaggerated to advance narrow, even venal political agendas. In numerous letters published in the January–February 2007 issue—the one in which the magazine's board announced that it was moving its famous Doomsday Clock from seven to five minutes before midnight—several distinguished nuclear policy professionals agreed with Arkin's thesis of manipulation, but took him to task for underestimating the real nuclear terror menace.[37]

A couple of months after the Allison-Arkin exchange, John Mueller published his book *Overblown: How Politicians and the Terrorism Industry Inflate National Security Threats, and Why We Believe Them*.[38] He argued, not unconvincingly, that what he saw as America's overreaction to 9/11 (and to several previous incidents as well) probably did more harm to our society and economy and national security (not to mention our collective mental health) than did the terror attacks themselves. He pointed out that more Americans die each year from lightning strikes and toilet drownings, let alone from robberies and auto accidents, than from terror attacks.

Brian Michael Jenkins entered this debate in 2008 with his book *Will Terrorists Go Nuclear?*[39] Jenkins provided a thorough examination of the difficulties terrorists face and will continue to encounter if they aspire to go nuclear, though he acknowledged that Al Qaeda and probably other groups clearly do harbor such aspirations. His main contention, however, was that long before the execution of an actual nuclear terror attack, Al Qaeda had already succeeded in terrorizing America by generating, through shrewd publicizing of its own aspirations, continuous and irrational worries about the possibility of nuclear terror. Moreover, Jenkins asserted, the Bush administration aided and abetted Al Qaeda in this regard by promoting, at least partially for its own political ends, a climate of fear in the wake of 9/11.

But for all its faults, much of Bush's "global war on terror" was focused prospectively, not retrospectively. And the overriding prospective danger remains that some group of terrorists, at some point down the road, will pull off a successful nuclear terror attack. Mueller, Arkin, and Jenkins all recognize this possibility but argue that such an attack would be difficult to execute. Others, however, emphasize that there is a great deal of difference between "difficult" and "impossible." A successful nuclear terror attack would be catastrophic, not only for the city or nation in question, but for the entire human community. There can be little doubt that those collective consequences would be far greater than the collective consequences of all the lightning strikes and toilet drownings in America in a year. It seems reasonable, then, even vital, to devote a good deal more attention to the one than to the other.

OUR NUCLEAR ARSENAL AND
THEIR NUCLEAR TERROR

Our nuclear arsenal not only does nothing to protect us from nuclear terror, but on the contrary, makes nuclear terror more likely. In the November–December 2006 issue of the *Bulletin of the Atomic Scientists*, Nick Schwellenbach and Peter D. H. Stockton presented another nuclear terror nightmare: the possibility that suicide terrorists might launch a lightning paramilitary operation on an American nuclear laboratory, barricade themselves inside, and quickly improvise a nuclear detonation fully half the size of Hiroshima. How? Believe it or not, perhaps simply by holding one heavy plate of HEU six feet above another and then letting go—an act that would give disturbing new meaning to the phrase "dropping the atom bomb." More than two decades ago, Luis Alvarez, a Nobel laureate in physics, said, "With modern weapons-grade uranium . . . terrorists, if they have such material, would have a good chance of setting off a high-yield explosion simply by dropping one half of the material onto the other half. Most people seem unaware that if separated U-235 is at hand, it's a trivial job to set off a nuclear explosion."[40] Such an event could take place at Los Alamos National Laboratory in the New Mexico desert. It could take place at Oak Ridge National Laboratory in the Tennessee woods. Or it could take place at Lawrence Livermore National Laboratory in the San Francisco Bay Area, where more than 7 million people live within a fifty-mile radius of the facility.

But aren't American nuclear laboratories the most extraordinarily secured facilities on the planet? Not according to the people responsible for testing such security. In 2004, a U.S. government team of mock terrorists breached the boundaries of Oak Ridge and managed to "kill" the entire lab security force in ninety seconds. Similar episodes, numerous times, have apparently taken place at Los Alamos as well. Richard Levernier, who led several such mock attacks, says, "In more than 50% of our tests . . . we got in, captured the plutonium, got out again, and in some cases didn't fire a shot because we didn't encounter any guards."[41] This remarkable revelation suggests that the "drop the uranium" scenario would not have to take place inside a nuclear weapons laboratory, but could just as easily be carried out in your neighbor's garage.

One obvious solution would be to consolidate all weapons-usable nuclear materials into a few facilities where the very best security procedures could be implemented and continually refined. According to Schwellenbach and Stockton, however, local political interests have resisted such consolidation for many years because of the adverse effect that local closings would have on local economies.[42] An improvised nuclear detonation, of course, in one of these laboratories or in your neighbor's garage, would likely have an adverse impact on the local economy as well.

Screw-ups happen in complex systems managed by fallible human beings. So long as there are thousands of American nuclear weapons, they will provide both a temptation and an opportunity for someone to figure out a way to purchase, purloin, or commandeer one. So long as we hold on to a vast American stockpile of weapons-grade plutonium and HEU, we provide both a temptation and an opportunity for someone to figure out a way to penetrate that stockpile. The longer we insist that we (but not others) must retain nuclear weapons indefinitely, the more possibilities will exist for theft, bribery, mishandling, infiltration, missing hard drives turning up behind copying machines (as they did at the Los Alamos lab in 2000), 1,500 pages of classified material turning up next to methamphetamine pipes in a residential trailer (as they did in a trailer park just outside the Los Alamos lab in 2006) . . . name your Armageddon scenario.

The likelihood that our own nuclear warheads or materials might somehow end up in the hands of terrorists is probably very low. Nevertheless, these disturbing reports indicate that the probability is surely greater than zero. And over a long enough period of time, even a virtually impossible event becomes virtually inevitable.

THE CONSEQUENCES FOR WORLD CIVILIZATION

The classic definition of *risk* is the probability of an event times the likely consequences of that event. And regardless of the probability of a successful nuclear terror attack, it is difficult to overstate the catastrophic consequences that would ensue. In a large urban area of the United States, a single nuclear detonation would pose an existential threat both to our nation and to the world.

Nikita Khrushchev, the Soviet premier from 1953 to 1964, famously observed that, after a nuclear exchange, "the survivors will envy the dead." The Los Angeles office of Physicians for Social Responsibility (PSR), the American affiliate of the Nobel peace laureate organization International Physicians for the Prevention of Nuclear War (IPPNW), projected the results of an atomic warhead the size of the Hiroshima bomb (about 13 kilotons) detonating at noon on a weekday in downtown Los Angeles. It concluded that more than 117,000 people would perish instantly, more than 15,000 others would die from intense radiation exposure within a few hours, and more than 96,000 survivors would slowly wither away as victims of deadly radioactive fallout.[43]

Similarly, the RAND Corporation released a study in August 2006 calculating the effects of a ten-kiloton device exploding shortly after unloading onto a pier at Los Angeles–Long Beach Harbor, the busiest port in the United States. It concluded that 60,000 people would die at once, 150,000 would be directly exposed to hazardous radiation, and 2 to 3 million would have to relocate immediately because their homes would be hopelessly contaminated.[44] Another 2006 study came to even more disturbing conclusions (and also illuminated the large measure of uncertainty regarding such assessments). A highly technical analysis in the journal *Atmospheric Chemistry and Physics Discussions* estimated the number of immediate deaths from a fifteen-kiloton nuclear detonation in various major cities around the world: Los Angeles, 700,000; New York, 2 million; Tehran, 2.5 million; Cairo, 3.5 million; Moscow, 3.7 million.[45]

Many of the city-busting hydrogen bombs produced during the protracted cold war, however, are still in service today, and they are far more potent than ten or fifteen kilotons. Consider, for instance, the 550-kiloton warhead still common in the Russian arsenal or the B-83, America's largest warhead, which weighs in at 1,200 kilotons (1.2 megatons—nearly one hundred times the explosive power of the bomb dropped on Hiroshima). Now raise those estimates from PSR, RAND, and *Atmospheric Chemistry and Physics Discussions* accordingly.

The RAND study also suggested that the economic losses resulting from such an attack would quickly soar into the trillions of dollars and would resonate throughout the global economy for years thereafter. The World Bank concluded that the 9/11 attacks cost the world economy 80 billion dollars and cast 10 million people into poverty.[46] The Royal Institute of International Affairs, defining *cost* more broadly, found that the burden of 9/11 on the United States alone was at least 500 billion dollars.[47] In a November 2004 video (perhaps after reading that study), Osama Bin Laden pointed out the cost-effectiveness of his operation, which inflicted half a trillion dollars' worth of damage on us yet cost him only half a million dollars to carry out.[48] The Dow Jones Industrial Average fell more than 7 percent on the first day of stock trading after the 9/11 attacks. How much would it fall on the day after a nuclear terror attack? The broad and cascading economic costs could plunge the world into deep depression and perhaps cause large segments of the global economy to collapse into chaos.

In addition, as our government endeavored to track down the perpetrators and prevent future incidents, we might well see the rapid and remorseless imposition of martial law and military rule into virtually every sphere of American life. General Tommy Franks, commander of the American military force that toppled the government of Saddam Hussein, speculated on the second anniversary of 9/11 about the possible domestic consequences of another "massive, casualty-producing event" in the United States, "this time employing the potential of a weapon of mass destruction." According to Franks, it might well cause "our population to question our own Constitution and to begin to militarize our country . . . [and] to unravel the fabric of our Constitution."[49]

In the wake of a nuclear terror attack, would any American politicians muster the temerity to object? If it happened in the weeks or days before a presidential election, would the election be canceled? For those who worry about the degradation of American civil liberties in the wake of Guantanamo, the Patriot Act, extrajudicial detentions, warrantless National Security Agency spying, ghost prisons, the September 2006 Military Commissions Act, and the disturbing Department of Justice Office of Legal Counsel memos issued within weeks of 9/11 but revealed to the public only after President Bush left office, only one thing can be said about the nuclear terror scenario: you ain't seen nothing yet.

Moreover, how might an incensed United States react in the international sphere? Even if virtually no evidence emerged to indicate who was behind the deed, enraged citizens and demagogic politicians would bay for retaliation—perhaps on Tehran, perhaps on Pyongyang, perhaps on Mecca and Medina. It is difficult to imagine any American president resisting such pressures indefinitely. It is hard to envisage such reprisals being undertaken with anything other than our substantially more powerful nuclear weapons. And it is hard to fathom the magnitude of conflagration toward which such responses might ultimately lead. "And what then?" asks Pervez Hoodbhoy. "The world shall plunge headlong into a bottomless abyss of reaction and counter reaction whose horror the human mind cannot comprehend."[50]

Following the end of the Second World War, the great British military historian B. H. Liddell Hart wrote incisively about this pattern of reaction in another context. The usual pattern in history, he said, is for the initial aggressors to tend "to avoid widespread destruction, whereas the incensed victims of aggression tend to be far more reckless. . . . [Aggressors] plan to achieve their gains with the least possible damage, both to themselves and to their acquisitions, whereas the victims of aggression are driven by an uncontrollable impulse to hit back regardless of consequences." Liddell Hart went on to discuss the recently completed war, maintaining that because Berlin had been the aggressor and Britain the victim, both Britain and America (when it later came into the war) were bent on not just the defeat of Nazi Germany but its utter devastation. "We were dominated by the impulse to destroy Nazism whatever else was destroyed in the process."[51]

Liddell Hart's description of the mindset of aggressors will likely not apply to the mindset of modern-day nuclear terrorists, whose ambition may well be to inflict the most damage possible on our nation and society. Indeed, almost by definition a terrorist would not choose the option of nuclear terrorism unless that was indeed the intent. But Liddell Hart's prescient portrayal of the psychological state of a victim of nuclear terror—us—could not be closer to the mark. In the hours and days after the sudden obliteration of a great American city and the deliberate mass murder of hundreds of thousands of Americans citizens, can there be any doubt that the American response will be "reckless," "driven by an uncontrollable impulse to hit back," and "dominated by the impulse to destroy"?

Moreover, here is a simple, cheap, easy way to unravel the American nation—politically, economically, and psychologically. Detonate an atom bomb in some American city on a Monday morning. Wait a week. Then detonate another atom bomb in another American city on the following Monday morning. Imagine the rapid, panicked exodus from every large American city once everyone grasps that the perpetrators have managed to acquire not just one, but God-knows-how-many nuclear bombs. Imagine how quickly basic essentials would disappear— food, gasoline, electricity, law and order—as the people charged with providing such essentials tried, like everyone else, to flee for their lives. Would you stay in your city, waiting impotently for the third bomb?

Maybe the reason we have not yet seen a nuclear terror attack is because the terrorists have already gotten their hands on one atom bomb . . . but they're waiting until they can obtain a few more.

THE FIRST WORD OF THE *ILIAD*

During the Vietnam War, people often said that every time we killed a Vietcong guerrilla, we created two more. During the Bush era, the world community witnessed the unveiling of a doctrine of preventive, unilateral, and illegal first strikes against "forces of evil" that had not attacked us. We witnessed an obsession with U.S. military superiority maintained into perpetuity, and an insistence that everyone else adhere to rules of international order that we did not intend to follow ourselves. We saw condemnations of the nascent nuclear arsenals of others but not one word about our own. We heard contempt for international organizations and any multilateral constraints whatsoever on the reach of American power. We listened to rhetoric declaring that other nations must follow our lead or become "irrelevant." And we watched our leaders display their unconcealed aspiration to build a twenty-first-century American empire. These foreign policy actions, and America's military empire, frightened and antagonized both the councils of other governments and the hearts of ordinary citizens all around the world. With regard to its international reputation, the United States, during the Bush years, became its own worst enemy.

Even some Republicans recognize how harmful American international behavior became for American national security. Texas congressman Ron Paul, running for president, told his audience at the University of South Carolina presidential debate in May 2007 that the 9/11 attacks were driven not by some blind hatred of American liberty but by rational objections to American foreign policy and to our enormous military presence abroad. An outraged Rudy Giuliani called on Congressman Paul "to withdraw that comment, and tell us that he didn't really mean it," while the other debate participants clamored to be heard. Paul, however, refused to budge: "They don't come here to attack us because we're rich and we're free. They come and they attack us here because we're over there."[52]

The humiliations inflicted on the German people in the 1920s are what prepared the soil for the emergence of Adolph Hitler in the 1930s. Nations have long memories, especially of the reverses they suffer during times of war, occupation, oppression, and great power arrogance. The repeated humiliations inflicted on peoples around the world today will not simply make new individuals angry. They will not just motivate previously uncertain sixteen-year-old boys to choose the terrorist path. They will not only move committed terrorists to endeavor to step across the nuclear threshold. No, they will prepare the soil for the emergence of new Osama Bin Ladens, self-appointed saviors who will build a constituency by expressing their determination to wreak great vengeance upon the west. New demagogues who will exploit those humiliations toward their own malevolent ends.

SHORT-TERM STRATEGIES

In the short term, we must do everything possible to ensure that no nuclear warheads or materials find their way into the clutches of Al Qaeda or anyone else with similar mass murder ambitions. The Obama administration, to its credit, on its very first day in office, indicated its intent to "lead a global effort to secure all nuclear weapons materials at vulnerable sites" by the end of its first term.[53]

Michael Levi's important 2007 book *On Nuclear Terrorism* provides grounds for optimism.[54] Like Mueller, Arkin, and Jenkins, the author, a physicist, argues that nuclear terror will be much more difficult to pull off than some have maintained. He says that while the "you have to be lucky every single time, but we have to lucky just once" framework is sound when considered over the course of many plots, each individual plot can be tackled from precisely the opposite perspective. Aspiring nuclear terrorists have to succeed at every step of a complex and difficult process, but the authorities only need nab them once. In addition, while it is not easy to imagine a single terror team bringing supreme proficiency to every aspect of that process, we can certainly demand that those tasked with protecting us from nuclear terror do so. Consequently,

Levi advocates a systematic, interactive, many-layered strategy of prevention, one that integrates "controls over nuclear materials and weapons, military power, diplomacy, intelligence, covert action, law enforcement, border security, and consequence management" with the goal of disrupting the aspiring nuclear terrorist at many potential chokepoints along the way.[55]

Some have suggested that governments in states such as North Korea and Iran might choose surreptitiously to slip a couple of atomic bombs into the hands of terrorists. We cannot, of course, entirely rule out such a possibility. We should engage in intensive intelligence monitoring to search for the earliest signs of such a development, and be alert to political developments that might make such an act appear rational to the government in question. But in the end, this possibility seems extremely remote. To the best of our knowledge, no state has ever transferred any weapon of mass destruction to a terrorist. The increasingly precise science of nuclear forensics means that no matter how carefully a state covered its tracks, the radiological residue of a nuclear detonation would allow scientists to trace a path directly back to the state in question. (It would be hard to imagine a more practical investment than to continue to develop that science.) Moreover, autocratic regimes are unlikely to place such a crucial and rare asset into hands they cannot directly control. The leaders of these nations are interested above all in preserving their positions and power, and being caught in such a malevolent act would spell their certain doom. Thus, it is difficult to see how any benefits they might seek from such a transfer would exceed the virtually infinite risks they would face as a consequence.

Rogue individuals within these regimes, however, are another issue entirely. Despite our strident disapproval of the nuclear course that North Korea and Iran have chosen, we probably ought to quietly offer such nations some technical expertise to improve their internal security over all things nuclear. Indeed, in late 2007, the *New York Times* reported that the Bush administration had spent more than 100 million dollars on a secret program to enhance the abilities of the Pakistani government to secure its nuclear weapons and facilities. The program has been hindered, however, by Pakistan's understandable resistance to revealing everything about its nuclear infrastructure to any other state, and its fear that the United States might surreptitiously implement a remote-controlled kill switch that would enable it to disable Islamabad's nuclear force.[56]

Yet for all our worries about Pakistan, North Korea, Iran, and the several states that may eventually follow their lead, priority number 1 in the nuclear terror realm has to be Russia. This heir to the vast arsenal of the Soviet Union still possesses several thousand nuclear weapons stored at roughly two hundred sites, as well as hundreds of tons of nuclear material stockpiled at an estimated fifty sites.[57] The Nunn-Lugar Cooperative Threat Reduction Program, instituted almost immediately after the December 1991 dissolution of the USSR to help secure and to some extent dismantle the Soviet nuclear stockpile, has done much to alleviate these dangers. So has the more recent U.S. Global Threat Reduction Initiative, an umbrella program established by the Department of Energy in 2004 to identify and secure dangerous nuclear materials of Soviet or American origin that had found their way into civilian nuclear programs of countries such as Serbia, Romania, Bulgaria, Libya, Germany, Vietnam, and the Czech Republic. By the fall of 2007, this program had succeeded in locking down more than 80 percent of the HEU at former Soviet-origin sites outside of Russia.[58] Nonetheless, Robert G. Gard, Jr., a retired U.S. Army lieutenant general and now chair of the Center for Arms Control and Nonproliferation, laments that the Bush administration delayed establishing the program and displayed no sense of urgency about it. And because it concerns only materials of U.S. or Soviet origin that exist outside of those two countries, the program probably covers only about a third of the amount of materials in the world.[59]

The Global Initiative to Combat Nuclear Terrorism, which President Bush and Russian president Vladimir Putin unveiled at the G-8 summit in St. Petersburg, Russia, in July 2006, was intended to improve bilateral cooperation on nuclear security, and it is certainly another promising step. Given the outrages perpetrated by Chechen separatists in recent years—blowing up apartment buildings, massacring hundreds of schoolchildren, taking an entire theater hostage—Moscow has at least as much incentive on this score as does Washington.

The urgency of this task is probably most crucial with regard to Russia's tactical nuclear warheads. In 1997, retired Soviet general Alexander Lebed claimed that, when the USSR unraveled at the end of

1991, Soviet authorities lost track of nearly one hundred nuclear weapons, some no larger than a suitcase.[60] Lebed's widely publicized claim has never been conclusively confirmed or refuted, but his statement was hardly implausible.

Russia currently deploys more than 3,000 such tactical nuclear weapons, with several thousand more in storage.[61] Because they are smaller, they are relatively portable. These weapons are forward-deployed rather than stored in one or two central arms depots with extraordinary security procedures. They are not mated to a hundred-foot-long ballistic missile, which obviously would be difficult for a thief to snatch. They do not have the same kinds of rigorous codes and locks and double keys that exist on larger intercontinental strategic weapons. And, though matters have undoubtedly improved since 1991, they are almost certainly not fully inventoried by the Russians, or fully maintained, or fully protected. They just sit there, waiting for the wrong character to get his hands on just one.

Nevertheless, the Russian-American arms control agreement signed by Bush and Putin in the spring of 2002 contained not a single word about tactical nuclear inventories, despite the dangers that must have been starkly evident to American policymakers during the year following 9/11. The Nunn-Lugar Program, for all its successes, has always been constrained by Moscow's natural fear, accurate or otherwise, that the United States aspires not only to secure Russia's loose nukes, but also to spy on its nuclear arsenal. The fissure between Moscow and Washington that abruptly opened in August 2008, following the brief but furious war between Russia and Georgia, can hardly be expected to ease this tension, or to enhance the prospects for cooperation in securing loose nuclear weapons or materials on the ground.

Russia, obviously, is not the only country where we have to worry about loose nuclear weapons and materials. The now infamous A. Q. Khan network's long history of transfers of nuclear technology and expertise suggests that Pakistan could serve as a source for aspiring nuclear terrorists. And the political turmoil that has prevailed inside Pakistan since late 2007, when President Pervez Musharraf declared martial law, assassins struck down former prime minister Benazir Bhutto, Musharraf himself resigned, Bhutto's widower Asif Ali Zardari assumed the presidency, and deadly terror attacks were immediately launched as apparent attempts to assassinate him, set off a flurry of commentaries about the possible unraveling of the nuclear-armed nation, a potential takeover by Islamic jihadists, and the several worrisome nuclear scenarios that still might ensue.

Washington should promote the establishment of an international accounting system for all nuclear weapons and fissile materials. It should agree, in conjunction with other countries, to dispose of the enormous surplus stockpiles of materials no longer needed for weapons, under IAEA verification. It should end the use of weapons-usable materials in all research reactors, power reactors, and naval reactors and encourage other nations to do likewise. And it should move to produce a verifiable and enforceable fissile material cutoff treaty, which would halt the production of all nuclear weapons materials in both military and civilian facilities so that eventually none would ever be produced again. On its first day in office, the Obama administration indicated an intent to enact such a treaty, and a great deal of nuts-and-bolts conceptual work has already proceeded on these scores.[62]

The enhancement of U.S. port and border safeguards must remain a high priority, and the Bush administration made commendable progress in this regard after September 11, 2001. Before 9/11, not a single container crossing our border was screened for radioactivity; but by 2006, probably more than 80 percent were.[63] On July 15, 2006, the Department of Homeland Security announced a major new program to install highly sensitive new radioactivity sensors at 370 ports and border crossings, and on October 13, 2006, President Bush signed the Safe Ports Act, which further enhances our abilities in this arena.

Still, the sheer volume of global commerce makes this job almost impossibly big. To find smuggled nuclear materials in the sea of consumer goods shipped around the world is to seek the proverbial needle in a haystack. An article in the October 2006 issue of *Risk Analysis* magazine reported the results of a rigorous statistical evaluation of U.S. container screening capabilities and concluded, "The likelihood that the current screening system would detect a shielded nuclear weapon is quite low (around 10 percent)."[64] Scarcely a month into office, new Obama Homeland Security secretary Janet Napolitano told Congress that her agency could not possibly meet a 2012 deadline mandated by Congress for 100-percent screening of all cargo coming into the United States.[65]

So it is fatuous to imagine that these kinds of short-term steps, no matter how elaborate, can forestall the fateful day forever. Strict control over all things nuclear may well save us in the short term. But in the medium term, we need to reduce not just the availability of nuclear weapons and materials, but also the motivations for nuclear terror.

MEDIUM-TERM STRATEGIES

On January 19, 2006, White House press secretary Scott McClellan blithely dismissed Osama Bin Laden's truce overture, indicating that President Bush had not given it a nanosecond of consideration. "We do not negotiate with terrorists," he said. "We put them out of business."[66] The Bush administration consistently and categorically rejected any suggestion that we should consider what might motivate either Al Qaeda or the impressionable young Muslim men who show up on the organization's doorstep.

But if we cannot consider negotiating with Al Qaeda, can't we at least try to recast some of our international behavior so it does not so enrage so many? Bin Laden has made numerous offers similar to the one he made on January 19, 2006, indicating that the United States could avoid further terror attacks if it changed specific foreign policy behaviors. He has mentioned Hiroshima in his statements on more than one occasion and has argued that, just as the atomic bombings delivered a sudden shock to imperial Japan and persuaded it to surrender quickly, a similar shock to the United States could quickly persuade Washington to withdraw completely from the Middle East.[67] Even the presumed mastermind behind the 9/11 attacks, Khalid Sheikh Mohammed, who spent nearly four years at a university in North Carolina in the 1980s, told U.S. interrogators after he was captured in March 2003 that his "animus to the U.S. stemmed not from his experience there as a student but rather from his violent disagreement with U.S. foreign policy."[68]

We may say we do not want to give in to terror. But how important are the things that we are determined to stand behind? On the Arabian peninsula alone, the American military presence during the Bush era increased after 9/11 from 12,000 combat troops to more than 150,000.[69] That figure does not include the similar number of American troops in Iraq. Presumably, someone made a judgment that such a troop presence enhances American national security. But how much security do they bring, if they also enhance the danger of an atomic detonation in MacArthur Park, or Grant Park, or Lafayette Park, or Central Park?

There are undoubtedly hardcore terror types out there who are determined to attack us no matter what. Obviously, we must do everything we can to prevent them from acting and make every effort to get them before they get us. Nevertheless, thousands more, undoubtedly, are still only thinking about it. These Muslim teenage boys may have spent their childhoods in *madrasa* Islamic religious schools. Their families have lived long in desperate poverty, and the boys are unemployed and idle. They are looking within themselves at this moment, trying to decide whether to take a stab at becoming a citizen of the world community, or to join the enemies of peace. And like intense young people always, they are looking for some purpose in life, some meaning, perhaps even some cause worth dying for.

During the Bush era, our incentive program for these boys was a singular, one-dimensional, all-negative message: if you seek to do us harm, we will pound you. President Bush offered them nothing other than the incessant drumbeat of war. His message was all stick and no carrot. But if history has anything to teach us at all, it is that all stick and no carrot strategies generate nothing more than an endless cycle of action and reaction. We must do more than simply threaten and frighten those on the fence with severe punishment if they choose to become outlaws against the human community. We do not need to be tough on terror so much as we need to be tough on the causes of terror. Perhaps President Obama could talk in a more serious way about the globalization of economic inequality, and the cultural humiliations at the root of the so-called clash of civilizations. Our nation might actually seek to dry up some of the swamps of hopelessness, despair, exploitation, and degradation around the world. It might offer the poor and dispossessed members of the human community some rewards for the better choice, some hope and opportunity, some promise of full participation in a prosperous and peaceful global civilization. It might act on the world stage with less hubris and more humility. We might recall the admonition of President Abraham Lincoln as our own Civil War wound to its bitter close: "the only lasting way to eliminate an enemy is to make him your friend."[70]

Nevertheless, even these kinds of steps, important though they are, are unlikely to save us from the nightmare of nuclear terror indefinitely.

We need to do more than prevent the bad guys from gaining access to nuclear devices in the short term. We need to do more, too, than reduce the motivations for seeking access to nuclear devices in the medium term. In the long term, our only real hope for saving ourselves from the nightmare of nuclear terror is to get rid of the nuclear weapons themselves. Every last one.

THE ONLY LONG-TERM STRATEGY

"The slow and hard-to-discover spread of atomic weapons," wrote former *New York Times* executive editor Max Frankel, "will end either in nuclear catastrophes or in the eventual surrender of nuclear arms and fuels to a genuine world authority."[71] This book advocates the latter course. Both the magnitude and the immediacy of the nuclear peril mean that a comprehensive nuclear policy agenda, one that fully integrates nonproliferation with disarmament, should become the most important foreign policy priority for the new American president. Such an agenda should contain many of the short- and medium-term steps I have described to diminish the danger of nuclear terror. But it must also describe abolition not as some utopian fantasy but instead as a concrete political goal. And it must set the course toward negotiating a universal, verifiable, and enforceable nuclear weapons elimination treaty. Aspiring nuclear terrorists will not be able to steal a nuclear bomb if there are no nuclear bombs. And they will find it immeasurably more difficult to steal nuclear materials if such materials are placed under the rigorous controls that will necessarily accompany any post-abolition architecture (see Chapter 9). In the long term, our best shot at ending the nuclear terror danger forever is to get serious now about moving toward a world free of nuclear weapons.

Our vulnerability to nuclear terror is surely one of the great paradoxes of the modern age. America's military supremacy over any conceivable combination of adversaries has never been greater. Our nuclear supremacy over all other nuclear actors is even greater still. Yet, arguably, we have never been so threatened, so endangered, or so exposed to nuclear annihilation.

The American government can choose to go down something like the path this book advocates. If it does not, the American people will simply have to await their fate. Walt Kelly's comic-strip character Pogo, in another context, said famously, "We have met the enemy, and he is us." Today, in this context, we might say that we have met the eventual victims of the device that we ourselves unleashed upon the world. And they are us.

We are the ones who devised these weapons in the past. We are the ones who contemplate the use of these weapons in the present. We are the ones who vaingloriously insist that we—but not others—must continue to possess these weapons long into the dim mists of the human future.

Now, in what must surely be one of the greatest ironies in all of human history, we are the ones who may soon feel the *menis* of our own invention. We are the ones who may turn out to be the authors of our own annihilation. We are the ones who may, in the end, be devoured by our own creation.

CHAPTER 4

Accidental Atomic Apocalypse

ONE OF THE BEST BOOK TITLES of recent years was *Lethal Arrogance: Human Fallibility and Dangerous Technologies*, released in 1999 by Lloyd J. Dumas of the University of Texas.[1] You almost don't need to read the book after seeing that title. You know how it's going to come out in the end. Dumas issues a stark warning about the hubris of believing that we can control anything we can invent: "We have vastly more power to affect the physical world than we had even 60 years ago. Yet humans are no less error-prone. The clash between our growing technological power and our enduring fallibility has laid us open to disaster on an unprecedented scale."[2] If we expect imperfect human beings to manage infinitely high-risk technologies, we are eventually going to get infinitely cataclysmic results.

No technology yet invented by fallible human beings, of course, is more lethal than nuclear weapons. If anything calls for extraordinary efforts at elimination, it is our arsenal of the apocalypse. Yet, astonishingly, the human race, long after the cold war's end, still faces the real possibility of an accidental nuclear launch, an accidental nuclear detonation, even an accidental nuclear war.

According to Mikhail Gorbachev, the last leader of the USSR, this risk was his chief concern when he pursued nuclear weapons abolition. "I was quite sure for some reason that the people in the White House were not idiots," he said in 1998. "I thought that they definitely knew what *any* nuclear war would mean. . . . More likely, I thought, was that nuclear weapons might be used without the political leadership actually wanting this, or deciding on it, owing to some failure in the command and control systems. . . . That fear motivated me to seek an end to the arms race . . . Nuclear weapons, a colossal threat to humankind, could run out of the control of politicians."[3]

As I maintained in Chapter 3, over a long-enough period of time, even a virtually impossible event becomes virtually inevitable. Surely, this truth applies not only to nuclear terror, but just as much to the possibility that our nuclear weapons might somehow be employed accidentally. As California governor Arnold Schwarzenegger says, "mistakes are made in every other human endeavor. Why should nuclear weapons be exempt?"[4] Accidents happen, and no matter how secure the systems or how foolproof the procedures, eventually something is going to go wrong.

And here, that something could be cataclysmic on a scale beyond imagination. In Chapter 3, I argued that a single atomic bomb detonating in a single American city would be an utterly transformative event, with consequences that would reverberate throughout the human community for many years to come. Now imagine thousands of nuclear-tipped missiles, each more powerful than anything a nuclear terrorist could procure or construct, launched somehow by mistake. The full-scale global thermonuclear war that we so precariously avoided for four-and-a-half cold war decades could now come about by accident, with consequences for life on earth beyond calculation.

"LAUNCH ON WARNING" MEANS "LAUNCH BY ACCIDENT"

Although many contemporary nuclear threats are very different from the scenarios we worried about during the cold war, this one is remarkably similar. On the day that Barack Obama was sworn in as president, nearly two full decades after the fall of the Berlin Wall, the strategic nuclear arsenals of both Russia and America were still probably operating on the enduring cold war principle of "launch on warning." Our ground-based intercontinental ballistic missiles (ICBMs), each armed with powerful nuclear warheads and scattered throughout the farmland of the midwest, are poised to launch at a point after American radar detects incoming nuclear warheads directed at these missiles, but before the enemy warheads strike. The idea is that an adversary will be dissuaded from launching a nuclear first strike on our land-based nuclear missiles if that adversary knows that our missiles will get off the ground before they can be hit. In this way, according to the argument, deterrence is enhanced.

But what if the radar warning is a mistake? What if the system thinks it's detecting incoming nuclear warheads but is in fact detecting a training exercise, or a satellite launch, or a flight of Canada geese on an unconventional trajectory? That couldn't ever happen, could it?

Actually, it already has.

In 1980, President Carter's national security advisor Zbigniew Brzezinski was awakened in the middle of the night, and told that 220 Soviet missiles were heading our way. One minute before he intended to wake the president, he learned that an overeager recruit had mistakenly put nuclear war game tapes into the North American Air Defense Command (NORAD) computer system.

Three years later, on the night of September 26, 1983, Soviet Lieutenant Colonel Stanislav Petrov was commanding a Russian early warning bunker just south of Moscow. Suddenly, without warning, every alarm bell in the place began to blare. "I felt as if I'd been punched in my nervous system," said Petrov years later. "There was a huge map of the States with a U.S. base lit up, showing that the missiles had been launched." According to procedures, he was supposed to alert higher authorities immediately, and advise them to initiate the launch-on-warning response sequence. But Petrov hesitated. He could not believe what the equipment was telling him; he could not believe his own eyes. And his instincts proved correct: after several minutes, he discovered that a computer error, not an incoming American nuclear first strike, had triggered the alarms. "After it was over," said the colonel, "I drank half a liter of vodka as if it were only a glass, and slept for 28 hours." Speaking about the incident, Global Zero's Bruce Blair, a former nuclear missileer and perhaps the world's foremost authority on nuclear command and control, said, "I think that this was the closest we've come to accidental nuclear war."[5]

A dozen years later, in 1995, long after the cold war had come to a peaceful close, Russian technicians at the Olengrosk early warning radar site detected what appeared to be a nuclear-tipped ballistic missile headed directly at them, apparently fired from a U.S. submarine in the Arctic Sea. President Boris Yeltsin spent eight frantic minutes deliberating on whether or not to launch-on-warning before the incoming weapon arrived. Fortunately, Russian radar officers were able to determine that the rocket was carrying not a nuclear warhead but a Norwegian weather satellite. With three minutes to spare.

Hundreds of similar, well-documented mishaps have occurred over the years on both sides.[6] One Defense Department count listed 563 incidents of nuclear mistakes, malfunctions, and false alarms.[7] How long must we wait before one of them is resolved not with three minutes to spare, but three minutes too late?

Launch on warning does, admittedly, carry some weight within the logic of deterrence. The Russian defense planner, who must decide every morning whether or not to advise his superiors to launch a massive nuclear first strike on the United States, is discouraged from doing so for many reasons. One of these must be his knowledge that American missiles will head toward Russia before the Russian missiles arrive over their targets in the United States. Nevertheless, if we were to eliminate our launch-on-warning policy tomorrow morning, would our breakfasting Russian defense planner likely conclude that Russian national interests would best be served by launching a nuclear first strike on the United States?

In 1995, I received a Ph.D. in public policy analysis from the RAND Graduate School of Policy Studies, with an accompanying certificate of specialization from the RAND/UCLA Center for Russian and Eurasian Studies. Now please do not tell my professors, my dissertation committee, or the dean, but I don't remember much from my qualifying exams. One thing I do remember, however, is how to perform a basic cost-benefit analysis. Most people misunderstand cost-benefit analysis, assuming it means only that one looks at a course of action (or policy option), compares the likely benefits to the likely costs, and if the benefits look likely to exceed the costs, go for it! But in reality, multiple courses of action are available as responses to almost any human circumstance. Each usually entails both likely benefits and likely costs. The word *likely* is crucial here. Because one is anticipating an uncertain future, one's assessments of those anticipated benefits and costs will also necessarily be uncertain. So the proper exercise is to examine all the alternative courses of action, calculate the anticipated benefits and costs for each, figure in some assessment of the confidence one has in those calculations, and then choose the course of action or policy option that appears most likely to offer the optimal net total of benefits and costs. (At my own wedding reception, I endeavored to describe my decision to ask for my new wife's hand in marriage as the product of such a cost-benefit analysis. In retrospect, it was possibly not the most romantic portrayal of our courtship I might have chosen.)

Let's perform a rudimentary cost-benefit analysis on the launch-on-warning posture.

- *Policy A: Launch on Warning.* Benefit: Adversaries are deterred from launching a "bolt from the blue" nuclear first strike. By how much? Say, by a factor of 99 on a scale of 100. Cost: Some possibility of global thermonuclear war by accident, which would certainly kill hundreds of millions of human beings, and possibly bring about the extinction of life on earth.
- *Policy B: No Launch on Warning* (with everything else about our nuclear weapons posture and policies remaining constant). Benefit: Adversaries are deterred from launching a "bolt from the blue" nuclear first strike. By how much? Say, by a factor of 98 on a scale of 100. Cost: No possibility, at least from this, of global thermonuclear war by accident, which would certainly kill hundreds of millions of human beings and possibly bring about the extinction of life on earth.

Most of you probably do not possess a Ph.D. in public policy analysis. Nevertheless, I bet that each of you can discern the optimal net total of benefits and costs if making a choice on that.

NUCLEAR SUBMARINES MAKE
LAUNCH ON WARNING POINTLESS

One of the most perplexing things about the launch-on-warning doctrine is that, even without it, no nuclear first strike on our arsenal could wipe out America's entire nuclear deterrent. The reason lies in the military potency and virtual invulnerability of the American nuclear submarine force. People often misunderstand the term *nuclear submarine*. It can mean a submarine propelled and powered by an onboard nuclear reactor, whether or not nuclear weapons are deployed on board as well. Alternatively, it can mean a submarine carrying submarine-launched ballistic missiles (SLBMs) tipped with nuclear warheads, whether or not the submarine is propelled and powered by an onboard nuclear reactor. For both the Russians and the Americans, the third arm of the traditional nuclear triad (land-based nuclear missiles, nuclear bombs delivered by warplane, and sea-based nuclear missiles) has long been submarines that deploy both nuclear reactors and nuclear weapons.

In 1954, the United States christened the USS *Nautilus*, the world's first submarine propelled and powered by a nuclear reactor and a masterful feat of naval engineering. Six years later, the nation deployed the USS *George Washington*, the world's first submarine with the capability to launch nuclear-tipped ballistic missiles. It, too, was propelled and powered by a nuclear reactor. One might suppose that, for purposes of nuclear deterrence, the crucial variable is the presence on these submarines of nuclear weapons, not nuclear reactors. But the opposite is arguably the case.

The *Nautilus* was unprecedented in its ability to cruise the world's oceans by stealth. It did not have to surface or refuel nearly so often as a conventional diesel-powered submarine, it made far less noise, and it emitted no conventional engine exhaust at all. These features made the *Nautilus*, for all practical purposes, invisible. And such stealth abilities have vastly improved in the ensuing half century. No one (including us) has yet figured out how to destroy nuclear submarines traveling deep under the surface of the sea, primarily because no adversary can tell exactly where they are in the single great ocean that encircles our planet. "These submarines are undetectable," said French defense minister Hervé Morin in early 2009. "They make less noise than a shrimp."[8]

Nevertheless, the "nuclear deterrent" function of nuclear submarines is performed not by their nuclear reactors, but their nuclear warheads. A submarine armed with nuclear-tipped SLBMs contains more destructive power than anything the human race has ever constructed. A single U.S. *Ohio*-class vessel can obliterate every large city in any country in the world, even in the largest countries like Russia or China. America's nuclear submarine fleet today consists of fourteen submarines carrying in total more than 1,700 operational and deliverable nuclear warheads. During the second half of the past decade, more than half of these (primarily those patrolling the Pacific) upgraded their missiles from Trident I C4s to Trident II D5s. Although the differences between the two are complex and highly classified, the Trident II D5s can apparently be employed over a longer range, are considerably more accurate, and can carry considerably more powerful nuclear warheads.[9]

Therefore, even if a nuclear first strike on the United States wiped out all of our ICBMs and nuclear-armed heavy bombers, the nation would retain a nuclear submarine force with the capacity to launch a massive nuclear retaliatory strike. This force makes launch on warning completely unnecessary. In the language of the NUTS, America's nuclear submarine force provides the United States with an "assured nuclear second-strike capability" to respond to any kind of nuclear first strike against American territory, military forces, or interests. In the language of ordinary folks, our nuclear submarine force means that, if anybody hits us, we can hit back. Guaranteed.

OTHER STATES, OTHER MISTAKES

Very little research and analysis has been performed about accidental nuclear launch scenarios in states other than the United States and Russia. It is reasonable to suppose, however, that less technologically sophisticated nuclear weapon states may well have less reliable safeguards against accidents. That danger will only increase as the number of nuclear weapon states increases. For all its faults, the United States probably has the best command and control technologies and procedures in the world. So if our nation has already made so many nuclear mistakes, how many more can we expect from the tenth, fifteenth, and twentieth nuclear weapon states?

Only a few other states possess nuclear submarines, and no other state possesses anything like our arsenal's robust capacity for survival after a hypothetical nuclear first strike. One might argue, then, that other states do indeed need launch on warning, or something very much like it, if their nuclear deterrent is to be both survivable and credible. But such an argument only enhances the need for the United States and Russia to end launch on warning, if only because it would enable both nations to effectively pressure other states to do likewise. It also enhances the argument for abolishing nuclear weapons.

THEY "GRABBED THE WRONG ONES"

Two worrisome nuclear accidents that had nothing to do with launch on warning took place during President Bush's second term. In August 2007, six AGM-129 cruise missiles, each armed with nuclear warheads ten times as powerful as the Hiroshima device, were mounted on B-52s and transported from North Dakota's Minot Air Force Base to Barksdale Air Force Base in Louisiana. The only problem? No one in the U.S. government knew this transfer was taking place. For thirty-six long hours, no one in charge knew where these nuclear weapons were.

According to Air Force secretary Michael W. Wynne, the issue was not bad procedures, but a failure to follow procedures. According to Wynne, the officers involved had five separate opportunities to examine the bundle of missiles, which should have alerted them to the fact that they were armed with live nuclear warheads instead of dummies. It was "an erosion of adherence to weapons-handling standards," said Major General Richard Newton, the Air Force's deputy chief of staff in charge of operations. Then, straying briefly from bureaucrat-speak, he admitted that the officers had simply "grabbed the wrong ones."[10]

The episode, when revealed, received widespread public attention. In response, Secretary of Defense Gates instigated both an internal Air Force investigation and two independent review commissions. The commissions issued their reports in early 2008 and concluded that, since the end of the cold war, the U.S. military had lost considerable focus on management of its nuclear arsenal, and had seen a decline in nuclear training, alertness, and expertise. One commission, led by retired Air Force general Larry D. Welch, said that the cold war's conclusion had led to "markedly reduced levels of leadership whose daily focus is the nuclear enterprise and a general devaluation of the nuclear mission and those who perform the mission." It warned that, without immediate improvements, nuclear accidents far worse than the errant B-52 flight were looming.[11]

Just a few weeks after the release of these reports, word emerged of yet another nuclear fiasco. The government of Taiwan had purchased a set of helicopter batteries from the United States, but received instead fuses that trigger the nuclear warheads loaded into the nosecones of American Minuteman ICBMs. The mishap apparently had something to do with a mistaken computer barcode entry in a Defense Logistics Agency warehouse in Utah. Moreover, although Taiwan informed the United States about the misdirected delivery almost immediately, the Pentagon took more than a year to respond.[12] When they finally did, they immediately informed Beijing of the inadvertent error as well. "In an organization as large as the [Department of Defense], the largest and most complex in the world," said Secretary Wynne, "there will be mistakes."[13]

On June 5, 2008, in response to the mistaken shipment, the Pentagon released a report that was again critical of the Air Force's nuclear leadership. It indicated that, even after the Minot-to-Barksdale nuclear misadventure and its widespread public disclosure and comment, Air Force brass had failed sufficiently to tighten its nuclear maintenance, handling, and security procedures.[14] A senior Air Force official, speaking on condition of anonymity to the newspaper *Stars and Stripes*, put it more bluntly: "When it comes to nukes, we suck."[15] So Secretary Gates, in an unprecedented move, simultaneously fired the highest civilian and military officials in the Air Force on the day that report came out: Secretary Wynne and Air Force chief of staff General T. Michael Moseley.

It is admittedly difficult to sketch a scenario in which either the mistaken nuclear flight or the mistaken nuclear fuse shipment could have led to the accidental launch of a nuclear weapon. Nevertheless, both episodes serve as stark warnings of nuclear mishandling, nuclear mistake, and nuclear error. As Lloyd Dumas might put it, they vividly illuminate the lethal arrogance of combining human fallibility with dangerous technologies.

When discussing the Minot-to-Barksdale flight, Secretary Wynne said that the U.S. military's standard operating procedure with regard to nuclear weapons was never to discuss the transport or location of its nuclear assets. He claimed that he had ordered an exception in this case because the accident was both so serious and so abnormal.[16] The *Los Angeles Times* said that the episode was "the first known incident in which the military lost track of its nuclear weapons since the dawn of the atomic age."[17] But how many such incidents remain unknown to all but those with the very highest security clearances? How many other times have nuclear weapons officers become lackadaisical, failed to follow procedures, and missed five opportunities to get the call right? Moreover, although the incident received an enormous amount of attention both inside and outside the Air Force, won't it eventually be forgotten? Can anyone seriously argue that, thanks to this single episode, we can maintain a vast nuclear arsenal for decades to come, and never again worry about "an erosion of adherence to weapons-handling standards"?

UNAUTHORIZED ATOMIC APOCALYPSE

One can easily conjure up dozens of scenarios involving not an accidental but an unauthorized launch of nuclear weapons, perhaps by someone with inside access harboring malevolent motives, or perhaps someone simply mentally unbalanced. A nuclear launch decision might be delegated to field commanders. Confusion could arise about who possesses the power to make such a decision. Despite numerous safeguards (which are undoubtedly more sophisticated in more technologically advanced nuclear weapon states), a military pilot might take off on a rogue nuclear bombing run, for whatever imagined rationale. Through miscommunication or misunderstanding, an underling might sincerely believe that she is carrying out the will of the government, and press the button.

Perhaps the most likely scenario (touched upon in Chapter 3 with regard to Pakistan) is what Lehigh University international relations professor Rajan Menon calls nuclear fragmentation: the possibility that governmental command and control over a state's nuclear weapons could dissipate during a civil war, revolution, or governmental disintegration. Currently Pakistan, North Korea, and Iran (if it acquires nuclear weapons) seem to be candidates for such an unraveling. But who knows which nations will top that list several decades down the road? As Menon says, "the specter of lots of nuclear weapons that are unaccounted for, that are poorly protected and that could therefore be stolen by nasty groups or that could be fired accidentally or willfully because anarchy destroys chains of command was [once] the stuff of sci-fi thrillers."[18] But as any science fiction aficionado knows, the things authors speculate about today often turn out to be what newspaper reporters write about tomorrow—after they happen.

HACKATTACK

In 1998, a *Los Angeles Times* article on computer security made a remarkable assertion. It claimed that it is "probably" impossible for hackers to launch the U.S. nuclear arsenal, "although even this is not completely certain."[19] The newspaper's editors placed that observation on page D3, in their "Cyberculture" section. Apparently it did not occur to them that the possibility, however remote, that your thirteen-year-old geek nephew might initiate global thermonuclear war might be of interest to more than just the readers of the newspaper's computer column.

"U.S. nuclear control is . . . far from fool-proof," said Bruce Blair
in 2003.

> For example, a Pentagon investigation of nuclear safeguards con-
> ducted several years ago made a startling discovery—terrorist
> hackers might be able to gain back-door electronic access to the
> U.S. naval communications network, seize control electronically
> over radio towers such as the one in Cutler, Maine, and illicitly
> transmit a launch order to U.S. Trident ballistic missile submarines
> armed with 200 nuclear warheads apiece. This exposure was deemed
> so serious that Trident launch crews had to be given elaborate new
> instructions for confirming the validity of any launch order they
> receive. They would now reject a firing order that previously would
> have been immediately carried out.[20]

In April 2009, U.S. military officials said that the Pentagon had
spent more than 100 million dollars in the previous six months repair-
ing the damage wrought by external cyber attacks. The perpetrators
ranged from "the bored teenager all the way up to the sophisticated
nation-state," said Air Force general Kevin P. Chilton, and the incur-
sions took place, astonishingly, millions of times each day.[21] It is far from
difficult to envision circumstances in which other states, or non-state
actors, may conclude that their interests would be served by initiating a
launch—against the will of the U.S. government—of the U.S. nuclear
arsenal. Computer hardware, software, and programming technologies
change extremely rapidly, and there are always geek geniuses out there
trying to figure out some razzle-dazzle way to defeat the latest institu-
tional security systems. Most of the time they fail. How long are we
willing to bet the fate of the earth that they will never succeed?

SUBMARINE SCENARIOS

I've noted that the lethality and survivability of our nuclear submarines makes launch on warning essentially pointless. Unfortunately,
however, the very existence of our nuclear submarines opens up yet
another opportunity for catastrophic nuclear error. Many worrisome
accidents, most of them never made public, have taken place aboard
American and Soviet (now Russian) nuclear submarines. Although much
of the information is highly classified, there are dozens of confirmed

cases where nuclear submarines have mistakenly collided with civilian vessels, and friendly or enemy naval vessels (both submarines and surface ships).[22] In the midst of a hot political crisis, such an accidental collision might easily be misinterpreted, and set off a cataclysmic response.

Moreover, nuclear submarines sink. At the beginning of this century, at least eight nuclear submarines—one French, two American, and five Russian—were rotting at the bottom of the sea. Together, they contained nearly fifty nuclear warheads and several hundred human bodies.[23] Setting aside for the moment both the human tragedy and the danger of accidental nuclear launch, consider the ecological damage being wrought by these nuclear reactors and warheads right now, as they almost surely leak uranium and plutonium onto the ocean floor.

In case you think these accidents were all the product of earlier, less-sophisticated generations of submarine technology, recall that in November 2008 more than twenty people died aboard Russia's brand-new nuclear-powered submarine *Nerpa* on its initial performance trial in the Sea of Japan. Apparently, a sailor set off a fire-extinguishing system by mistake, emitting deadly Freon gas into sealed compartments and killing those trapped inside.[24] In February 2009, the British submarine HMS *Vanguard* and the French submarine *Le Triomphant*, each of them nuclear-powered and nuclear-armed, collided in the Atlantic, causing heavy damage to both vessels.[25] Scarcely a month later, on March 20, the day of the Persian New Year, the American nuclear-powered submarine USS *Hartford* collided with the American amphibious vessel USS *New Orleans* in the Strait of Hormuz at the entrance to the Persian Gulf. Fifteen sailors aboard the *Hartford* were injured, and the collision ruptured the fuel tank on the *New Orleans*, spilling 25,000 gallons of marine diesel fuel into the strait.[26]

Perhaps the most disturbing known episode took place in the summer of 2000, when the Russian nuclear-powered submarine *Kursk* (which apparently did not carry nuclear weapons) suffered a torpedo explosion while submerged off Russia's Kola Peninsula, and sank to the bottom of the sea. I remember this episode vividly because it took place during the Democratic National Convention in Los Angeles, and everyone there was talking about it. Over the course of a week, the submarine's oxygen supply dwindled and then ran out, and all 118 seamen aboard perished. Apparently, suffocation is not only an excruciating way to die, but it literally drives a human being out of one's mind. So what might those doomed submariners have done if nuclear-tipped missiles had been aboard? As with so many things nuclear, we are betting the fate of the earth on the assumption that a submarine's dangerous technology will always remain under rational control. Is it really inconceivable that somewhere, sometime, under the sea—especially if we eventually see ten or twenty or fifty nuclear weapon states—some disturbed sailor might just push the button?

THE DOOMSDAY MACHINE

Although its existence has never been definitively proven in the unclassified literature, some allege that during the cold war, the Soviets constructed a nuclear dead-man switch. Its purpose was purportedly to ensure that, after a U.S. nuclear first strike on the USSR, a retaliatory strike would be launched on the United States even if the entire Soviet leadership had been killed or cut off from command and control. Within the internal logic of nuclear deterrence, such a mechanism contained a certain sort of sense. If American leaders ever did contemplate a nuclear first strike, especially one that aspired to decapitate the Soviet political leadership, the existence of a guaranteed retaliatory device should indeed make pulling the trigger less appealing. But for the system to work as a deterrent, Washington would have to know about it. As Dr. Strangelove exclaims to Soviet Ambassador Kissoff in Stanley Kubrick's 1964 film, "Yes, but the . . . whole point of the doomsday machine . . . is lost . . . if you keep it a secret! Why didn't you tell the world, eh?"[27]

Whatever a doomsday machine's effect on deterrence might be, however, it also gives rise to easy-to-conjure scenarios in which the preprogrammed device mistakenly concludes that the USSR—and now Russia—has suffered a nuclear first strike and that its leadership is incapacitated. Perhaps there is a cascade of errors in the computer code. Perhaps only one of the two instigating events—leadership incapacitation or American nuclear first strike—has taken place. Perhaps a rogue individual has manipulated the computers to mistakenly draw those triggering conclusions. Perhaps a limited American nuclear first strike has indeed occurred and has temporarily cut off the Russian leadership, but the situation is an accident that no one on either side wants to escalate. No matter: the doomsday machine launches the massive nuclear retaliatory strike anyway. And ensures that doomsday rains down upon us all. By accident.

IN SPACE, NO ONE CAN HEAR YOU SCREAM

In 2002, U.S. Air Force brigadier general Simon P. Worden told a House science subcommittee about yet another scenario that could lead to accidental atomic apocalypse: asteroid explosions in the earth's atmosphere. Yes, you read that last sentence correctly. Most people are vaguely aware that, however long the odds, on any particular afternoon a collision between our planet and an asteroid of sufficient mass (say, the size of Manhattan) could spell doom for life as we know it. After all, paleontologists now believe that just such a collision suddenly ended the age of dinosaurs some 65 million years ago, and many similar episodes have occurred over the 4.5-billion-year life of our planet. But fewer people know that smaller celestial bodies (say, the size of your neighbor's garage) closely approach earth two or three dozen times per year. As they slash across our atmosphere, they blow up. Those detonations, said General Worden, contain roughly the same explosive force as your average atomic bomb.

The United States possesses sophisticated satellite instruments that can quickly distinguish between an asteroidal blast and an atomic blast. The problem, according to the general, who was then deputy director for operations in the U.S. Strategic Command, is that no one else does. Other nuclear weapon states might mistake a space-rock explosion for an atomic attack, and consequently might launch an atomic retaliation. General Worden offered a specific example. In August 2001, tensions were high between India and Pakistan, and both states were at full military alert, prepared for nuclear war. Just a few weeks before the crisis reached its peak, American satellites detected the explosion of an asteroid fifteen to thirty feet wide over the Mediterranean Sea, a blast that produced "an energy release comparable to the Hiroshima burst." What if the explosion had occurred a few weeks later? What if it had taken place not over the Mediterranean, but over the Indus or the Ganges? "The resulting panic in the nuclear-armed and hair-triggered opposing forces," said the general, "could have been the spark that ignited a nuclear horror we have avoided for over half a century."[28] It sounds like a blockbuster summer disaster movie. Someone may already be working on the screenplay. But the possibility—however long the odds on any particular afternoon—is not fiction.

It really is quite ironic when you think about it. At least it took an impact with something the size of Manhattan to drive the dinosaurs to extinction. Yet an impact with something perhaps as small as your neighbor's garage could quite possibly do exactly the same thing to us. Perhaps we should reconsider just which we should call smarter— dinosaurs or human beings. Dinosaurs, after all, at least knew how not to bring about their own demise by their own hands.

We don't.

A Finger in the Dike

The possibility of accidental atomic apocalypse can be immediately and dramatically reduced if President Obama and the leaders of other nuclear-armed states (notably Russia) take several steps to ensure that no nuclear weapon stands poised to be fired in a matter of minutes. These include:

- End the pointless policy of launch on warning.
- Separate nosecones and nuclear warheads from ballistic missiles and store them in separate facilities. This would dramatically increase the time between a decision to launch and an actual launch, and enhance opportunities for a sober consideration of alternatives. Moreover, it would enhance deterrence because it would create twice as many targets for an adversary to take out on the ground. Pakistan, with far fewer nuclear weapons and far greater vulnerabilities, has already taken this step.[29]
- Similarly, separate air-dropped gravity bombs and air-launched cruise missiles from the aircraft equipped to deliver them and store them at separate airfields.
- Take technical measures to reduce submarines' ability to launch nuclear weapons at short notice. If our nuclear submarines are intended to act only in retaliation for some heinous act of aggression, why does the retaliation have to take place within minutes? Is the deterrent diminished if a devastating retaliation

can be brought about in days rather than minutes—but with every bit as much certainty?

By the time this book is published, President Obama may already have initiated some of these actions. (If not, please ask him why he hasn't.) On the day he took office, the official White House website stated that the new administration intended to "work with Russia to end dangerous Cold War policies like keeping nuclear weapons ready to launch on a moment's notice, in a mutual and verifiable manner."[30] Nonetheless, even if he implements every one of those steps, the possibility of accident will not disappear. As long as nuclear weapons exist, so, too, will possibility of some kind of nuclear cataclysm—by mistake.

ACCIDENTAL LEGACIES AND
ACCIDENTAL DESTINIES

The danger of accidental atomic apocalypse is hardly new. Just as with nuclear terror, it is inherent in the nature of the technology itself. After interviewing several nuclear experts in the Kennedy and Johnson administrations, *New Yorker* writer Daniel Lang said, "Our own officials are haunted by the thought that we may all be ambushed by error, human or mechanical, Soviet or American. They are in almost continuous conclave about this, I learned, their sessions being devoted to imagining what could possibly go wrong."[31]

Albert Schweitzer, whom President Kennedy called "one of the transcendent moral influences of our century," became deeply involved in the nuclear policy debate during the last decade of his life.[32] After awarding Schweitzer the 1952 Nobel Peace Prize—which they could not deliver until 1954 because the recipient refused to take a break from his work at the modern hospital he built at Lambaréné in French Equatorial Africa (now Gabon)—the Nobel committee and Radio Oslo arranged for him to deliver a series of three radio addresses in April 1958, to be broadcast over shortwave radio around the world under the title "Peace or Atomic War?"[33] In the second of these broadcasts, Schweitzer discussed the possibility of nuclear accident with long-range bombers, the delivery technology of the day:

> The necessity for a round-the-clock alert against attack carries with it the extreme danger of an error in interpreting what appears on a

radar screen, when immediate action is imperative, resulting in the outbreak of an atomic war. Attention was drawn to this danger by the American General Curtis Le May when recently the world was on the brink of such a situation. The radar stations of the American Air Force and American coastal command reported that an invasion of unidentified bombers was on the way. Upon this warning the General in command of the strategic bomber force decided to order a reprisal bombardment to commence. However, realizing the enormity of his responsibility, he then hesitated. Shortly afterwards it was discovered that the radar stations had made a tactical error. What could have happened if a less balanced General had been in his place?[34]

A few years later a popular work of fiction elaborated on the real-world situation that Schweitzer had described. The 1962 novel *Fail-Safe*, by Eugene Burdick (co-author of *The Ugly American*) and Harvey Wheeler, may be the single most frightening work of literature ever to spring from the human mind. In 1964, it was made into a film produced and directed by Sidney Lumet; written by Walter Bernstein; and starring Henry Fonda, Dan O'Herlihy, Larry Hagman, and Walter Matthau. Both book and film describe, with excruciating tension and complete plausibility, how a single squadron of American "Vindicator" strategic bombers is ordered to proceed across its "fail-safe" point in the Bering Strait, with each warplane directed to drop two twenty-megaton hydro-gen bombs on Moscow.

But the order is a mistake, conveyed as a result of minor technical mishaps related to an unidentified aircraft flying over the Arctic toward the United States, which is eventually identified as a wildly off-course civilian airliner. American officials in the Strategic Air Command (SAC) in Omaha and in Washington discover the mistaken order long before the bombers reach their target. So the commanding general of SAC gets on the radio, explains the error, and orders the pilots to turn around. The president of the United States gets on the radio, explains the stakes, and orders them to turn around. The wife of the Vindicator squadron commander is rushed to the nearest Air Force base, gets on the radio, and begs her husband to turn around. "There's no war, Jack," she says, weeping. "There's no war."

But the Vindicator pilots have been trained, and ordered, and drilled and drilled and drilled, to accept no kind of recall order once they have passed their predesignated fail-safe point. So the couriers of nuclear doom plunge onward, through the dark Siberian night, as both American and Soviet officials frantically try to improvise ways to stop them—and to avoid a full-scale nuclear war if they fail. I will not reveal how the novel comes out, in case you want to read it. But I will tell you that, once you pick it up, you will not be able to put it down.

"There is substantial agreement among experts that an accidental war is possible, and that its probability increases with the increasing complexity of the man-machine components which make up our defense system," wrote Burdick and Wheeler in the prescient preface to their novel. "The accident may not occur in the way we describe, but the laws of probability assure us that ultimately it will occur. The logic of politics tells us that when it does, the only way out will be a choice of disasters."[35]

Whether Murphy's Law—anything that can go wrong will go wrong—applies to our nuclear fate remains an open question. By the time the world finds out, no one, neither Mr. Murphy nor anyone else, may be around to appreciate the answer. In 2008, the venerable international relations scholar John Steinbruner described the essence of modern strategic nuclear realities: "The countervailing deterrent operations of U.S. and Russian nuclear forces still dominate international security arrangements in operational reality, if not in public consciousness. . . . Both countries continuously maintain several thousand nuclear weapons on alert status, and they are programmed to initiate bombardment within minutes and to complete it within hours. As an objective matter, that situation presents what is by far the greatest physical danger to both of the societies in question, and to all others as well."[36]

This chapter has examined several different scenarios by which nuclear weapons might be launched and detonated by accident. Those with professional technical expertise about nuclear weapons delivery systems and launch authorization procedures could probably construct several more. If such an accidental launch ever takes place—either of a single nuclear weapon or of several hundred—the victims of the accidental nuclear strike might react in many possible different ways. The response of other members of the international community, too—especially those with their own nuclear armaments—could go in any number of directions. Many alternative scenarios could be constructed regarding how events, after one or 101 accidental nuclear launches and detonations, might subsequently unfold.

Some of them might not result in the end of the world.

CHAPTER 5

Nuclear Crisis Mismanagement

"THERE WOULD BE NO LEARNING CURVE"

IN NOVEMBER 2008, about a week after the horrific terror attacks in Mumbai, India, an astonishing episode came to light. The Pakistani newspaper *Dawn* reported that, during the waning hours of the sixty-hour-long siege, the president of nuclear-armed Pakistan, Asif Ali Zardari, took a phone call from the foreign minister of nuclear-armed India, Pranab Mukherjee. The message from Delhi was blunt, directly threatening Islamabad with military action in response to the Mumbai attacks. Immediately following the call, Pakistan placed its air force on its highest alert level and directed its warplanes to patrol the skies with live weapons.

There was only one problem: the telephone call was a hoax.[1] A prank call. A splendid gag!

We might have all died laughing.

Nuclear miscalculation is a scenario that almost no one talks about anymore. It is as if we got through the Cuban missile crisis, so we don't ever have to worry about something similar ever happening again. But in a nuclear-armed world there remains the singular danger that some-time, somewhere, some head of state, in the midst of some kind of political beef with some other state, is going to misjudge the adversary, or the geopolitics, or the political winds, or the veracity of a prank caller, or his mistress's mood, and abruptly decide that the only option is to fire off a few nuclear missiles—right now. It is easy to imagine a pair of national leaders in a hot political crisis: under extraordinary pressure, haven't slept for three days, sweating, taking advice from five sides at once. And then one of them begins to engage in an insidious logic—deciding that the other leader must be planning to launch a nuclear first strike, and concluding that the only way to forestall that is to launch a nuclear first strike first. So he pushes the button.

The danger that a deteriorating political crisis will go nuclear is probably increased by the accidental-launch danger discussed in Chapter 4. In a hot political crisis, with both tempers and uncertainties escalating, one side might be more likely to conclude that the other side is planning a nuclear first strike if the other side's nuclear forces could be launched within minutes of decision. In such a case, one side may decide to roll the dice, and strike first.

People don't think straight when they are bombarded with uncertainty, or when then they are wound up in anger, or when they are filled with fear. Crises can spin out of control; decision makers can misunderstand, miscommunicate, and misjudge. In matters of war and peace, political events take on a momentum of their own, and even the instigators may not be able to turn them around. "Any fool can start a war," said Khrushchev, "and once he's done so, even the wisest of men are helpless to stop it—especially if it's a nuclear war."[2]

In 1959, when the nuclear age was not yet two decades old, philosopher Bertrand Russell wrote about the importance that pride, honor, and self-esteem might play in such a context: "The game may be played without misfortune a few times, but sooner or later it will come to be felt that loss of face is more dreadful than nuclear annihilation. The moment will come when neither side can face the derisive cry of 'Chicken' from the other side. When that moment is come, the statesmen of both sides will plunge the world into destruction."[3] Decades later comedian George Carlin, more coarsely, made much the same point. Speaking about India and Pakistan, he said, "I'm telling you, somebody is going to fuck somebody's sister and an atom bomb is going to fly. . . . Tune in and watch the human adventure. It's a cursed, doomed species."[4]

Astronomer Carl Sagan also wrote about the irrationality that lies so close to the human surface and the circumstances that cause it to emerge. Nuclear deterrence proponents, he said, contend "that hydrogen bombs keep the peace, or at least prevent thermonuclear war, because the consequences of warfare between nuclear powers are now too dangerous."

We haven't had a nuclear war yet, have we? But all such arguments assume that the nuclear-armed nations are and always will be, without exception, rational actors, and that bouts of anger and revenge and madness will never overtake their leaders. . . . [But] whenever our ethnic or national prejudices are aroused, in times of scarcity, during challenges to national self esteem or nerve, when we agonize about our diminished cosmic place and purpose, or when fanaticism is bubbling up around us—then, habits of thought familiar from ages past reach for the controls.[5]

The human instinct to strike first and ask questions later is probably deeply coded in our genetic makeup. Nicholas Wade's marvelous book *Before the Dawn: Recovering the Lost History of Our Ancestors* emphasizes the incessant warfare and extreme intraspecies violence that apparently plagued virtually all human communities throughout prehistory.[6] In the ancestral environment, the act of quickly killing other humans, especially strangers, before asking questions arguably carried a strong survival value. Those who showed an ability to ruthlessly and remorselessly kill the other guy first were more likely to procreate, and to keep their progeny alive long enough so that they could procreate themselves. Those who were less violent and more cautious, who hesitated at countless ancestral moments of truth, often did not succeed in passing on their genes to the next generation.

However unpleasant it may be to contemplate, every living human likely carries more genes from the "hit fast and hit hard" type rather than the "we can work it out" type. So how likely is it that every living human facing a perilous, fast-moving, potentially nuclear crisis will, in every instance, act slowly and cautiously? Isn't it far more likely that, eventually, someone will act quickly and ruthlessly when facing a nuclear moment of truth?

COLD WAR NUCLEAR CRISES

Few individual international political events have been examined in more excruciating detail than the Cuban missile crisis.[7] And with good reason: historian Arthur Schlesinger, Jr., who served as an aide in the Kennedy White House during the crisis, has justly called it "the most dangerous moment in human history."[8] By the fall of 1962, the United

States and the Soviet Union possessed numerous nuclear weapons within their own borders, and each country was capable, from its own homeland, of striking the other. But unlike Moscow, Washington had also deployed nuclear weapons in European countries very close to the USSR border. Khrushchev badly wanted to match that capability. Therefore, he surreptitiously tried to install nuclear-tipped missiles in Cuba, the USSR's new communist ally.

Midway through the installation process, Washington learned about the plan. During an unbearably tense thirteen-day period in October, the Kennedy administration grappled with its options. (It was arguably the first overt appearance of a nuclear double standard. The essential American position at the outset of the crisis was "We can deploy nuclear-tipped missiles adjacent to your borders, but you cannot deploy nuclear-tipped missiles adjacent to ours.") According to Secretary of Defense Robert McNamara, "the majority of Kennedy's military and civilian advisors" recommended some kind of military strike.[9] In such an event, the Soviets would undoubtedly have responded with some kind of military action of their own. And any such response could easily have escalated to nuclear confrontation. It was the closest the United States and the Soviet Union ever came to directly shooting at each other. And it was the closest the human race has ever come to global thermonuclear war.

Perhaps the most disturbing element of the Cuban missile crisis is that nothing essential to the security of either side was really at stake. The presence of a few dozen Soviet nuclear-tipped missiles in Cuba did not fundamentally affect the strategic balance between the two great cold war antagonists. On both sides, the strategic calculations and tangible actions undertaken during the crisis centered more on psychology, prestige, and posture—the urge to stand up to an opponent and maintain an image of strength, resolve, and credibility among domestic and foreign audiences. Both needed a resolution that would save face, that would avoid "the derisive cry of 'Chicken' from the other side."

Yet those intangible considerations produced astonishing tangible decisions. Philosopher John Somerville wrote about the crisis in the mid-1980s, when cold war tensions and fears of nuclear escalation were once again in the air:

> In some ways the most important and incredible fact [of the entire nuclear age] is that the executive leaders of the Kennedy

administration in 1962 . . . deliberately made a decision which they admittedly expected to result in the annihilation of the human race. . . . President Kennedy's brother Robert . . . wrote a small book about it . . . [that] was also printed in a popular family magazine. . . . But the strange thing was that neither the book nor the magazine publications caused any outcry of indignation, though the text demonstrated, in the most explicit detail, that the president and the other leaders "expected" the ultimatum they sent to the Soviets would not be obeyed, and that the resulting world conflict would be "the end of mankind." . . . I concluded that the reason there was no outcry of public indignation . . . was the fact that the readers could not really believe it happened that way.[10]

In the fall of 1983, the human community stood at the abyss of atomic annihilation once again, this time for a different reason. Even with the massive apparatus of the American intelligence establishment, and despite the brainpower exerted by professional Sovietologists, this time we simply had no idea what was going on in the minds on the other side.

In March of that year, when President Ronald Reagan announced his Strategic Defense Initiative in March (popularly known as Star Wars), Soviet leaders took it very seriously. Their fear was that the United States might create a missile defense capability that would enable it to launch a nuclear first strike on the USSR and then defend itself against the few remaining Soviet missiles that might survive such an attack. Soviet defense planners worried that, for American defense planners, a surprise nuclear strike might come to seem like a rational policy option. By the fall, according to cold war historian John Lewis Gaddis, Soviet fears regarding such a scenario "approached panic."[11]

The first extraordinarily dangerous consequence occurred on September 1, when a South Korean airliner inadvertently strayed over Soviet airspace above Sakhalin Island. Military officials in Moscow, on edge, rapidly gave the order to shoot it down, killing 269 civilian air passengers, including sixty-nine Americans. Millions in the United States were outraged and demanded retaliation. But the Soviets never admitted any mistake. In fact, general secretary Yuri Andropov claimed that the incident had been a "sophisticated provocation organized by the U.S. special services." It is not hyperbole to say that for the next few weeks, the two superpowers were on the brink of military confrontation.

Then, two months later, something infinitely more perilous ensued, although virtually no one in the west knew about it at the time. Every previous autumn for many years, the United States and its NATO allies had conducted military exercises in Europe. For whatever reason, the 1983 maneuvers, called "Able Archer 83," engaged high-level western officials to an unusually large extent. Soviet intelligence learned of this heightened interest, and Andropov and his high command became convinced, at least for a short time, that an American nuclear first strike on the USSR was imminent. "It was probably the most dangerous moment since the Cuban missile crisis," says Gaddis, "and yet no one in Washington knew of it until a well-placed spy in the KGB's London headquarters alerted British intelligence, which passed the information along to the Americans." Washington quickly ratcheted down its military maneuvers. But even the greenest Hollywood screenwriter could pen an alternative ending to Able Archer 83, one in which Andropov, convinced that the Americans were determined to strike first, concluded that his only responsible action to defend Soviet national security was to order his own commanders to launch a nuclear first strike first. Which, in all likelihood, would have also been the last.

FOR WANT OF A NAIL THE SHOE WAS LOST

One might argue that both the Cuban missile crisis and the Able Archer episode took place during the heart of the cold war, when the central political problem of the age was the danger that a minor east-west dispute might escalate to global thermonuclear war. And the cold war has long since passed. Surely there is no possibility now that a minor international political misunderstanding could escalate to global thermonuclear war. What could possibly lead to that today?

Try a mistaken computer barcode entry in a Defense Logistics Agency warehouse in Utah. The previous chapter discussed the inadvertent shipment of nuclear ICBM nose cone fuses to Taiwan, in the context of nuclear accident. For nearly four decades, Taipei has aspired to obtain nuclear weapons, and China and the United States have worked in tandem to prevent it from doing so. Few things could do more to shake up the status quo between China and Taiwan than if the latter were to obtain nuclear weapons. The People's Republic of China (PRC) on the mainland has maintained since its birth in 1949 that the

Republic of China (ROC) on Taiwan is legitimately and historically a province of China and that the two parties will one day to be reunited. Because matters of historical integrity and deep national pride are at stake, the PRC is intransigent about this issue to an extremely irrational extent. China has always maintained the option of undertaking a full-scale military assault on the ROC in order to restore Beijing's sovereignty over the island. A nuclear-armed Taiwan would eliminate that option, by giving the ROC the capability to inflict cataclysmic damage on the Chinese mainland before capitulating to a Chinese assault.

NBC News producer Robert Windrem has elaborated on the history of Taiwan's efforts to obtain nuclear capabilities, and of Washington's and Beijing's intensive pressures to keep that from taking place.[12] According to Windrem, Beijing knows that such an eventuality would fundamentally change the balance of power as well as its available options, while Washington wants at all costs to avoid war with China over the fate of the island republic. So let's return to the accidental shipment of nuclear nosecone fuses. Consider how the United States might have reacted if we had discovered that, say, China had sent nuclear detonation devices to Syria, or that India had sent them to Venezuela. "This is really unbelievable," said Joseph Cirincione when the Taiwan incident became public. "If the Russians had shipped triggers to Tehran, we would be going nuts right now."[13]

On the other hand, consider how Beijing might have misinterpreted the mistaken fuse shipment if its intelligence sources had revealed it before Washington itself had alerted Beijing. Imagine this alternative history: The PRC discovers that the United States has shipped crucial components of its largest nuclear weapons to Taiwan—before the United States does. This is hardly implausible. Beijing undoubtedly undertakes elaborate intelligence operations on Taiwan and knows infinitely more about what is happening on the island than we do. After intensive consultations at the highest levels of the Communist party leadership, perhaps incorporating intelligence reports on other matters and the Chinese-American political winds of the hour, the PRC high command concludes that Washington intends to slip Taiwan a few nuclear weapons. As a consequence, they also decide that they must act to avoid that eventuality. Immediately.

The next morning, Chinese warplanes launch massive conventional airstrikes on all Taiwanese military facilities. On a per capita basis Taiwan is one of the most heavily militarized places on earth, yet a land of 22 million people is no match for a PRC of 1.3 billion. Taipei frantically reminds the United States of its repeated pledges to defend Taiwan against Chinese aggression, promises that date back to the inception of the two states in 1949. The White House administration, whether Democrat or Republican, immediately finds itself under intense pressure from the right—especially since not a single American official has any idea about the mistaken nuclear fuse shipment.

So America responds, but in a precise and limited way. U.S. naval aircraft, armed only with conventional weapons, begin to take out Chinese warplanes in the air over the Straits of Taiwan, and on selected airfields on the Chinese mainland. The president announces that America intends no aggression against the PRC, but is acting only against those Chinese forces directly attacking the ROC. Nevertheless, leaders in Beijing know they cannot back off now, especially since they genuinely believe that Taiwan is about to become a nuclear weapon state. Because their air force is no match for the technologically superior American juggernaut, they conclude that their only defense is to escalate.

Despite the PRC's longstanding pledge of "no first use" of a nuclear weapon, suddenly the entire American aircraft carrier battle group that had been launching attacks on Chinese aircraft and airfields from the East China Sea is vaporized by the detonation, from 3,000 feet overhead, of a single Chinese nuclear warhead.

Within minutes, long-dormant U.S. nuclear contingency plans swing into action. Massive assaults, both nuclear and conventional, rain down upon every known Chinese nuclear weapon installation and facility. But before the United States can succeed in eliminating the entire Chinese nuclear arsenal, a single Chinese Dong Feng 31-A nuclear-armed intercontinental ballistic missile successfully launches into the stratosphere. No real decision was made by the Chinese leadership to fire it. Instead, low-level Chinese missile officers, executing longstanding orders for how to react if the country's nuclear missile silos are under direct attack, push the button.

Less than an hour later, at about 3,000 feet above Griffith Park in the middle of Los Angeles, the four-hundred-kiloton nuclear warhead contained in the nosecone of the Dong Feng 31-A detonates. More than 1 million Southern Californians die instantly. More than 10 million others receive an instant death sentence, as catastrophic radioactive contamination rains down upon them.

No real decisions are made by the American political leadership after this point either. Massive retaliation commences almost automatically. Less than an hour after the disappearance of Los Angeles, American nuclear submarines deep under the surface of the Pacific launch dozens of powerful nuclear-tipped ballistic missiles toward China. Less than a half hour later, they detonate over dozens of Chinese cities. More than 100 million Chinese die instantly. Nearly a billion—practically the whole population of China and nearly one-sixth of all living humans—are exposed to radioactive fallout, receiving an instant death sentence of their own.

All, narrowly, for want of a nail. Or, more precisely, for want of a correct computer barcode entry in a Defense Logistics Agency warehouse in Utah. All, broadly, because our leaders still had failed to grasp the most fundamental truth of the nuclear age—that any benefits nuclear weapons may bring for our own national security are exceeded by the virtually infinite risks. For our own national security, and for humanity as a whole.

CRISIS AND CONSEQUENCE

"Allen Funt Lets President Kennedy in on Hilarious 'Cuban Missile Crisis' Prank," declared the October 29, 1962, headline of the *Onion*. "JFK a Good Sport, Says Host of TV's *Candid Camera*." The faux news story elaborated:

> Following a briefing by the "Joint Chiefs of Staff" (in actuality, professional actors) . . . Kennedy was surprised by a loud knock at the Oval Office door. Funt, who has passed himself off as Nikita Khrushchev for the last two weeks in a series of increasingly implausible televised speeches, walked unimpeded through a phalanx of "Secret Service agents" and approached the president. . . . According to Arthur Schlesinger Jr., special advisor to the president and one of the prank's principal conspirators, the confused Kennedy then turned to his brother, Attorney General Robert Kennedy, who had "turned beet-red and was biting his knuckle" to keep from bursting into laughter. "At that point," Schlesinger said, "I think Jack figured something was up."[14]

In Chapter 4, I compared the catastrophic consequences of a nuclear terror attack to the incomprehensibly greater consequences of an accidental nuclear war. The identical point must surely be made about the possibility that an ordinary international political crisis might escalate to nuclear war. Writer and ecologist Jane Shevtsov attempts to quantify these consequences, and suggests that doing so ought to guide us in choosing how much effort to devote to alternative preventative priorities:

> When we evaluate risks, we must look at both probability and magnitude. Let's look at the most basic level of threat, that of lives lost (ignoring the consequences of a major terrorist attack for democracy and the possibility of civilizational annihilation in all-out nuclear war). At worst, a nuclear terror attack could kill millions, although tens to hundreds of thousands seems more likely. However, the worst-case scenario in a nuclear war is the death of billions, although tens to hundreds of millions may be more probable. That is a difference of about three orders of magnitude—a thousand times. Nuclear terrorism, even with several million deaths, is probably much more likely over the next 20, 50, or 100 years than nuclear war. But is it a thousand times more likely?[15]

Robert McNamara, again drawing upon his experience as U.S. secretary of defense during the Cuban missile crisis, has made a similar point. Nuclear crisis mismanagement, he said in 1998, "is a risk I don't believe the human race should accept. . . . Many people don't understand . . . that, quite unintentionally, we can maneuver ourselves into a position where these things would be used. They don't understand the fog of war."[16] McNamara elaborated in 2005: "Among the costs of maintaining nuclear weapons is the risk . . . of use of the weapons either by accident or as a result of misjudgment or miscalculation in times of crisis. . . . In conventional war, mistakes cost lives, sometimes thousands of lives. However, if mistakes were to affect decisions relating to the use of nuclear forces, there would be no learning curve. They would result in the destruction of nations."[17]

Of course, after one side in an international political showdown actually does pull the nuclear trigger, when we find ourselves on the other side of the nuclear moment of truth, that rage, fear, and less-than-fully-rational thinking will only intensify. Misunderstandings, miscalculations, and miscommunications will likely become even more chaotic and unpredictable, driven not so much by the irrationalities of the people in charge, but by a victimized population that has been transformed, in an instant, into an angry, hyperventilating, hypernationalistic mob. As in the case of nuclear terror, it is difficult to imagine any national leader resisting such pressures indefinitely.

Jaroslaw Anders has written eloquently about the primal forces that overtake *homo sapiens* at such moments:

> War, as a tool of rational policy, does not make much sense. . . . It would be hard to mention one war whose results neatly coincided with the designs of its architects and advocates. It was known since the times of Homer that war is a costly, unwieldy and capricious instrument. . . . None of this, however, prevented wars from happening, perhaps because war never was deployed in a fully rational manner. . . . War draws much of its energies, and much of its perverse allure, from mythology, hubris, fear, religious frenzy, moralist zeal and grandiose historical visions.[18]

As is the case with near accidental nuclear launches, the few known episodes of nuclear crisis mismanagement examined in this chapter are probably only the tip of the iceberg. Was 2006 really the only time that a nuclear weapon state shipped key components of nuclear weapons abroad by mistake? Was 1983 really the only time that some adversary concluded that its opponent's military maneuvers were in reality preparations for nuclear war? More importantly, can we really expect, if we retain nuclear weapons for another twenty or thirty or fifty years, that not a single nuclear crisis will ever descend into nuclear war? Perhaps when Arthur Schlesinger, Jr., insisted that October 1962 was "the most dangerous moment in human history," he should have added two words: so far.

CHAPTER 6

Intentional Use

THE NUCLEAR LEGACY
OF GEORGE W. BUSH

A NUCLEAR TERROR ATTACK, executed by a non-state actor, is one terrifying scenario by which an actual nuclear detonation might take place. An accidental nuclear launch or even an accidental nuclear war, from the potent nuclear arsenal of a state, is another. And an international political confrontation between nuclear-armed states spinning wildly out of control, and escalating from nuclear crisis to nuclear war, is another still. This chapter explores a fourth scenario: a government's conscious employment of nuclear weapons. Unlike the previous three scenarios, this one has already occurred. The U.S. bombings of Hiroshima and Nagasaki were the result of rational decision, not a rash, ill-considered, heat-of-the-moment act. And someday the leadership of another nuclear state may make a similar decision, concluding, not from fear and panic but after a sober, calm, detached cost-benefit analysis that they ought to start a nuclear war.

Which state, in recent years, has seemed most likely to make such a decision? You only get one guess. Because the administration of George W. Bush, throughout its tenure, publicly contemplated and codified both new nuclear weapons development plans and a new nuclear war fighting doctrine that proffered just that possibility. The administration announced its radical shift away from traditional American nuclear doctrines in several documents that received astonishingly little public comment or attention: the "Nuclear Posture Review" (NPR) of December 2001, the "National Security Presidential Directive 14" of June 2002, the "National Security Strategy of the United States of America" of September 2002 (with a revised version released in March 2006), the "National Security Presidential Directive 17" of September 2002, the

"National Security Strategy to Counter Weapons of Mass Destruction" of December 2002, the "Nuclear Weapons Employment Policy" signed by Secretary of Defense Rumsfeld in 2004, and the "Doctrine for Joint Nuclear Operations" of September 2005. These documents insisted that American national interests might require American nuclear first strikes and maintained that the United States must be prepared to initiate nuclear war. They articulated several new scenarios in which American nuclear weapons might be employed in new military situations, and even identified seven particular states as possible targets of a nuclear first strike.

Several books have already comprehensively reviewed Bush's nuclear legacy, including James Wirtz's *Nuclear Transformation: The New U.S. Nuclear Doctrine*, Amy Woolf's *U.S. Nuclear Weapons: Changes in Policy and Force Structure*, and Steven Weinberg's *Glory and Terror: The Growing Nuclear Danger*, all of which elaborately describe and analyze his administration's nuclear weapons policies, especially the landmark "Nuclear Posture Review" of December 2001.[1] Jonathan Schell's *The Seventh Decade: The New Shape of Nuclear Danger*, goes even further.[2] Schell emphasizes just how great a departure Bush's nuclear policies were from those that precariously evaded nuclear catastrophe during the first half century of the nuclear age. He examines the administration's efforts to modernize nuclear weapons, its doctrine of preventive war (including the possible first use of American nuclear weapons), and its pursuit of a military hegemony spanning the whole planet. Schell makes the case that these policies, on balance, enhanced the likelihood of continuous nuclear proliferation, and eventual nuclear catastrophe.

But we must briefly examine the nuclear weapons policy record of George W. Bush here because the nuclear weapons employment doctrines promulgated by the previous administration do, indeed, constitute a fourth scenario for nuclear weapons use. They show how tempting it was for policy analysts to conclude that launching nuclear weapons might be a rational policy option. And they suggest how easy it might be for other defense planners, in the years to come, in the United States or elsewhere, to arrive at the same conclusion again. As long as the human race holds on to nuclear weapons, the possibility will persist that someone, someday, will soberly conclude that good things will result from their use.

PERPETUAL POSSESSION

In 2005 Jeffrey Sachs of Columbia University published a book boldly insisting that we can eradicate extreme poverty from the face of the earth by 2025.[3] During his 2000 presidential campaign, Vice President Al Gore talked about eliminating the internal combustion engine by the same date. "Why is it so hard," asked Dan Plesch of the British American Security Information Council, "for the U.S. to think about how we could get rid of nuclear weapons in that same time frame?"[4]

The Bush Administration did in fact demonstrate a capacity for thinking about such time frames. However, they did not think about getting rid of nuclear weapons during that period, but rather about prolonging our reliance upon them.

The administration advanced a multi-decade, multibillion-dollar plan to rebuild the nation's nuclear weapons production infrastructure. The idea was both to modernize existing nuclear weapons production facilities and to construct new ones, thus enabling the United States to mass-produce new nuclear weapons for the first time since the end of the cold war. Administration officials initially called the plan Complex 2030. Then, in a shift overlooked by opposition political figures as well as the peace community, they changed the name to Complex Transformation, apparently in order to de-emphasize the fact that the plan ensured that the United States would retain thousands of nuclear weapons for at least the next three decades. The administration sought to build "mini-nukes" (an oxymoron if there ever was one), with the explicit intent of removing the "self-deterrent" that a U.S. president might perceive in launching nuclear weapons with a larger yield. Officials sought to develop a new "bunker buster" nuclear weapon that would burrow deep into the earth before detonating, with the goal of destroying hardened underground command posts and weapons caches. They sought to construct a plant to produce new "plutonium pits"—the fissile core of most nuclear warheads—that was scheduled to commence operations in 2020.[5]

It is important to distinguish between nuclear weapons delivery systems and the nuclear weapons or warheads themselves. An intercontinental ballistic missile, for example, is the system that delivers the powerful nuclear warhead contained in its nosecone to a desired target. A combat warplane, or bomber, is the system that delivers a gravity-dropped nuclear bomb or a nuclear cruise missile to a desired target. Both a submarine-launched ballistic missile and the submarine are delivery systems themselves.

A nuclear weapons modernization program might begin to develop new versions of nuclear weapons delivery systems but not new nuclear warheads, or vice versa. Not surprisingly, however, the Bush administration did both. Complex Transformation and the NPR contained plans to construct a brand new ICBM that would come on line in 2018. They envisioned unveiling a brand new SLBM in 2029. They anticipated the christening of a new intercontinental heavy nuclear bomber in 2040.[6] Moreover, all would be equipped to deliver various incarnations of a new nuclear weapon—what the nuclear weaponeers called the "reliable replacement warhead." And everything would be ready by 2045—just in time for the centennial of the dawn of the atomic age.

"The Bush Doctrine": Not Just Preemption but Nuclear Preemption

It would be one thing if the Bush administration had only put forth elaborate plans for modernizing and expanding the American nuclear arsenal for many decades to come. It is another thing entirely to advance new nuclear weapons employment doctrines that envision actually using American nuclear weapons first, in a wide variety of unprecedented military situations. Not surprisingly, the Bush administration did both.

Yet Bush was not the first president to begin contemplating the use of nuclear weapons as war-fighting tools in the post–cold war era. That person was President Bill Clinton. Almost immediately after the end of the cold war, Defense Department NUTS naturally began to think about a new role for nuclear weapons in American national security strategies. A concept emerged, which soon became official Clinton administration doctrine, that nuclear weapons could serve as a counterproliferant—that is, be used in preemptive first strikes to prevent rogue states or non-state actors from acquiring weapons of mass destruction.[7]

Nevertheless, two dates—Bush's inauguration on January 20, 2001, and the terrorist attacks in Pennsylvania, Washington, and New York on September 11, 2001—mark the most significant turning points in post–cold war American nuclear history. The Bush administration not only followed the Clinton administration's lead in installing such thinking as official doctrine, it also "rattled the nuclear saber," making quite explicit nuclear threats. And it apparently thought very seriously, in at least one case, about carrying those nuclear threats out.

The NPR of December 2001 specifically contemplated the use of American nuclear weapons against non-nuclear threats. It envisioned launching them both in response to a chemical or biological attack and preemptively against suspected chemical or biological weapons depots or development facilities. More disturbingly, the NPR stated that it might become necessary to use American nuclear weapons in response to "surprising military developments" and "unexpected contingencies." Rather than trying to specifically delineate possible use scenarios and forcibly proscribe all others, this catchall language conspicuously proffered no limitations at all.[8] The NPR was soon followed by other confirmations of American nuclear doctrinal transformation. In late 2002, the *Washington Post* revealed that the president, in the highly classified document "National Security Presidential Directive 17," specifically authorized preemptive nuclear first strikes if U.S. intelligence could conclude that specific targets might contain chemical, biological, or nuclear weapons.[9]

Three years later, the Pentagon released its revised nuclear weapons employment principles in its "Doctrine for Joint Nuclear Operations." This document envisioned using nuclear weapons for "attacks on adversary installations including WMD [and] deep hardened bunkers containing chemical or biological weapons" and said that the United States must be prepared to use nuclear weapons "to prevent" other states from using or even acquiring weapons of mass destruction.[10]

The doctrine of using nuclear weapons as a tool of preemption was breathtaking in its audacity. Traditionally, the United States had threatened to use nuclear weapons primarily to deter others from using nuclear weapons. Now we were threatening to use them to deter others from using chemical and biological weapons as well. Moreover, nuclear preemption proposed nuclear first strikes to prevent others from even building such weapons. Secretary of State Powell voiced the change explicitly: "For those nations that are developing these kinds of weapons of mass destruction, it does not seem to us to be a bad thing for them to look out from their little countries and their little capitals and see a United States that has a full range of options."[11] Few statements could more plainly be construed not just as a preemptive threat, but as a direct nuclear threat. Thinking of developing nuclear weapons, little country? Or even chemical or biological weapons, little capital? If so, be warned. The United States may call upon its "full range of options" to keep you from doing so.

THE BUSH DOCTRINE, NUCLEAR PREEMPTION, AND IRAN

Most informed Americans will remember that the question of whether or not to launch a preemptive military strike on Iran was the central foreign policy question of George W. Bush's second term. But fewer people know that numerous reports indicated that the administration was contemplating not just a preemptive military attack to prevent Iran from acquiring nuclear weapons, but a preemptive nuclear attack. This news became public in the April 17, 2006, issue of the *New Yorker*, where investigative journalist Seymour Hersh alleged that, to prevent Iran from acquiring nuclear weapons perhaps five to ten years down the road, Pentagon planners were preparing nuclear strikes upon Iran. According to Hersh, some U.S. analysts insisted that our use of tactical nuclear warheads was the only way to eliminate Tehran's nascent nuclear capability.

President Bush had the opportunity to disavow Hersh's stunning charge on April 18, when a reporter asked him directly if his administration was planning a nuclear strike on Iran. His reply was the exact formulation he had used many times before: "All options are on the table."[12] Later Bush referred to the Hersh reports as "wild speculation," and White House spokesman Scott McClellan said the United States intended to press ahead with "normal military contingency planning."[13] But as Matthew Rothschild of the *Progressive* observed at the time, those were "hardly categorical denials."[14] Six weeks later, when Secretary of State Condoleezza Rice announced that Washington was willing to negotiate directly with Tehran if it suspended enrichment and reprocessing, she was asked if this meant that plans to attack Iran, with conventional or nuclear weapons, had been shelved. Mr. Bush, replied Rice, "was not going to take any of his options off the table."[15]

In the July 10, 2006, issue of the *New Yorker*, Hersh reported that, after lengthy and heated internal Pentagon debates, the military brass had persuaded the president that, for the time being, a nuclear attack on

Iran would be "politically unacceptable." But then, on January 7, 2007, the *Sunday Times of London* reported that Israel had begun laying the groundwork for a series of nuclear strikes of its own on the Iranian nuclear infrastructure—perhaps using tactical nuclear weapons supplied by the United States, and perhaps also in conjunction with American forces. In addition, Robert S. Norris and Hans M. Kristensen reported in the March–April 2008 issue of the *Bulletin of the Atomic Scientists* that the "national nuclear war plan" of October 2004 included "executable, scenario-based [nuclear] strike options against regional states, including North Korea and Iran."[16] If all this were not worrisome enough, in a CNN presidential debate on June 5, 2007, four of the Republican presidential candidates indicated that, to prevent Iran from acquiring nuclear weapons, they would consider launching an American nuclear first strike against it.[17]

In response to these reports and ruminations, the nuclear disarmament advocacy group Physicians for Social Responsibility conducted a study of the likely medical consequences of a nuclear first strike on Iran. PSR has a long history of such analyses: in 1961, it published groundbreaking research on the medical results of nuclear detonations and nuclear war in the *New England Journal of Medicine*. Using unclassified software developed by the U.S. Department of Defense, PSR concluded that a U.S. nuclear attack on the Iranian facilities at Isfahan and Natanz would kill 2.6 million people within forty-eight hours. Soon thereafter, 10.5 million more would be exposed to catastrophic radioactive fallout in Iran, Afghanistan, Pakistan, and India. Much of that fallout could make vast areas uninhabitable for decades.[18]

Death penalty opponents often display an unanswerable bumper sticker: "Why do we kill people who kill people to show that killing people is wrong?" In the nuclear context, we might ask, "How can we contemplate nuking people who might nuke people to show that nuking people is wrong?" The United States, during the Bush administration, apparently considered using nuclear weapons to keep another state from obtaining nuclear weapons. In this way, we would have demonstrated the illegitimacy and unacceptability of nuclear weapons in the modern world. And we would have delivered a message of irony so towering, so bald, and so unsubtle, that not a single member of the world's Islamic community would have failed to take notice.

Once anyone actually uses a nuclear warhead, there will be no turning back. The taboo against using nuclear weapons that has prevailed since Hiroshima and Nagasaki will prevail no more. The distinction between conventional and nuclear war will forever be lost. The nuclear Pandora's box, kept so precariously closed since August 9, 1945, will never be shut again.

INTERLUDE: THE FOLLY OF PREEMPTION ITSELF

During George W. Bush's first term, guerilla political artist Robbie Conal drew a popular caricature sketch of Secretary of Defense Rumsfeld with the simple caption "Secretary of Offense." The previous four chapters of *Apocalypse Never* focus on four scenarios in which the possession of nuclear weapons could result in the detonation of nuclear weapons, with cataclysmic consequences. However, perhaps the reader will indulge a slight departure from that focus here. The Bush administration formally instituted a doctrine of preemptive war, with either conventional or nuclear forces, and carried out that doctrine (with conventional forces only) in the sands of Mesopotamia with terrible consequences. Moreover, the Obama administration has hardly taken preemptive war categorically off the table—most especially, again, with regard to Iran. So it is well worth exploring why any kind of preemptive war can be catastrophic, not only for the human community as a whole, but specifically for American national security.

First, it is necessary to distinguish between the terms *preemptive war* and *preventive war*. The former traditionally connotes undertaking military action when a threat is imminent. Israel offers a classic example: it preemptively fired the first shots in the Six Day War of 1967, but only after Arab governments had overtly thrown out U.N. peacekeeping "tripwire" forces along the Israeli border and begun to mass Arab armies there instead. The latter traditionally connotes undertaking military action against a threat that is distant, speculative, and hypothetical. By this reckoning, then, what the Bush administration really instituted was a doctrine of preventive war. Nevertheless, most of the commentary about conceptual national security shifts equated the Bush doctrine with the doctrine of preemption; so I will continue to use that term here, even though in most cases *preventive* is more accurate.

Few have spoken more eloquently against the folly of preemptive war (albeit in a different historical context) than American diplomat and U.N. official Ralph Bunche when he accepted his Nobel Peace Prize at the University of Oslo on December 11, 1950: "There are some in the world who are prematurely resigned to the inevitability of war. Among them are the advocates of the so-called 'preventive war,' who, in their resignation to war, wish merely to select their own time for initiating it. To suggest that war can prevent war is a base play on words and a despicable form of warmongering. . . . The world has had ample evidence that war begets only conditions which beget further war."[19]

It is worth drawing a distinction between different kinds of goals that preemptive war might be undertaken to achieve. One might be preemptive military action to remove the government of a state that is, in our judgment, pursuing nuclear weapons or other weapons of mass destruction, harboring terrorists, or committing some other defined-by-us sin. This is the kind of preemptive war that the Bush administration launched in March 2003 against Iraq. A fundamentally different goal of preemptive war would be military action directed simply at removing a state's actual or potential nuclear or WMD capabilities, or perhaps at degrading its overall military capabilities. Arthur Schlesinger, Jr., pointed out repeatedly that the administration never entirely clarified how these kinds of preemptive strikes would differ from what the Japanese did to us at Pearl Harbor.[20]

Not surprisingly, the Bush administration, in its nuclear doctrines and its broader national security doctrines, declared its intent to undertake both forms of preemptive war. Yet it never undertook the second, though it probably would have done so if had it chosen to pull the trigger on Iran. (Israel has done so, at least twice, in its air assault on Iraq's Osirak nuclear reactor on June 7, 1981, and in its air assault on alleged Syrian nuclear facilities on September 6, 2007.) Even the darkest interpretations of the administration's plans for Iran rarely suggested that a regime-changing invasion was in the cards. For one thing, the American military was massively overstretched by Iraq, Afghanistan, and the global war on terror. It probably did not possess the capability, after the Iraq invasion, even to remove the regime in Iran, let alone to occupy and endeavor to stabilize the country afterward. Not only does Iran contain more than twice the population and more than three times the land mass of Iraq, but our misadventure in Iraq didn't prove to be quite as quick and easy as its neoconservative architects had anticipated in early 2003.

Yet the Bush administration did not necessarily plan on limiting itself to inflicting "surgical" air operations on Iran's nuclear facilities either. "They're about taking out the entire Iranian military," said Alexis Debat, director of terrorism and national security at the Nixon Center, somewhat breathlessly in late 2007.[21] Indeed, the likeliest scenario was a massive and prolonged series of U.S. air and missile strikes carried out continuously for at least a couple of weeks, directed at destroying the nascent Iranian nuclear infrastructure and degrading its broader military capabilities for many years to come.

Bush's preemption doctrine was eerily reminiscent of Phillip K. Dick's 1956 short story "The Minority Report," which Steven Spielberg turned into a 2002 feature film starring Tom Cruise. In the story, government officials operate a Department of Pre-Crime and act in advance to prevent crimes that, they claim, will occur in the future. (Unlike the film, the story also explores the dangers of an excessively influential military during peacetime.)

One of the most perplexing aspects of Bush's preemption doctrine was that, even though it was set in motion largely as a response to 9/11, it was directed not only at the shadowy non-state terror networks responsible for the attacks, but at traditional state adversaries as well. Yet the administration put forth no evidence or argument to explain why states would no longer be subject to traditional principles of deterrence.

Indeed, in his speech to the West Point graduating class of 2002, President Bush openly bragged about the overwhelming ability of the United States to deter any states from actions that might directly threaten American national interests, thus revealing a glaring inconsistency in the preemption doctrine itself: "America has, and intends to keep, military strengths beyond challenge."[22] But if America possessed—and, in Bush's rendering, intended to possess indefinitely—overwhelming military superiority over every other state, why weren't we then able to deter any other state in virtually any conceivable circumstance? Why, if we had successfully deterred a powerful (and nuclear-armed) USSR, were we suddenly unable to deter a puny (even if nuclear-armed) Iraq or Iran or North Korea?

Perhaps the most troubling aspect of the Bush administration's preemption doctrine was that it suggested that U.S. perceptions of its own vital interests should always trump its obligations to operate within the world rule of law. The preemption doctrine overthrew, in a stroke, the U.N. Charter's 1945 rule about the use of force in the international arena. Under the charter, all such use of force is prohibited, save for two circumstances. First, a state may act to defend itself "if an armed attack occurs against a Member" (article 51). Poland, for example, would not have been prohibited from endeavoring to fight off the German forces that crossed its borders on September 1, 1939. Iraq, to choose another example, was not prohibited from defending itself against the U.S. forces that illegally crossed its borders on March 20, 2003. Second, the U.N. Security Council may authorize states to employ their military forces on behalf of the United Nations if it determines that such action is necessary "to maintain or restore international peace and security" (articles 39 and 42). (It did not authorize that 2003 U.S. attack on Iraq, which is why the attack was illegal under international law.) That is the core notion of collective security. In Bush's conception, however, preemption was to be deliberated on and undertaken by one state alone.

Former vice president Al Gore, in a seminal speech before the Commonwealth Club in San Francisco in October 2002, opposed the looming invasion of Iraq well before most other leading Democrats did. Moreover, he did so largely on these grounds. According to Gore, "what this doctrine does is to destroy the goal of a world in which states consider themselves subject to law, particularly in the matter of standards for the use of violence against each other. That concept would be displaced by the notion that there is no law but the discretion of the president of the United States."[23]

The consequence, of course, is that if one nation insists on such a standard, other nations acquire a cheap and easy excuse to follow suit. If we abandon the law of nations, we are left only with the law of the jungle, with Hobbes's state of nature extended to the widest possible stage. The only constraint then on the use of violence will be the power and ruthlessness of those who would employ it. And rest assured: on that wide stage, the United States would not be the only one to employ it.

The authors of the Bush administration's preemption doctrine admittedly had a point. In endeavoring to create postwar rules regarding the use of force, the framers of the U.N. Charter were clearly contemplating traditional acts of aggression against states by the military forces of other states. They clearly did not anticipate the conditions of the early twenty-first century—when non-state actors pose significant challenges to national security, when direct and consequential attacks on a state may be launched by entities other than the armies and navies and air forces of other states. But if international law, international rules governing the use of force, and perhaps even the U.N. Charter are to be modified so that states can act to protect their national security within the rule of law, those modifications for the world community must be deliberated and decided upon by the world community. One state cannot simply create new rules for itself. Yet the Bush administration did precisely that. It declared, openly and contemptuously, that it would make ad hoc, sui generis judgments about when the United States could violate the rules—the same rules it expected everyone else to follow.

"A rule-based international society may seem a lackluster phrase, but it describes, for those who wish organized life on this planet to survive in a decent form, the most important of all the long-term international objectives mankind can have," wrote former U.N. undersecretary general Brian Urquhart in 2006. "The United States should reengage in respecting and developing the rule-based system that it largely initiated after World War II and which has for many years served it well. Such an approach could certainly not have worse consequences than the recent attempt to abandon the idea of international restraint and go it alone."[24]

A New Definition of American National Security

At the beginning of this chapter, I mentioned that one of the many new nuclear weapons systems the Bush administration pursued was a new "bunker buster" nuclear weapon. Known as the Robust Nuclear Earth Penetrator (RNEP), it would have possessed seventy times the explosive power of the Hiroshima device. The RNEP was designed to burrow deep into the earth before detonating, in order to guarantee the destruction of subterranean command or weapons complexes. Because it would have detonated underground, the bunker buster would have hurled thousands of tons of radioactive rock, dust, and debris high into the sky, in far greater quantity than an aboveground nuclear burst. Thus, it would have exposed many more thousands of people to slow and agonizing deaths from radioactive fallout. Some have estimated that one use of a bunker buster could cause more than a million fatalities.[25]

Thankfully, the U.S. Congress killed the RNEP plan. And in any case, the American nuclear arsenal already contains a bunker busting nuclear weapon, the B61-11, which can burrow six meters underground before detonating.[26] The RNEP was just a modern, more robust version of the same military idea. Yet it is fair to say that there was an underlying political idea behind the weapon as well.

Most observers simply took the RNEP plan at face value: that because some potential adversary states were constructing elaborate underground command posts or weapons caches, we should develop nuclear weapons that can burrow underground to destroy them. In reality, though, the quest for the bunker buster exposed no less than a new definition of national security, or, more precisely, of American national security alone.

Combined with the Bush administration's missile defense plans, the quest for the RNEP meant that our national security strategy was twofold. First, no one can hold any American asset at risk anywhere on earth. All American persons, properties, and interests must be absolutely invulnerable. Second, no non-American people or assets, anywhere on earth, can be allowed to defend themselves from the awesome might of the American military. The United States must be able to annihilate every asset of every country anywhere on the planet. Indeed, defense official Linton Brooks revealed this precise rationale for the bunker buster weapon when, in making the case for it in April 2005, he told a Senate panel, "It is unwise for there to be anything that's beyond the reach of American power."[27]

According to Hans Kristensen of the Federation of American Scientists, these policies, taken together, sought "to create near-invulnerability for the United States by forcing utter vulnerability upon any potential adversary."[28] Jennifer Nordstrom and Felicity Hill have made the same point in a different way: "In personal interactions, this sort of fearful controlling is called abuse, but from a realist geopolitical perspective, it is called 'hard security' and wise policy."[29] No other nation today has such a national security strategy, capability, or "need." Arguably, no other nation in history ever has. Every other country has lived with some vulnerability from potential adversaries and some inability to destroy all potential adversaries anywhere, anytime. Perhaps we might consider whether American national interests are actually served by our country, alone, pursuing such an unprecedented concept of national security.

JUST ANOTHER WEAPON OF WAR

In the opening years of the nuclear age, one of the most intoxicating appeals of the new atom bomb was that it might become just another tool to achieve military superiority, just another rung on the ladder of escalation, just another weapon of war. This impression was reinforced by the way in which the bomb was introduced into the world: as the mechanism for abruptly ending the greatest conflict humanity had ever known. While some recognized that the dawn of the nuclear age had changed everything about the ultimate consequences of warfare and perhaps the fate of the human race, others saw it primarily as a new and potent means to achieve an ancient goal—victory on the field of battle.

The late George F. Kennan, arguably one of the greatest sages of the nuclear age, wrote eloquently about the enduring tension between these views:

> When the first nuclear weapon was exploded over Hiroshima, and in the years immediately following, a number of weighty and impressive voices could be heard, pointing out that the emergence of destructive power of this magnitude invalidated the greater part of traditional thinking about the relationship of war to national policy. . . . All of these men perceived the suicidal quality of the nuclear weapon. . . . Unfortunately . . . these warning voices have been disregarded in every conceivable respect. . . . [The nuclear weapon has] been made subject to the primitive assumption that the value of a weapon is simply proportionate to its destructiveness, and that the more you have of any weapon . . . the more secure you are. . . . People have gone on, in other words, behaving as though this were 1916 instead of 1986, and as though the nuclear weapon were only some new species of artillery. This was, of course, precisely what the Einsteins and the Eisenhowers had tried to warn about.[30]

Nevertheless, the hawks who believed that nuclear weapons could be rationally employed as one of many military tools pushed for their position throughout the cold war. The lead author of the December 2001 NPR, in fact, was Keith Payne, who had been a leading proponent during the early Reagan administration of the idea that nuclear war might be "winnable."[31] He even set forth this thesis in a landmark article, co-authored with Colin Gray, entitled "Victory Is Possible."[32] Yet President Reagan himself eventually felt compelled to denounce this line of thinking, saying famously, in a joint statement with Mikhail Gorbachev at their first meeting in Geneva in 1985, "A nuclear war cannot be won and should never be fought."[33]

Perhaps the single most frightening thing about the nuclear legacy of George W. Bush was that he seemed determined to disassociate himself from this element of the Reagan legacy. If humanity had made any progress, since the dawn of the nuclear age, in getting through its thick collective skull that nuclear weapons were not just another weapon of war but the most dangerous creations ever to spring from the human mind, that progress came to an abrupt halt with the election of President Bush. The conviction that nuclear weapons could be employed on the battlefield, and that doing so might actually benefit American national security, had beguiled those charged with defending that security once again. It happened at the very outset of the new century, for the first time in the new century.

There is very little reason to suppose that it will not happen again.

The Grand Bargain of the Nuclear Nonproliferation Treaty and the Rules of the Nuclear Game Today

THE YEAR 2008 was filled with anniversary commemorations and remembrances of the many epochal historic events that had taken place four decades earlier, during the seminal year of 1968: The Tet offensive in Vietnam, which for the first time caused many Americans to comprehend that this was a war we might actually lose; the assassination of Martin Luther King, Jr., and the riots that ensued around the country; the assassination of leading presidential candidate Robert F. Kennedy two months later; the melee at the Chicago Democratic convention; the black power salutes of Tommie Smith and John Carlos at the Mexico City Olympics; the tumultuous three-way November presidential election and the victory of Richard M. Nixon. And—at the very end of the year, on Christmas Eve—the flight of Apollo 8 from the earth to the moon, and the first view that any humans had ever been granted of our single, borderless, breathtaking planet, lonely and fragile and whole, suspended among the blazing stars.

Not to mention the 1968 opening of John Hersey High School in Arlington Heights, Illinois.

Yet one anniversary, that largely escaped public notice in 2008, may have consequences in the end greater than any of these.

THE 1968 DEAL

After you finish reading this chapter, try an experiment. Visit a Starbucks, or some locally owned alternative, and talk to a hundred people waiting in line. There are always people waiting in line at these places. Tell them that on July 1, 1968, world leaders in Washington, London, and Moscow signed something called the Treaty on the Nonproliferation of Nuclear Weapons, commonly known as the NPT. Then ask each person to tell you what it says. In this era of vast civic disengagement, probably about ninety will respond, "I don't know. I never heard of it. But my mocha grande yaya is ready and I've got to go get my dry cleaning now." Of the remaining ten, probably eight or nine will tell you, "It's about preventing the spread of nuclear weapons. It's about keeping countries like North Korea and Iran from getting the Bomb."

Those eight or nine respondents will be half right. In the NPT, the human race endeavored to offer a permanent solution to the great problem of the nuclear age. The grand bargain of the treaty was that the many nuclear have-nots agreed to forego nuclear weapons, while the few nuclear haves agreed to get rid of their nuclear weapons.

No, that is not a misprint. More than forty years ago, the U.S. government really did commit itself to eliminate its entire nuclear arsenal, and, in conjunction with the other nuclear weapon states, to abolish nuclear weapons from the face of the earth forever.

The NPT does not just impose nonproliferation obligations on countries such as Iran, Syria, and Libya. It also imposes disarmament obligations on us. The treaty requires all nuclear weapon states "to pursue negotiations in good faith on effective measures relating to a cessation of the nuclear arms race at an early date, and to nuclear disarmament . . . under strict and effective international control" (article 6). If anyone perceives any ambiguity in those words, she needs only turn to the treaty's preamble, which states that the signatories are "desiring to further the easing of international tension and the strengthening of trust between States in order to facilitate the cessation of the manufacture of nuclear weapons, the liquidation of all their existing stockpiles, and the elimination from national arsenals of nuclear weapons." It was the first time since the dawn of the age of atomic weapons, nearly a quarter-century earlier, that the human race had formally expressed its intent to bring that age eventually to a close.

"The NPT is supposed to lead to a nuclear-free world," says Ben Sanders, a member of the Dutch delegation to the 2000 NPT Review Conference. "The non-nuclear countries see it as a bargain which the weapons states have failed to keep."[1] "The NPT does not simply aim to maintain the nuclear status quo," says Ambassador George Bunn, who served on the original U.S. negotiating team in the late 1960s. "Article VI . . . requires that the original five nuclear weapon states pursue effective nuclear disarmament measures."[2] "The NPT is based on a core bargain under which all the non-nuclear-armed countries have agreed they would not acquire nuclear weapons," says former president Jimmy Carter. "In exchange, the five nuclear-armed countries have agreed to take good faith disarmament steps, with the eventual goal of the complete, worldwide elimination of nuclear weapons. The Treaty has been remarkably successful on the first part of the bargain, but not so successful on the second."[3]

THE NPT FOR DUMMIES

The NPT was signed in 1968 by three nuclear weapon states—the United States, the USSR, and the United Kingdom—and by fifty-nine non-nuclear weapon states. For various reasons the nuclear weapon states France and China did not sign the treaty until 1992, though they did pledge in 1968 to adhere to its terms and, for the most part, did so.

By 1992, the signatories had expanded to not only these five nuclear weapon states but a total of 183 non-nuclear weapon states. It is the most nearly universal treaty in all of human history, surpassing even the U.N. Charter. Only four states remain outside the treaty regime, and all possess nuclear weapons: India, Pakistan, Israel, and North Korea, which was once a member but withdrew in 2003. Article 10 permits such withdrawal if a state party concludes that "extraordinary events . . . have jeopardized the supreme interests of its country." As I will argue in Chapter 8, North Korea could make quite a good argument that for them, during the Bush era, that was indeed the case.

The full bargain of the NPT is actually a bit more complicated than "we won't get them if you'll get rid of them." One way to grasp the essentials of the treaty is to examine what both sides put forth as their part of the deal. What do the non-nuclear weapon states give or give up? Two things. Two enormous concessions.

- The non-nuclear weapon states pledge to remain non-nuclear weapon states indefinitely into the future. That, of course, is what many believe to be the only goal of the treaty: to prevent nuclear weapons from passing into more and more hands. The pledge appears in article 2, which says that the non-nuclear weapon states commit not to "receive," "manufacture," or "otherwise acquire" nuclear weapons.

- In addition, the non-nuclear weapon states pledge to provide reports on all their peaceful nuclear activities to the IAEA, allow international authorities to inspect peaceful nuclear work to ensure that it doesn't become nuclear weapons work, and allow significant intrusions upon their sovereignty. It is crucial to recognize that this duty applies only to the non-nuclear weapon states. The treaty imposes no obligation upon the nuclear weapon states to report anything about their nuclear activities, peaceful or otherwise, or allow any intrusions upon their sovereignty. Article 3 commits non-nuclear weapon states "to accept safeguards . . . for the exclusive purpose of verification of the fulfillment of its obligations assumed under this Treaty with a view to preventing diversion of nuclear energy from peaceful uses to nuclear weapons."

The nuclear weapon states make several pledges in return.

- They agree that the non-nuclear weapon states can pursue civilian nuclear programs. According to article 4, the non-nuclear states possess an "inalienable right" to develop "nuclear energy for peaceful purposes."
- The nuclear weapon states agree to assist the nuclear programs of the non-nuclear weapon states, by providing technologies for nuclear energy and other commercial nuclear products. Article 4 says that the nuclear weapon states commit "to facilitate . . . the fullest possible exchange of equipment, materials, and scientific and technological information" for non–weapons-related nuclear projects, and that they "shall cooperate" with the non-nuclear weapon states for the "further development of the applications of nuclear energy for peaceful purposes."
- The nuclear weapon states also agree not to launch a nuclear attack on any non-nuclear weapon state. (I will discuss the agonizing history of this promise later in the chapter.)

- Finally, the nuclear weapon states agree that they will eventually eliminate their nuclear arsenals entirely in order to bring about a nuclear weapon–free world. This provision appears in article 6. As your experiment at Starbucks will tell you, it remains widely unknown to the public to this day.

The Grand Bargain: Repeatedly Reaffirmed

The parties to the NPT have formally and frequently restated their intentions to fulfill these promises. The treaty entered into force in 1970, two years after it was signed, but did not commit the parties to its terms forever. Instead, it was set to be reviewed and reaffirmed twenty-five years later, in 1995. Otherwise, by its own terms, it would expire.

According to everyone who attended the 1995 NPT Review Conference, the dissatisfaction with the nuclear status quo was quite palpable among both the non-nuclear weapon states and the many civil society advocates who showed up to agitate. These parties sensed that the NPT's two-tier structure was in danger of becoming permanent, and that the nuclear weapon states did not ever intend to fulfill their article 6 obligation to engage in nuclear disarmament. Both the non-nuclear weapon states and the peace agitators were determined to let the nuclear weapon states know that they would not stand for this attitude, and that nuclear apartheid was not indefinitely sustainable.

For their part, the nuclear weapon states desperately wanted the treaty to be extended indefinitely. That was the ace in the hands of the non-nuclear weapon states, and they played it well. By agreeing to extend the treaty, they were able to extract several tangible commitments in return. As a way to pursue the implementation of article 6, the nuclear weapon states agreed to a set of "Principles and Objectives for Nuclear Nonproliferation and Disarmament." (Recall the emphasis in Chapter 2 on the unbreakable connection between non-proliferation and disarmament.) These included completing the negotiation of a Comprehensive Test Ban Treaty (CTBT) within one year; commencing the negotiation of a new treaty to ban the worldwide production of weapons-grade fissile materials; and working to establish a zone in the Middle East that would be free of nuclear weapons, other weapons of mass destruction, and their delivery systems.

Five years later, at the 2000 NPT Review Conference, the nuclear weapon states again found themselves on the hot seat. A group of seven non-nuclear weapon states calling themselves the New Agenda Coalition—Ireland, Brazil, Egypt, Mexico, New Zealand, South Africa, and Sweden—this time led the charge. These are not trivial countries but what some today refer to as influential middle powers. (One of the most important civil society nuclear disarmament organizations today calls itself the Middle Powers Initiative.) The group intended to pressure the nuclear weapon states to take tangible steps toward fulfilling their article 6 obligations. It was widely reported that their agenda had mobilized the support of about 120 of the 155 non-nuclear states in attendance.[4]

In response, the nuclear weapon states again committed to thirteen "practical steps for the systematic and progressive efforts to achieve nuclear disarmament." Those steps included a reiteration of all the commitments made in 1995, and added measures such as applying principles of verification, transparency, and irreversibility to nuclear arms reduction agreements; reducing the operational readiness of standing nuclear forces; preserving and strengthening the Anti-Ballistic Missile (ABM) Treaty; and diminishing the role of nuclear weapons in any state's national security strategies.[5]

As I made clear in Chapter 6, most of those commitments, which were adopted only months before George W. Bush's election, were baldly violated, by commission or omission, during his tenure as president. Indeed, the 2005 NPT Review Conference ended without adopting any substantive final statement at all—mostly because the United States refused to allow even any mention of these commitments that our own government had made at earlier conferences.

Perhaps even more important than the practical steps that the nuclear weapon states agreed to pursue in 1995 and 2000 was their reaffirmation of article 6 itself. The conferences convened in those years emphasized more clearly than ever that the 1968 commitment to pursue nuclear disarmament was not intended as merely a distant dream (or, one might say now, as a commitment to be fulfilled only after the end of the lifetime of someone—Barack Obama—born only seven years earlier!). At the 1995 conference, the nuclear weapons states reiterated that the NPT required them to undertake "systematic and progressive efforts to reduce nuclear weapons globally, with the ultimate goal of eliminating those weapons." Five years later, at the 2000 conference, the nuclear weapon states recommitted themselves again to "an unequivocal undertaking . . . to accomplish the total elimination of their nuclear arsenals."

These statements could hardly be plainer. Their unadorned and unqualified language indicates that, regarding the abolition of nuclear weapons, the NPT requires them to do it, and the nuclear weapon states in fact intend to do it. Four long decades ago, they promised to do it. Twice since, they promised to keep their promise to do it. All that remains is for them actually to do it.

THE WORLD COURT WEIGHS IN

The International Court of Justice (ICJ), also known as the World Court, issued a formal advisory opinion on July 8, 1996, describing the present state of international law regarding virtually all aspects of the possession, possible use, and possible threat of use of nuclear weapons. The verdict it rendered on the specific requirements of the international legal obligation to engage in nuclear disarmament, created by article 6 of the NPT, was unambiguous:

> The Court appreciates the full importance of the recognition by Article VI . . . of an obligation to negotiate in good faith on nuclear disarmament. The legal import of that obligation goes beyond that of a mere obligation of conduct; the obligation involved here is an obligation to achieve a precise result—nuclear disarmament in all its aspects—by adopting a particular course of conduct, namely, the pursuit of negotiations on the matter in good faith. This twofold obligation to pursue and to conclude negotiations formally concerns . . . the vast majority of the international community.[6]

Although the World Court claimed a "twofold" obligation, its paragraph on the matter really identifies three requirements:

- The nuclear weapon states must enter formal international "negotiations" on nuclear disarmament. Moreover, the last sentence indicates that these negotiations should be multilateral; indeed, they should aspire to be universal.
- The nuclear weapon states must not only initiate, but must also "conclude" such negotiations—that is, not drag them out indefinitely into the future.

- The negotiations must "achieve a precise result—nuclear disarmament in all its aspects." This, unambiguously, means abolition.

Yet a quick glance at the historical record demonstrates that the nuclear weapon states have not come close to complying with any of these requirements. Although the United States and the Soviet Union (and later Russia) have engaged in many negotiations over the years regarding their nuclear arsenals, these negotiations have always been bilateral. The two leading nuclear states have never commenced anything like formal multilateral negotiations aimed at transforming the global nuclear status quo. Obviously, then, if they have not even commenced such negotiations, in more than forty years since the signing of the NPT, they cannot have concluded them. Finally, even when east-west arms control negotiations have taken place, they have always focused on the size and composition of each party's nuclear arsenal. They have never had abolition as a goal. At Reykjavik, Iceland, in October 1986, Ronald Reagan and Mikhail Gorbachev came close to agreeing that they might set such a goal. Presumably, had they managed to strike an agreement, bilateral and eventually multilateral negotiations would have followed. But the moment passed, the opportunity was missed, and, so far, it has not yet been seized again.

In the last paragraph of its long and complex opinion, the World Court concluded: "Unanimously: There exists an obligation to pursue in good faith and bring to a conclusion negotiations leading to nuclear disarmament in all its aspects under strict and effective international control." Those last six words arguably create a fourth requirement. Whatever nuclear abolitionist architecture might ultimately be created by the conclusion of such negotiations, that architecture must move beyond pure national sovereignty and exclusive national control over nuclear weapons—the most sensitive components of any state's military and national security establishments. States must find a way to cede the management, verification, and enforcement of nuclear disarmament to some kind of international institution, global structure, or mechanism of transnational governance.

It hardly needs saying that a quick glance at the historical record demonstrates that the nuclear weapon states have not come close to complying with this requirement either.

THE U.N. GENERAL ASSEMBLY WEIGHS IN

The World Court is not alone in emphasizing that the nuclear weapon states have long been obligated to eliminate nuclear weapons, and in insisting that they get busy fulfilling their obligation. Shortly after the 1995 Review Conference and the 1996 World Court opinion, the U.N. General Assembly, frustrated by decades of stall and delay, decided to enter the fray. On December 10, 1996, it adopted resolution 51/45 M, which, after approving the verdict rendered by the World Court earlier that year, "call[ed] upon all States to fulfill that obligation immediately by commencing multilateral negotiations in 1997 leading to an early conclusion of a nuclear-weapons convention prohibiting the development, production, testing, deployment, stockpiling, transfer, threat or use of nuclear weapons and providing for their elimination."[7]

The UNGA language is excruciatingly specific, even more so than the World Court's. It not only calls upon the nuclear weapon states to fulfill their article 6 disarmament obligation "immediately," but also announces that *immediately* means "1997." Like the World Court opinion, it also demands that these states commence negotiations on an actual nuclear weapons elimination treaty, and bring those negotiations to a conclusion. But unlike the World Court, the UNGA details exactly what such a treaty should do.

The General Assembly has passed similar resolutions every year since 1996. Ten years later, again expressing extreme frustration, this time with the 2005 Review Conference fiasco, it expressed its feelings once more. This resolution was sponsored by the only state ever to have been attacked with nuclear weapons—Japan. Tokyo called the resolution "Renewed Determination," and the Japanese delegation drafted language that focused on the tangible commitments made in 1995 and 2000: transparency, irreversibility, verification, diminishing the role of nuclear weapons in national security strategies, reducing the operational readiness of deployed nuclear weapons, entry into force of the CTBT, and commencing negotiations on a fissile material cutoff treaty. Moreover, it emphasized that the point of all these measures was to engage "in the process of working toward the elimination of nuclear weapons." When the members of the UNGA cast their votes, the resolution passed 167 to 4.[8] Weary observers will be unsurprised to learn that the United States was one of the four.

THOU SHALT NOT ATTACK NON-NUCLEAR
STATES WITH NUCLEAR WEAPONS

I have already emphasized that there is more to the NPT's grand bargain than simply a pledge not to get nuclear weapons in return for a pledge to get rid of nuclear weapons. When the treaty was originally under negotiation in the 1960s, the non-nuclear states asked, in return for their promise to remain non-nuclear, that the nuclear states promise never to attack them or threaten to attack them with nuclear weapons. This, said Robert McNamara and Thomas Graham, Jr., "could be the most reasonable request in the history of international relations."[9] Nonetheless, the nuclear states refused, prostrating themselves before the altar of military flexibility.

The issue arose again twenty-five years later, shortly before the 1995 NPT Review Conference. Under the intense pressures described above, France, Russia, the United Kingdom, and the United States issued "harmonized security assurances," declaring that they would not use or threaten to use nuclear weapons against non-nuclear weapon states (although they did introduce a slight caveat regarding nuclear retaliation against non-nuclear states aiding and abetting any kind of attack by a nuclear state). On April 11, 1995, the states incorporated these security assurances into U.N. Security Council Resolution 984. And in the final document adopted by the NPT Review Conference a few weeks later, the signatories noted their hope that the resolution could eventually "take the form of an internationally legally binding instrument."[10] That's quite a convoluted process, and admittedly not as good as if such an unambiguous promise had made it into the original text of the NPT itself (or been added later as an amendment). Nevertheless, most international legal experts now agree that the promise not to launch or threaten to launch a nuclear attack against non-nuclear states has become an integral part of the NPT bargain.

Flash forward half a decade or so from 1995. As Chapter 6 revealed, this promise was completely disregarded by the administration of George W. Bush. The administration's general nuclear policy documents explicitly envisioned attacking non-nuclear states with nuclear weapons. Moreover, the administration specifically contemplated attacking the non-nuclear weapon state of Iran with nuclear weapons.

That chapter illuminated the broad irony of a state acting to prevent another state from acquiring nuclear weapons by employing nuclear weapons of its own. However, in this context another more specific irony emerges: In 2003, the United States itself defied the United Nations, to show Saddam Hussein that he could not get away with defying the United Nations. Now we also know that the Bush administration actually breached the NPT (by making the explicit nuclear threats described in the last chapter) to show Mahmoud Ahmadinejad that he could not get away with allegedly breaching the NPT (by building nuclear weapons, which, of course, Iran had not yet done).

Perhaps instead of the ladder of nuclear escalation discussed so often during the cold war, we might talk instead today about climbing ever more rungs on a ladder of nuclear irony.

THE NPT AND IRAN

As indicated above, Article 3 of the NPT imposes specific obligations on the non-nuclear signatories: they must disclose their peaceful nuclear activities to the international community and open themselves to IAEA inspections and verification. There is no question that Iran, soon after the 1979 inception of the Islamic Republic, began pursuing many of the basic technologies involved in enriching uranium, and that it failed to disclose those activities to the international community and the IAEA. Tehran has openly admitted as much.

It seems reasonable to assume that a party's article 4 rights (to develop nuclear energy) would be conditioned upon compliance with its article 3 responsibilities (to disclose its development of nuclear energy). Why, then, doesn't Iran's clear violation of article 3 cause it to forfeit its "inalienable right" under article 4 to pursue a nuclear energy program? Let's explore the question point by point.

First, the NPT itself does not explicitly condition the exercise of article 4 rights on compliance with article 3 responsibilities. In fact, the text of article 4 suggests the opposite: "Nothing in this Treaty shall be interpreted as affecting the inalienable right of all the Parties to the Treaty to develop research, production and use of nuclear energy for peaceful purposes without discrimination and in conformity with articles I and II of this Treaty." Michael Spies of the Lawyers' Committee on

Nuclear Policy argues that, according to the terms of the treaty, a non-nuclear weapon state forfeits its article 4 rights only if that state violates its article 2 non-acquisition responsibilities, and endeavors to produce or acquire nuclear weapons.[11] After all, the treaty explicitly states that to be the case. But it does not state that a non-nuclear weapon state forfeits its article 4 rights if it violates its article 3 reporting responsibilities.

Second, Spies points out that "this argument could be undermined" by language in the statement adopted by the 1995 Review Conference, in which parties to the treaty said, "Particular importance should be attached to ensuring the exercise of the inalienable right . . . without discrimination and in conformity with articles I, II, as well as III of the Treaty." The parties agreed on similar language at the 2000 Review Conference. It is almost as if the participants in 1995 and 2000 concluded that there had been a flaw in the original 1968 text, and that the exercise of article 4 rights should indeed have been conditioned upon compliance with article 3 responsibilities. One might have expected the Bush administration would have cited these statements in regards to Iran. But it did not. Why not? Probably because if the United States had talked too explicitly about these 1995 and 2000 statements, Iran, and others, might have begun to talk explicitly about the administration's complete disregard of the obligations that the U.S. government itself had committed to at the 1995 and 2000 conferences.

Third, during its tenure, the Bush administration repeatedly demanded not just that Iran fully comply with IAEA inspection requests, but that it actually cease its enrichment of uranium. Yet the administration never made the argument that Iran must cease doing something it is entitled to do under article 4 because of its deficiencies in complying with article 3. Why not? Probably because if the United States talked too explicitly about articles 3 and 4, Iran, and others, might well have replied by talking explicitly about article 6.

Fourth, Iran has not only admitted that it failed to disclose its nuclear activities between 1981 and 2003, but has attempted to explain why. And it is difficult not to give some credence to their explanation. Tehran claims that if it had divulged that it was seeking nuclear technologies during this time, Europe, Israel, and the United States would have endeavored to keep them out of Iranian hands—even though Iran was legally entitled to them. Iran feared the consequences if it did in fact, as it was required to do, reveal its nuclear activities to the world. After all, it had weathered Iraq's direct invasion of its territory in 1980, which escalated into an eight-year war in which Iraq, with American support, killed hundreds of thousands of Iranians. During that war, Iraq employed chemical weapons supplied by German, British, and American companies against Iranian soldiers and civilians. In addition, in 1981 the Israeli air force destroyed Iraq's Osirak nuclear reactor, with little international condemnation. However geostrategically sensible the action might have been, under the NPT, the Iraqi reactor was perfectly legal, while, under the U.N. charter, the Israeli airstrike was perfectly illegal. Was it entirely unreasonable for Iran to suppose that, if it were to disclose its legal nuclear activities to the IAEA, as required under article 3, it might suffer a similar fate?

It is crucial to distinguish between the two NPT violations that Iran might or might not have committed. If Iran had actually worked on designing and developing nuclear weapons, then it would have clearly violated its article 2 obligation not to "receive," "manufacture," "or otherwise acquire" nuclear weapons. (This is an open question. American intelligence concluded in December 2007 that Iran had engaged in such work prior to 2003—and then stopped. But the IAEA has never made such a finding.) If Iran undertook research and development of civilian nuclear energy only, yet failed to report it to the IAEA (which Iran admits), then it was in clear violation of its article 3 obligation to disclose its nuclear activities to the international community. But if Iran's nuclear activities between 1981 and 2003 did not involve nuclear weapons work, then Tehran was in violation of the NPT not because its nuclear activities themselves were illegal, but only because it did not report activities that it was, in fact, fully entitled to undertake.

One might compare this to the situation with Major League Baseball's recently crowned all-time home run champion, Barry Bonds. According to both the federal investigators who indicted him and to Major League Baseball itself, Bonds's crime was not taking steroids, but lying to federal investigators about taking them. During the time period for which prosecutors allege that he took steroids, Major League Baseball had no rule forbidding players from taking them. His record-breaking home run season, in which he slugged seventy-three dingers to surpass Mark McGwire's record of seventy, took place in 2001. But

Major League Baseball's players and owners did not agree to ban steroids until September 2002. Allegedly, Bonds told lies about doing something pharmaceutical that he had no reason to conceal, because it was not in fact against the rules.

And the state of Iran failed to disclose the whole truth about doing something nuclear that it had no reason to conceal, because it was not in fact against the rules. Because under the terms of the NPT, if Iran has not engaged in actual nuclear weapons development work, all its nuclear activities have been perfectly legal.

A GRAND BARGAIN DELAYED IS
A GRAND BARGAIN DENIED

In Chapter 2, I highlighted the world's enduring and increasing resentment about the nuclear double standard. Now, we can inject another crucial element into the situation: the NPT specifically rejects that double standard, and demands that it be brought to an end. Certainly one of the overriding reasons for the bitter and enduring resentment over the nuclear double standard is that the nuclear weapon states have committed themselves, legally, numerous times, to getting rid of their entire atomic arsenals. The grand issue facing the NPT regime today is how much longer the nuclear have-nots will keep to their end of the contract, if the nuclear haves do not seriously begin to move toward keeping theirs. They, say they, have met their end of the bargain. When are we going to meet ours?

Four long decades after the grand bargain of the NPT was forged, one could argue that the fate of the treaty may hinge on the name of the treaty itself. If the drafters had chosen to call it the Treaty on the Nonproliferation and Elimination of Nuclear Weapons, and it was commonly known as the NPET, the name might not only have ameliorated the public's vast ignorance about the treaty's true terms; it would have more accurately reflected them as well. There is, it seems, a fundamental disconnect between the NPT's purpose and its name. If the framers had identified the twin goals of nonproliferation and abolition in the treaty's name, the human race today might be well on the way to preventing proliferation, and achieving elimination. However, by limiting the name (and, in the ensuing four decades, the emphasis of most nuclear weapons policies) solely to the one goal, the drafters may have ensured, ultimately, that we will fail at both.

CHAPTER 8

Nuclear Weapons Are Militarily Unnecessary and Militarily Useless. For Us.

Ivo Daalder and Jan Lodal both served as nuclear policy advisors to the presidential campaign of Senator Barack Obama. During the transition period after his election, their article "The Logic of Zero: Toward a World Without Nuclear Weapons," appeared in the November–December 2008 issue of *Foreign Affairs*, the quintessential forum for America's foreign policy elite.[1] The article urged the new president to "make the elimination of all nuclear weapons the organizing principle of U.S. nuclear policy" and offered several promising suggestions about how the United States might persuade other states to follow a bold American initiative toward that end.[2] Because of its timing, its placement, and its authors' connection to the incoming president, the article was arguably comparable in importance to the *Wall Street Journal* op-eds, discussed in the opening chapter above, that issued from the pens of the Gang of Four in January 2007 and January 2008.

Concerning one point, however, Daalder and Lodal did not seem fully to appreciate the vast potential that America's conventional military might now holds to transform the global nuclear status quo. "Only one real purpose remains for U.S. nuclear weapons: to prevent the use of nuclear weapons by others," the authors wrote. "There is no way to defend reliably against a nuclear attack from the missiles or aircraft of a hostile state; such an attack can only be deterred through the certainty of devastating retaliation. Accordingly, so long as others have nuclear weapons, the United States must maintain a viable nuclear deterrent."[3]

Indeed, President Obama has put forth much the same sentiment. He, too, as indicated in the opening chapter, has called unambiguously for nuclear weapons abolition, most notably in his groundbreaking speech in Prague on April 5, 2009. However, not only did he declare in Prague that nuclear weapons elimination might take more than the remainder of his lifetime to complete, but he also said, "Make no mistake: As long as these weapons exist, the United States will maintain a safe, secure and effective arsenal to deter any adversary."[4] The presumption could hardly have been clearer. For Obama, such deterrence can apparently only be exercised by the United States through the continued possession of an "effective [nuclear] arsenal."

This chapter will offer a three-pronged thesis about the political and military utility of nuclear weapons for different actors in the contemporary international arena—and the different strategies required to persuade them to walk together down the road toward abolition. First is a specific contention quite different from that offered above by Daalder and Lodal and Obama. In the early twenty-first century, the United States, uniquely, can promise "the certainty of devastating retaliation," and consequently can "deter any adversary," with its conventional military power alone. To protect American national security, to defeat any enemy, and to dissuade any potential aggressor by threatening to inflict catastrophic retaliatory destruction upon it, America's conventional military power alone can fully do the job. For those missions, U.S. nuclear weapons are militarily unnecessary.

Second, nuclear weapons cannot accomplish the many other missions that American conventional weapons—for all their firepower—cannot accomplish for the United States. For those missions, U.S. nuclear weapons are militarily useless.

Third, unfortunately, today's geostrategic realities make these kinds of calculations very different for other, weaker states. For them, nuclear weapons hold a powerful appeal as an effective means—indeed, likely the only available means—to dissuade stronger states from attacking them. To persuade these states to sign on to the abolitionist project will require simultaneous initiatives on three parallel tracks. One would contain foreign and defense policies that assure weaker states that stronger states do not intend to attack them. Another would contain rhetoric and diplomatic overtures that convince weaker states that, on balance, their national security will best be served in a world where neither they nor anyone else possesses nuclear weapons, instead of a world where they do—but so, too, do many others. And a third would carry nuclear weapons policies that directly address the long-simmering resentments about the nuclear double standard, and that directly connect nuclear nonproliferation to nuclear disarmament.

Because the one thing we can probably say for sure about the prospects for universal nuclear disarmament is that no state will agree either to abjure or to dismantle nuclear weapons unless it believes that such a course is the best course for its own national security.

NUCLEAR WEAPONS ARE MILITARILY UNNECESSARY FOR US

The United States is the one state today that can defend itself, protect its interests, and exercise deterrence without resort to atomic weapons. As discussed in Chapter 2, when one figures in all the elements of American defense spending, our nation today spends more on its military prowess than all the other countries in the world combined.[5] As evidenced by our military successes in the Persian Gulf in 1991, Kosovo in 1999, Afghanistan in 2001, and Iraq in 2003, we can inflict overwhelming damage and impose our will upon hostile regimes without resort to our nuclear capabilities. Advances in satellite and surveillance technologies mean that we can know everything about an opponent's military preparations or actions. Electronic jamming, combined with overwhelming U.S. air dominance, means that an opponent can know nothing about our own. American warplanes and land- and sea-based missiles armed with conventional explosives can obliterate the bulk of virtually any opponent's military formations, command and control facilities, and transportation and communications systems. Many air and ground missions are now accomplished by robotic drones directed by stateside controllers—who actually go home for lunch.

Our country can station its military forces far away from any field of battle, yet manage to control it decisively. That also dramatically lowers the risk of American casualties, which makes the prospect that the United States will actually carry out such operations far more credible. If any country can deter all attacks and defeat any enemy without resorting to an atomic arsenal, it is our country. Consequently, the United States stands now in a prime position to both assure our national security and acquire vast international political capital by leading the way toward universal nuclear disarmament.

In a widely noted 1999 *New York Times* op-ed piece, the last he wrote before he died, Ambassador Paul H. Nitze, one of the great hard-line cold warriors, said that he could "think of no circumstances under which it would be wise for the United States to use nuclear weapons," that the "simplest and most direct answer to the problem of nuclear weapons has always been their complete elimination," and that America's vast nuclear arsenal had become "a threat mostly to ourselves."[6] Perhaps the main reason that Nitze could identify "no circumstances" where it would make any sense for the United States to employ nuclear weapons is the ever-increasing precision of our conventional weapons. The Pentagon has even coined a term to describe this development: precision-guided munitions (PGMs).

In 2005, the U.S. Air Force issued a "Prompt Global Strike Analysis of Alternatives," whose stated purpose was to examine "a range of system concepts to deliver precision weapons with global reach, in minutes to hours." It laid down an explicit marker of the aspiration: "Global is defined as the capability to strike any target set in the world."[7] A detailed technical analysis of America's latest and greatest conventional military capabilities is beyond the scope of this book, and such matters are highly classified in any case. Nevertheless, thanks to continual advances in space technology, computation, software, sensors, and navigational features, one broad, overarching truth can be asserted without hesitation. The U.S. military can launch a powerful conventional bomb today from almost anywhere in the world, and deliver it to within just two or three feet of most any designated target anywhere else in the world. The United States can destroy virtually anything, virtually anywhere, with conventional munitions alone.

The Pentagon already seems to recognize that improvements in accuracy mean that it can accomplish military missions without resort to nuclear weapons. In March 2005, for instance, the USS *Tennessee* test-launched an unarmed D-5 ballistic missile equipped with an accuracy adjunct developed by Lockheed Martin. According to the U.S. Navy admiral directing the test flight, "I had GPS signal all the way down and could steer it."[8] Two years later, the Department of Defense requested funding to reconfigure twenty-four Trident long-range SLBMs to enable them to carry conventional payloads instead of the nuclear warheads for which they were originally designed.[9] An independent panel convened by the National Academy of Sciences Naval Studies Board to study the Trident modification program stated that such an initiative "would be a valuable addition to U.S. military capabilities."[10] Clearly, downgrading the explosive power of the warheads atop these long-range missiles would make no sense unless American military planners were confident that the conventional warheads could be delivered exceptionally close to any desired target.

This development is not limited to SLBMs. By most accounts, measures of delivery accuracy for ground-, sea-, and air-launched cruise missiles, as well as for ground launched ballistic missiles, have increased dramatically in recent years. In fact, the independent panel of the Naval Studies Board also examined the possibility of replacing nuclear warheads with conventional warheads atop land-based ICBMs and air-launched cruise missiles.[11] Andrew Lichterman of the Western States Legal Foundation, one of the world's leading experts on delivery system technologies, says that the Pentagon envisions "exploiting advances in accuracy to deliver conventional weapons by missile at heretofore impracticable distances. . . . [The aspiration is] to develop conventional weapons that can strike anywhere on earth in a matter of hours. . . . The development of conventional weapons with global reach . . . will give the United States a capability to inflict devastation from afar that few states if any can match."[12] As General Richard Myers, chair of the joint chiefs, said in 2002, the continuing refinement of such systems could be so transformative that they "have the potential to change significantly the way we fight, and perhaps even the nature of warfare itself."[13]

In addition, in March 2009, the Pentagon announced plans to develop a giant dirigible that would float nearly twelve miles above the earth for ten years at a time and provide continuous and detailed radar surveillance of activities below. Because of its height, it would be virtually invulnerable to attacks from both surface-to-air missiles and fighter planes. Military officials indicated that the ultimate objective was a fleet of aerial spy ships that would give the United States an unprecedented ability to identify and locate anything its forces wanted to pinpoint.[14]

Indeed, in Nitze's landmark *New York Times* op-ed, the increasing precision of our conventional weaponry formed the centerpiece of his case that such weaponry could now fully protect American national security. "The technology of our conventional weapons is such that we can achieve accuracies of less than three feet from the expected point of impact. The modern equivalent of a stick of dynamite exploded within three feet of an object on or near the earth's surface is more than enough to destroy the target. In view of the fact that we can achieve our objectives with conventional weapons, there is no purpose to be gained through the use of our nuclear arsenal."[15] And that was more than a decade ago, in 1999, when the U.S. capability to deliver explosives with great precision was considerably less than it is today.

THE SECOND WORLD WAR PRECEDENT

Since the moment it happened, many people have debated the moral validity, political utility, and military necessity of the U.S. decision, in the conflict's final hours, to transform the Second World War into the First Nuclear War. Arguments justifying the decision usually assume that the only alternative to the atomic obliteration of Hiroshima and Nagasaki was a massive land invasion of the Japanese home islands, which would have resulted in many thousands of American casualties and perhaps more Japanese deaths than those that resulted from the atomic bombings themselves. Of course, alternative history is speculative by nature: more than sixty years later, we can still debate whether or not the Imperial Japanese government would have surrendered soon, or ever, without the sudden shock of the atom bombs. What is beyond dispute, however, is that Japan's military and industrial assets had already been completely destroyed prior to Hiroshima and Nagasaki. By August 5, 1945, American conventional air power had reduced the mighty Japanese empire entirely to ruins.

One of my sources for this information is my late father, Second Lieutenant Claude Daley, Jr., a tall, skinny Irishman from rural Georgia, who served at age twenty-one on one of the famed B-29 Superfortresses toward the end of World War II. He went straight from the ROTC program at Georgia Tech (where Jimmy Carter was a classmate) into the U.S. Army Air Forces (USAAF), predecessor of today's U.S. Air Force, which trained him as a B-29 navigator, bombardier, and radar observer. During June, July, and August 1945, his team, Crew 5B3 of the 355th Squadron of the 331st Bombardment Group (Very Heavy) of the 315th Bomb Wing of the 20th Air Force, flew repeatedly from faraway Guam in the Mariana Islands to attack what he always called "the homeland" of Imperial Japan. Second Lieutenant Daley's aircraft, named *Jus' One Mo' Time*, had the obligatory sultry beauty painted on the side, and the 331st's motto was *Imparido Pectore* ("with undaunted heart").

But my father, may he rest in peace, always told his three sons that, by the time he got into action, the USAAF was simply running out of targets. He vividly remembered talking to the mission planners on Guam, who admitted that by the summer of 1945 there was very little left to attack in the homeland from the air. Therefore, although the 331st was still flying missions against the few remaining targets of strategic consequence, it had also begun to train as a tactical air force that would support American ground operations after the imminent invasion. By this point in the war there was virtually nothing left in Japan to bomb.

Perhaps the reader will indulge me here to recount the story of my father's last bombing mission, which, it turns out, was also the last bombing mission of the Second World War. The vast waves of B-29s that had been pummeling Japan throughout 1945 mostly ceased operations after the atom bomb fell on Hiroshima on August 6. They continued to stand down through August 8 (when the USSR entered the war) and August 9 (when the Nagasaki bomb was dropped), all the way up until August 14. But at that point, when the Imperial Japanese government still had not surrendered despite the introduction of both a brand-new enemy and a brand-new weapon, President Truman ordered General Curtis LeMay to resume bombing operations. LeMay, commander and architect of the strategic bombing campaign against Japan, later became one of the most extreme hawks of the cold war, and the model for the character Jack D. Ripper in *Dr. Strangelove*.

The 315th was directed to attack what might have been Japan's last remaining target of military or industrial significance: the Nippon Oil Company at the far northern tip of Honshu, the last operational refinery in Japan. This meant that the mission was not only the last of the war but also, at seventeen hours, the longest, and also the largest, with nearly 1,200 planes in the air. The raid, according to my father, serving as the navigator on this sortie, set afire every designated target on the ground. But at almost the same instant that his aircraft released its heavy load, the *Jus' One Mo' Time* flew directly into a churning plume of smoke and heat rising furiously from one of the blazing refineries below.

Those simultaneous events caused the aircraft to ascend several hundred feet in just a few seconds. Then, seconds later, it descended just as rapidly, essentially in free fall before the pilot, First Lieutenant Frank J. Kawalec, could regain control. My father compared this violent up-and-down motion to the force of a nail being hammered into a piece of wood. In this case, the nail was my father's spine.

Two hours later, the 315th, en route to Guam, got word over their headsets that Japan had surrendered unconditionally. Emperor Hirohito, for the first time, had spoken to his subjects on the radio, telling them the time had come "to bear the unbearable." The worst conflict the human race had ever known at last had come to an end. My father, in severe pain and trying to sleep, was nonetheless awakened by the radio operator, Corporal Robert D. Clark: "The war's over, Lieutenant! The war's over!" And Dad, doing his best John Wayne impression, replied simply, "Good. We won't have to do *this* again." Then he rolled over and went back to sleep.

But the war was not yet over for Crew 5B3. Three hours later, the backup navigator awakened my father and told him that some of the navigational equipment had been badly damaged by the mishap, that no other planes were visible in the air, that to him the vast Pacific looked the same in all directions, and that they were lost. So my father, hurting badly, called upon the celestial dead-reckoning skills he had been taught at Georgia Tech, but never used in real life. With no tools other than the positions of the stars, he directed the aircraft's course accurately enough that eventually the pilot and the co-pilot were able to spot Guam emerging over the southeastern horizon.

Yet Crew 5B3's problems still weren't over. Seventeen hours after takeoff, with the aircraft running on fumes, they discovered that the heat from the burning oil refineries had melted their landing gear. So First Lieutenant Kawalec, or perhaps it was the co-pilot, First Lieutenant William L. Sliger, with great agility, raised the plane's nose as high as it would go, and managed to bring down the *Jus' One Mo' Time* flat on its belly. That didn't do my father's back any good either. But they were home.[16]

The back injury turned out to be so severe that my father was hospitalized on Guam for several months thereafter, during which time he was promoted to first lieutenant and then captain. He suffered from back trouble unremittingly until his death in 1997. Though he never pursued the point, I always wondered if he had been perhaps the last member of the American armed services injured in combat during the Second World War.

More authoritative sources than my father tell a similar tale of a prostrate and devastated Japan in the days before the bombings of Hiroshima and Nagasaki. The official opinion of the U.S. Strategic Bombing Survey, on the scene at the time, was that Japan probably would have surrendered during the summer or fall of 1945 even without the atom bombs or the Soviet offensive on Manchuria:

> Air supremacy over Japan could have exerted sufficient pressure to bring unconditional surrender and obviate the need for invasion. Based on a detailed investigation of all the facts, and supported by the testimony of the surviving Japanese leaders involved, it is the Survey's opinion that certainly prior to December 31, 1945, Japan would have surrendered even if the atomic bombs had not been dropped, even if Russia had not entered the war, and even if no invasion had been planned or contemplated.[17]

We were able to defeat both Nazi Germany and Imperial Japan with conventional weapons alone. Actually, the word *defeat* is an understatement. It is not just that we were able to persuade both countries to surrender unconditionally. It is also that we succeeded in destroying virtually every target of military or industrial value, through conventional weapons alone.

In the case of Nazi Germany, that devastation was accomplished by both air and ground assaults, and through our collaboration with many other nations—the Soviet Union paramount among them. In the case of Japan, the record is more unambiguous. That devastation was accomplished exclusively by American conventional air power. In addition, up until the final months of World War II, in both the European and Pacific theaters, American bombers met serious opposition from both enemy fighter planes and anti-aircraft fire from the ground. Hundreds of American (and British and Russian and other) aircraft were lost to enemy opposition.

Today, that is unlikely ever to be the case anymore. The U.S. Air Force now is virtually unchallengeable in the air. What happened to

John McCain over North Vietnam more than forty years ago almost never happens to U.S. aircraft today. During the brief campaign to depose the regime of Saddam Hussein in the spring of 2003, not a single Iraqi fighter pilot even left the ground—so sure were they that the U.S. Air Force would deliver their doom. The air supremacy of the United States is so pronounced today that in virtually any hypothetical theater, the U.S. Air Force can operate with practically zero risk to its aircraft and crews. Even Russia and China probably could not destroy American assets in aerial combat to the same extent as did Germany and Japan nearly two-thirds of a century ago.

Since 1945, then, we have both vast advances in the precision with which munitions can be delivered to their targets, and a vast diminishment in the ability of any conceivable enemy to take American warplanes out of action. So if the conventional air power available to the United States then could do what it did to Hitler's Germany and Imperial Japan in 1945, think of what the immensely more powerful might of the U.S. Air Force can do today. With conventional weaponry alone.

THE GULF WAR PRECEDENT

One usually thinks of deterrence as operating to prevent aggression from taking place. But actors may also be deterred from certain actions after a conflict has commenced. For example, during the first Gulf War in January and February 1991, Iraq's military forces both in Kuwait and on its own territory were under assault. Iraqis had been occupying Kuwait since their blitzkrieg invasion and conquest in August 1990, and the objective of the American-led coalition was to eject them. Yet both Iraq and the coalition held the potential to escalate the conflict.

After coalition attacks had commenced, Iraq responded by firing Scud missiles armed with conventional warheads at Israel, killing and wounding several Israeli citizens. But Iraq could have armed these missiles with chemical munitions rather than conventional warheads. After all, it had employed nerve gas repeatedly during its 1980–88 war with Iran. Why didn't it do so against Israel? Although George H. W. Bush's administration never officially confirmed the claim, many people believed that Washington had directly told Baghdad that any use of chemical weapons by Iraq would be met with an American nuclear retaliation against Iraq. Therefore, it was argued, Saddam Hussein was deterred from escalating the conflict.

So far so good. But the question then arises: was it necessary to threaten Iraq with nuclear retaliation to deter President Hussein from employing his own weapons of mass destruction? Not according to U.S. Air Force general Charles Horner, who commanded all aspects of the air war against Iraq. In a private conversation with Senator Alan Cranston a few years after the end of the Gulf War, General Horner persuasively argued that his capability to obliterate Baghdad was just as potentially devastating, and probably more credible, with conventional weapons. If Iraq had crossed the chemical threshold, said Horner, "I could have taken apart their entire country, brick by brick by brick, with American conventional air power alone." Washington could have conveyed that threat to Baghdad just as easily as it had apparently conveyed the nuclear threat. Consequently, we could have deterred Iraq from undertaking actions we were not willing to tolerate—without need for any nuclear saber rattling.

No less than General Colin Powell appeared to agree with Horner's conclusions. On September 27, 1991, just months after the end of the Gulf War, the first President Bush announced that the United States would unilaterally dismantle all its nuclear artillery, all its short-range nuclear missiles, and all its nuclear torpedoes and depth charges aboard naval submarines and surface vessels.[18] The action was spearheaded by Powell, then chair of the joint chiefs, who later wrote that he had concluded that such weapons were "trouble-prone, expensive to modernize, and irrelevant in the present world of highly accurate conventional weapons."[19]

Sweden's Rolf Ekeus, who led the U.N. special commission charged with verifying Iraq's compliance with its post–Gulf War agreement to relinquish its weapons of mass destruction, recognized the importance of America's advanced conventional weaponry in achieving victory: "The Gulf War was an enormous display of what can be done with the opposite of nuclear weapons—namely, high-tech, precision arms. The interest of military people now is chiefly in these. . . . [Nuclear weapons] have become rather absurd, esoteric, big, clumsy clubs—it is difficult to outline a scenario of use."[20]

In 1992, however, a special commission established by the U.S. Strategic Command (STRATCOM) offered the opposite view: "It is not difficult to entertain nightmarish visions in which a future Saddam Hussein threatens U.S. forces abroad, U.S. allies or friends, and perhaps even the United States itself with nuclear, biological, or chemical weapons. If that were to happen, U.S. nuclear weapons may well be a resource for seeking to deter execution of the threat."[21] But as General Horner argued, even in the early 1990s such a hypothetical adversary could probably have been fully deterred by U.S. conventional capabilities alone. That is certainly the case now, nearly twenty years later. The United States, with its conventional military capabilities alone, can threaten to inflict catastrophic retaliatory damage on any hypothetical adversary anywhere in the world, sufficient to deter such an adversary from carrying out any kind of nuclear, biological, or chemical "nightmarish vision." The United States, with its vast conventional military capabilities, simply no longer needs the nuclear weapons "resource" in order to "deter execution of the threat."

NUCLEAR WEAPONS ARE MILITARILY USELESS FOR US

Anthony Russo, who, along with Daniel Ellsberg, revealed the Pentagon Papers to the world, spent much of the Vietnam War years inside the country, working on a RAND Corporation project on Viet Cong motivation and morale. Russo's job was to interview Viet Cong prisoners of war. Speaking in his own defense in his 1973 trial for conspiracy, theft, and espionage about his role in releasing the Pentagon Papers, Russo recounted one of the sessions.

"He said he would never give up because he believed in something," Russo said of the Viet Cong captive. "I had thought up until then that these Viet Cong were indoctrinated. He told me what he was committed to, how the French had wiped out his whole village." Then, Russo testified, the prisoner recited him a poem, and sang him a song. "It was very moving. . . . Even now, when I'm thinking about it, it comes back to me," said Russo, breaking into sobs on the witness stand. "That Viet Cong prisoner, he recruited me."[22]

It is one thing to claim that we do not need nuclear weapons to accomplish our national security objectives. It is another to claim that nuclear weapons cannot achieve for us any national security objectives at all. Nevertheless, for today's United States, both statements appear to be true. Our conventional weapons can accomplish anything that nuclear weapons can accomplish. And for those objectives that conventional weapons cannot accomplish—such as winning the hearts and minds of Tony Russo's Viet Cong prisoner and his millions of comrades—nuclear weapons offer us no help at all.

Since the end of the Second World War, wars between the armed forces of states have become less significant, while low-intensity wars involving irregular insurgencies—sometimes called asymmetrical conflict—have become more so. In places as diverse as Vietnam, Afghanistan (twice), Lebanon, Northern Ireland, Namibia, and Sri Lanka, advanced modern militaries have found themselves stymied and often defeated by nimble guerilla bands with little central command structure and rudimentary weapons. These groups never take on their opponents in open battle, but resort to snipers, assassinations, booby traps, and roadside bombs. As warriors, they are everywhere and nowhere simultaneously.

If advanced modern militaries have not yet figured out how their vast conventional military superiority can defeat such enemies, they have been even less successful in using nuclear weapons to do so. One great lesson of the nuclear age is that atomic arsenals have provided their possessors virtually no political or military advantage in most of the actual conflicts of the nuclear age. They did nothing to enhance American military capabilities or political options in Vietnam; nor did they help us during the humiliation of the 1979–81 Iranian hostage crisis; nor did they make any difference to the exercise of American power in East Timor, Kosovo, and Somalia in the 1990s; nor did they cure our shameful impotence in failing to prevent the genocides in Bosnia and Rwanda.

And consider some of the major national security tests now confronting the Obama administration. Our nuclear weapons can do nothing to help us create a stable government and thriving society in either Afghanistan or Pakistan. As in Rwanda and Bosnia, they cannot help us end the genocide in Darfur. Nuclear weapons provide us with no tools to ameliorate the tragedy in Congo—what Gerard Prunier calls "Africa's world war."[23] They can neither bring an end to piracy off the Horn of Africa nor bring a stable government to Somalia.

In years to come, such low-intensity struggles will be, by most accounts, the kinds of conflicts that the U.S. military will most likely face. Secretary of Defense Robert Gates made this case in the January

2009 issue of *Foreign Affairs*. Because no one is likely to take on American forces in a direct conventional fight, he believes that the Pentagon should devote more of its attention to "tracking enemies down hilltop by hilltop, house by house, block by bloody block."[24] It is difficult to imagine what role nuclear weapons might play to help the U.S. military do that.

Indeed, these points have been made in succinct and persuasive fashion by no less than Iran's president, Mahmoud Ahmadinejad. Appearing on CBS's *60 Minutes* on September 23, 2007, he insisted that Iran has no interest in developing nuclear weapons, because the "nuclear bomb is of no use" in today's world. The USSR, he said, possessed tens of thousands of nuclear weapons, yet those weapons did nothing to prevent the empire's fall. The United States, he claimed, holds a vast nuclear arsenal, yet "if it was useful, it would have resolved the problems of the Americans in Iraq."[25]

Even given Ahmadinejad's faults, and all the harm his odious rhetoric has inflicted on international political stability, we can hardly dispute these contentions about Moscow and Washington. Regarding the single greatest Soviet security disaster since the dawn of the nuclear age—the dissolution of the Soviet Union itself—nuclear weapons were able to do nothing to stave off the fall. And regarding probably the single greatest American foreign policy disaster since the dawn of the nuclear age—the quagmire in Iraq—nuclear weapons have provided no military options or political advantage whatsoever.

Unfortunately, however, for smaller and weaker states, even just a few nuclear weapons do appear to provide decisive benefits and enhance their national security. In his interview, Ahmadinejad was obviously trying to score political points and convince Americans that Iran is not seeking nuclear arms. Yet while his analysis appears valid when applied to the two greatest cold war powers, the same analysis, when applied to his own country, yields very different conclusions.

ALTERNATIVE MODELS OF NUCLEAR DETERRENCE

During the cold war's long atomic arms race, we needed thousands of nuclear weapons, the argument ran, because the Soviets possessed thousands of nuclear weapons. And the Soviet Union needed thousands of nuclear weapons because we possessed thousands of nuclear weapons. Our atomic arsenal deterred the Soviets from using theirs, and their atomic arsenal deterred us from using ours.

There were at least three broad situations where our nuclear arsenal was intended to deter hypothetical Soviet aggression (and that were probably mirrored, on their side, against hypothetical American aggression). The first was a direct Soviet nuclear attack on American cities, the largest conceivable disaster for American national security. We threatened to respond to such a strike by launching an American nuclear attack on Soviet cities. "The Department of Defense," exclaimed an exasperated Ohio congressman in the early 1960s, "has become the Department of Retaliation."[26] In the lexicon of the NUTS, this scenario was known as both "strict deterrence" and "assured destruction," and when critic Donald Brennen added the word "mutual" it soon became universally known as "MAD." As Winston Churchill remarked succinctly in 1955, "it may be that we shall by a process of sublime irony have reached a stage in this story where safety will be the sturdy child of terror, and survival the twin brother of annihilation."[27]

Senator Cranston liked to point out a basic problem with MAD. The threat made some logical sense, he said, but would the action itself? If one side actually were to launch a nuclear first strike on the other side's cities, nothing could be accomplished by launching a nuclear response other than slaughtering millions of innocents. But if one side believed that the other would fail to carry through on its retaliatory threat, then the other's nuclear deterrent would no longer be credible. And what if both sides were saying it while suspecting that the other might not actually do it? This kind of logic could continue indefinitely, until one entered various psychological cul-de-sacs worthy of Lewis Carroll. Fortunately, neither of the great cold war adversaries ever chose to test the credibility of the other side.

The second broad scenario was a Soviet nuclear attack on the American nuclear missile fields spread throughout the Great Plains (and probably also on our nuclear-armed aircraft bases). The NUTS called this "counterforce targeting," as distinguished from "countervalue." We threatened to respond to such an attack by launching nuclear strikes from our invulnerable submarine fleet on all remaining Soviet nuclear assets and perhaps on Soviet cities as well. The reply to that, however, would probably have been Soviet nuclear attacks on American cities, using the weapons that they had retained on their own less advanced but still essentially invulnerable submarines. This, of course, threw the credibility of our second-strike threat into question, once again dropping us into Wonderland with Alice. Fortunately, neither side ever decided to roll these dice either.

The third broad scenario was a Soviet attack on Western Europe—perhaps only with conventional forces, perhaps also with tactical nuclear forces, and perhaps too with Soviet nuclear strikes on selected Western European cities. This was the classic fear (in retrospect, probably a phantom one) that Soviet tanks were poised to shoot across the bridges of the Elbe River dividing East and West Germany and conquer Western Europe in much the same kind of blitzkrieg that Hitler had used a generation earlier. We threatened to respond even to a conventional ground attack by attacking Soviet conventional forces with our own tactical nuclear weapons. That was a vital component of western defense strategy because NATO's conventional forces probably would not have been a sufficient match for the conventional forces of the Warsaw Pact—simply because the USSR was so much closer to the theater of operations than the United States. This is why American presidents, both Democratic and Republican, always refused to commit to "no first use." The NUTS called this "extended deterrence."

One problem with this scenario was that Soviet conventional forces on the ground would already be in Western Europe, and to attack them with American nuclear weapons, however "tactical," would mean destroying or poisoning much of what we were trying to save. So the answer was to threaten to respond to any kind of Soviet attack on Western Europe, conventional or nuclear, with American nuclear attacks on Soviet cities.

But such an attack would assuredly be met by Soviet nuclear attacks on American cities. And that posed a second, trickier problem: would we risk America to save Western Europe? No one was ever quite sure. French president Charles DeGaulle raised this question repeatedly with President Kennedy during his visit to Paris in May and June 1961, where he stopped en route to his first meeting with Soviet premier Nikita Khrushchev in Vienna. (This was the trip where JFK introduced himself to the French media at a press conference a couple of days in—after the French people had fallen hopelessly in love with his wife, fully fluent not only in the French language but also its culture and history—by saying, "I am the man who accompanied Jacqueline Kennedy to Paris.")[28] The United States may have held a vital interest in preserving Bonn and Brussels and Paris, but it certainly did not supercede our interest in preserving Boston and Baltimore and Pittsburgh. As Nigel Calder said in his 1979 book *Nuclear Nightmares,*

> The United States would regard a nuclear attack by the Soviet Union on any of its Allies as an attack on itself; if an H-bomb falls, say, on Amsterdam, the Americans are supposed to attack Soviet cities in retaliation. Presumed rationality goes out the window and is replaced by presumed American lunacy. The Russians are still supposed to be deterred, as reasonable chaps, by the threat of US destruction of Soviet cities, but the Americans pretend to be quite undeterred by the symmetrical threat of Soviet destruction of American cities. They promise to be so enraged by any nuclear bombing of their allies that, without thought for their own survival, they will let loose the final nuclear war. Really?[29]

Lewis Carroll again. Fortunately, no one ever chose to test these hypotheses either. Nuclear deterrence was too new in the affairs of humanity—too theoretical, too unpredictable—for either side to know for sure how it might play out in real life, and how the other side might react to the use of a nuclear weapon. So for nearly half a century, we dodged the bullet of global thermonuclear war.

Between the dawn of history and the dawn of the nuclear age, it appeared self-evident to most that the more military power one could amass relative to one's adversaries, the more security that party gained. But that all changed with Alamogordo and Hiroshima and Nagasaki. Strategic thinkers slowly began to realize that, in the nuclear age, security did not require superiority, but simply an ability to retaliate after an adversary had struck. To inflict what some called "unacceptable damage" on that adversary. According to the logic of nuclear deterrence, if an adversary knew the chances were good that it would take massive damage in response to a first strike (even if it were far less damage than it had inflicted as long as it was "unacceptable"), that adversary would be dissuaded from striking first.

Imagine a fanciful situation in which one state has 35,000 nuclear weapons (roughly the high point that the United States and the Soviet Union each reached during the cold war), while another holds only a single one. But if the latter state can absolutely guarantee that its sole nuclear weapon will survive any kind of first strike, and can be used to attack the first state's capital city or largest city in retaliation, then the first state could find no rationale to launch a nuclear first strike. What benefit could possibly outweigh the obliteration of its most important asset, and perhaps more than a million lives?

This hypothetical case may seem to be farfetched, but it actually parallels the logic behind the creation of the British and French nuclear forces in the 1950s and 1960s. Both states chose to develop nuclear submarine forces precisely because they were the delivery system most likely to survive a hypothetical Soviet nuclear first strike. Their forces never came close to matching the nuclear forces of the USSR. Nevertheless, if the United States and its nuclear umbrella were suddenly to disappear into thin air, as British and French leaders always feared it might at the moment of truth, these weapons were a guarantee that London and Paris could retaliate.

In an insightful 2008 article in the *Bulletin of the Atomic Scientists*, Jeffrey Lewis argues that something like this dynamic—which he calls "minimum deterrence"—has long been practiced not only by Britain and France, but also by China.[30] Beijing has never possessed the ability to ruin hundreds of American cities with Chinese nuclear warheads. Indeed, it has probably never had more than a couple of dozen nuclear warheads capable of reaching the United States at all. Yet even the possibility of one Chinese nuclear warhead detonating over a city in the United States has profoundly affected every calculation that American defense planners perform regarding any possibility of a security confrontation between the two nations. In *The Minimum Means of Reprisal*, Lewis's 2007 study of the evolution of Chinese nuclear forces and doctrines, he argues that Chinese defense planners concluded early on that the inexorable arms race between Moscow and Washington was essentially pointless, and that a few survivable Chinese nuclear warheads would more than serve to deter external aggression.[31]

However, the unassailable logic of the unacceptable damage model of nuclear deterrence failed to put the brakes on a Soviet-American nuclear arms race that accelerated rapidly after the USSR became the world's second nuclear weapon state in 1949. But those who engaged in a futile effort to slow it often employed the model in their attempts. As early as 1953, Robert Oppenheimer said, "Our twenty thousandth bomb will not in any deep strategic sense offset their two thousandth."[32] "Deterrence," said the great strategist Bernard Brodie in 1965, "does not depend on superiority."[33] Deterrence depends only on an ability to strike back. "There is no foreign policy objective today that is so threatened," said retired admiral and former CIA director Stansfield Turner in 1998, "that we would . . . accept the risk of receiving just one nuclear detonation in retaliation."[34] Indeed, as he caught his breath in the first days after the successful resolution of the Cuban missile crisis, President Kennedy remarked that the prospect that even one nuclear warhead might detonate over an American city was enough to deter him from launching any kind of attack on the USSR.

Philosopher Steven C. Patten made this case vividly in 1985, just before the ascension of Mikhail S. Gorbachev:

> It is tempting, but mistaken to think that if one warhead creates fear and thereby deters, two warheads will create even greater fear and more deterrence. (And then think what 4000 or 10,000 or 20 million warheads might do.) My argument is that the equation is false, even if we grant that fear is increased by nuclear multiplication. I am arguing that what is sufficient to deter can be, will be, far below the most fearsome possibility imaginable. As an analogy, suppose that I am thirsty. You can rationally deter me from drinking the glass of water before me if you tell me that it will give me two weeks indigestion. I don't also need to know that ingestion will cause hepatitis, or kill me, before I am rationally deterred. . . . Is there any reason to think things might be different with the laws of psychology as they apply to nation states?[35]

IRAN, NORTH KOREA, AND THE EMERGING MODEL OF NUCLEAR DETERRENCE

This brings us to the twin nuclear challenges that have dominated the headlines during most of the past decade and to the immediate nuclear proliferation issues now confronting the Obama administration.

The most persuasive argument for the nuclear quests of both Iran and North Korea is, indeed, the notion that deterrence does not depend upon superiority. Deterrence depends only an ability to inflict unacceptable damage upon an adversary.

Neither North Korea nor Iran can hope to defeat the United States in a direct military confrontation. They cannot repel an actual attack or shoot American planes and missiles out of the sky. Indeed, no country can. But North Korea and Iran can aspire to dissuade the United States from attacking them, by developing the capability to vaporize an American military base in South Korea or Qatar, or an entire U.S. aircraft carrier battle group in the Persian Gulf or the Sea of Japan, or even an American city on one coast or the other. The obliteration of an entire American military base, or an entire naval formation, or an entire city would seem to qualify as unacceptable damage for the United States.

To deter us, Iran and North Korea do not need thousands of nuclear warheads. They just need a couple of dozen, well hidden and well protected. American military planners might be almost certain of our ability to take out all the nuclear weapons in these countries by means of a dramatic surgical strike. But with nuclear weapons, "almost" is not good enough. Even the barest possibility that such a strike would fail, and that one or two nuclear weapons might make it into the air, is probably enough to dissuade the United States from undertaking it.

Iran and North Korea would not intend their nuclear arsenals to deter only nuclear attacks. With the overwhelming conventional military dominance of the United States (and the belligerent rhetoric and actions during the Bush administration), actors like Iran and North Korea don't just fear that America is going to attack them with nuclear weapons; they fear that America is going to attack them. If the entire nuclear arsenal of the United States disappeared tomorrow morning, but America's conventional military superiority and the political dynamics of the situation remained the same, the only possible military asset that these states could acquire to effectively deter an American military assault would be a nuclear one.

Although in the case of North Korea and Iran the United States appears to be the paramount threat, this phenomenon—of the weak feeling threatened by the strong and seeking to deter the strong by acquiring a few deliverable nuclear warheads—surely has a more general applicability. Iran also perceives a need to deter a stronger Israel. North Korea also perceives a need to deter a stronger South Korea, a stronger Japan, and perhaps even a stronger China. Pakistan perceives a need to deter a stronger India. Israel perceives a need to deter a combined attack from multiple regional antagonists. In July 2009, it was revealed that Saddam Hussein told his FBI interrogators that the main reason he falsely claimed between 1991 and 2003 that he possessed weapons of mass destruction had nothing to do with the United States: it was to deter a stronger Iran.[36] And in the years and decades to come, other examples will surely emerge as well.

North Korea today is one of the most desperate countries in the world. Most of its citizens are either languishing in gulags or starving. And yet—in contrast to the debate about whether the United States or Israel ought to launch a preemptive strike on Iran—no one has seriously proposed any kind of military strike on North Korea. Why not? As the government mouthpiece organization known as the Korean Committee for Solidarity with World Peoples stated plainly in the weeks after America's March 2003 invasion of Iraq, "The Iraqi war taught the lesson that . . . the security of the nation can be protected only when a country has a physical deterrent force."[37] Similarly, a few weeks earlier, just before the Iraq invasion began, a North Korean general was asked to defend his country's nuclear weapons program. With refreshing candor he replied, "We see what you are getting ready to do with Iraq. And you are not going to do it to us."[38]

Much like the North Korean general, Sadegh Zibakalam, head of the department of Iranian studies at Tehran University, said in early 2009, "A substantial reason for the Iranian insistence on the nuclear program is that they have realized that this is an insurance policy. . . . [E]very country that has a nuclear capability has not been invaded [or] attacked by any other state. . . . The psychological feeling of insecurity has driven Iranian leaders toward insisting on becoming nuclear."[39] When Tehran looks west, it sees an Iraq that abandoned its nuclear weapons program, opened itself to unprecedented intrusions on its sovereignty, did not in fact possess weapons of mass destruction—and got invaded for its trouble. When Tehran looks east, it sees a North Korea that is impoverished and puny, a pathetic excuse for a twenty-first-century nation-state. Yet because it chose to construct a small nuclear arsenal in secret and then whipped back the curtain to reveal that arsenal to the world, North Korea appears to be successfully deterring a military attack from the greatest military juggernaut in history.

So what would you do if you were Iran?

"Obviously we don't want Iran to have nuclear weapons, and I don't know if they're developing them," said Martin Van Creveld, an Israeli military theorist who teaches at Hebrew University in Jerusalem, speaking in 2005. "But if they're not developing them they're crazy." He elaborated in 2007: "Since the Americans went into Afghanistan, Iran's strategic situation has deteriorated sharply. Look at it from the point of view of Iran: You are surrounded by hostile forces, and in the White House is a guy who considers you part of the Axis of Evil, who has repeatedly threatened you and who has invaded your neighbor. . . . You can't match him conventionally. So you build nuclear weapons as fast as you can, and you try to get through the period before you have them by bluffing."[40]

His phrase "the period before you have them" requires elaboration. The prevailing dynamic has a cyclical character: America is threatening, and Iran feels threatened. Iran seeks a nuclear deterrent, or at least the uranium enrichment capability that would allow it quickly to acquire one. But pursuing that enrichment capability makes America and Israel feel threatened. So they become even more threatening, which gives Iran even more incentive to seek a nuclear deterrent, which causes America and Israel. . . .

This phenomenon will likely not be limited to the cases in today's headlines. If weaker states conclude that a nuclear deterrent is their best strategy to deter the attacks of stronger states, they must also recognize that the period between deciding to pursue a nuclear weapons deterrent and actually acquiring one will be their time of greatest vulnerability. The decision to pursue a nuclear deterrent, to diminish the possibility of being attacked, will increase the likelihood of being attacked during the period between that decision and its achievement.

Nonetheless, as the cases of North Korea and Iran seem to indicate, some states will choose to roll those dice and will seek to acquire a nuclear deterrent before it is too late. North Korea has apparently rolled double sixes and decisively won the gamble. The jury is still out on how the wager might ultimately play out for Tehran.

We Don't Need Them but They Do

So hence, we see perhaps the starkest paradox of the contemporary nuclear age. The country that has by far the most potent nuclear arsenal on the planet does not appear to need it. And the two countries that appear most desperately to need just a tiny nuclear arsenal to protect their own national security are the two countries that the international community has endeavored most insistently to consign to the other side of the nuclear divide.

The model of nuclear deterrence as practiced by Iran and North Korea differs from the traditional cold war model of MAD in several fundamental ways. In MAD, one big superpower deterred the other big superpower; now small states deter big states. In MAD, nuclear weapons existed primarily (though not exclusively) to deter the other side from using nuclear weapons; now nuclear weapons deter both conventional and nuclear aggression. In MAD, the opponent's entire country was put at risk; now a threat of far lesser magnitude is enough to act as a deterrent. In MAD, tens of thousands of nuclear weapons were deployed to deter the opponent effectively; now a few dozen well-hidden and well-protected warheads are sufficient to do the job.

Perhaps the most remarkable thing about the unacceptable damage model of nuclear deterrence, which we might as well call UD, is that it seems every bit as effective as MAD. If Iran, for example, were to obtain a dozen secure and deliverable nuclear weapons, it would not lead to anything like a "mutual" balance with the United States. Washington would still possess overwhelming military superiority, both nuclear and conventional. In addition, the threatened retaliation need not promise complete "assured destruction." To threaten to vaporize an American carrier group in the Persian Gulf is not at all the same as to threaten the annihilation of the entire American nation. Yet the threats seem to exercise deterrence in precisely the same way. Astonishingly, it seems that we would find ourselves every bit as deterred by an Iran with twelve nuclear weapons as we did by a Soviet Union with twelve thousand. Although UD hardly contains the rich acronymphomaniacal irony wrought by MAD, it appears now that Iran and North Korea intend to base their national security strategies solidly upon it.

There is very little reason to suppose they will be the last states to do so.

OUR COMPARATIVE ADVANTAGE

The good news is that the UD perspective enhances the argument that nuclear weapons are militarily unnecessary for us. Unlike with MAD, it is not necessary to assure the complete destruction of an adversary—for example, transforming every Soviet city with more than 100,000 residents into an irradiated ruin—in order to deter that adversary. We could not do that then with conventional weapons alone, nor could we do that now. (Though the precedents of WWII and the first Gulf War suggest that we could come close.) But if all that we need to deter an adversary is to guarantee the infliction of UD, then the United States is uniquely able to manage that task with conventional capabilities alone. Moreover, our overwhelming conventional military superiority can probably serve as a greater deterrent than our nuclear arsenal, because its potential use is more credible. As during the cold war, a potential adversary will only be dissuaded from undertaking hostile actions if it believes that threatened retaliation will actually be carried out. In most conceivable circumstances today, nuclear responses to hostile actions are less likely than conventional responses. Because of the taboo, thankfully, that has developed in two-thirds of a century of non-use. Because of the likely enormous political costs, tangible and intangible, that would likely follow for a state that employed nuclear weapons (even in retaliation to aggression). And because of the sheer uncertainty of how events might unfold after crossing the nuclear threshold.

A conventional military response to aggression would not entail those costs and risks, at least not in anything like the same magnitude. Consequently, the threat of such a response is more credible, more likely actually to be carried out. Therefore, it probably operates today as a greater deterrent than our nuclear arsenal ever has. And that deterrent capacity would endure in a nuclear weapon free world.

There might be one military mission that cannot be accomplished by America's conventional capabilities alone. It may well be that American conventional weapons, although quite precise and quite powerful, cannot penetrate the deepest underground command posts and storage facilities for weapons of mass destruction (nuclear or otherwise). Some of these may already exist in Iran, and perhaps in other states as well. In addition, it may turn out that advances by others in the techniques for constructing and hardening such deep underground facilities will outpace America's advances in the precision and power of its conventional munitions. This, of course, was the rationale for the Bush administration's quest to develop the robust nuclear earth penetrator. Without such a device, the administration claimed, such underground refuges would be invulnerable to American attack.

So does that settle the case against abolition? If there is a single potential target that the United States cannot destroy with anything else, does that necessarily mean that America must retain nuclear weapons perpetually? Let us consider two alternative futures.

In one, Washington retains nuclear weapons indefinitely, and thereby retains that ability to penetrate and destroy these deep underground military or leadership facilities, at any depth, anywhere on earth. Count that as a benefit for American national security. But consequently, the United States makes no move to abolish nuclear weapons. Therefore, in the next couple of decades we see both many more nuclear weapon states and many more nuclear weapons, especially insecure ones. And eventually, just one or two of those find their way into the hands of aspiring nuclear terrorists, for whom the United States is target number one. Count that as a cost to American national security.

In the other alternative, the world abolishes nuclear weapons—America's and everyone else's. The United States deprives itself of an ability to penetrate and destroy deep underground military or leadership facilities in any country on the planet. A few places, very few, stand as a refuge from American military might. Count that as a cost for American national security. However, the abolition of nuclear weapons brings with it meaningful international controls on all things nuclear, everywhere on earth. And that diminishes the likelihood of a nuclear terrorist strike—most especially on target number one—to about as low as fallible human beings can ever make it. Count that as a benefit for American national security. So which alternative future, on balance, will best serve the long-term interests of the people of the United States?

THEIR COMPARATIVE DISADVANTAGE

America's relative military advantage over any adversary would improve dramatically in a nuclear weapon–free world. In that world, no state would be able to threaten to impose UD on the United States. Yet Washington would continue to be able to threaten to impose UD on any adversary, with its conventional capabilities alone, and consequently to deter them from undertaking actions that directly challenged American interests.

That dynamic would likely be the case not only with weak states like North Korea, but also with America's strongest potential adversaries: Russia and China. The overall military power of the United States is clearly superior to that of either of these states today. However, Washington's relative superiority would be even greater still if all states did away with their nuclear arsenals. Put another way, if America ever has to take on Russia or China militarily, it will be much better for the United States if that confrontation takes place with neither side possessing nuclear weapons, rather than both.

Our conventional military superiority, however, leads to an obvious question: why would anyone else agree to give up or forego nuclear arsenals of their own?[41] For Moscow, the ability of its nuclear arsenal to deter a militarily superior United States was underscored during the war between mighty Russia and tiny Georgia that suddenly erupted in August 2008. For many reasons, no one in Washington seriously considered a military intervention in the conflict. Certainly one of those reasons, however, was the prospect that American military action, even if exclusively conventional, might meet a Russian nuclear reply. Contemporary Russian nuclear doctrines specifically contemplate employing tactical nuclear weapons in response to any use of American precision-guided munitions against Russian forces or interests. What if the exact same geostrategic situation had prevailed in the Caucasus, but without the presence of nuclear weapons on either side? Perhaps Moscow might have hesitated more before launching its offensive military actions against Georgia, and perhaps Washington might have hesitated less before eschewing any military response. From the Russian perspective, their nuclear deterrent gave them a freer hand to pursue their military objectives in Georgia.

Given the conventional military imbalance between the United States and Russia, then, how likely is Moscow to contemplate complete nuclear disarmament? Former Soviet leader Mikhail Gorbachev tackled that question directly in Rome in April 2009. The main barriers to nuclear disarmament for others, he said, are American defense expenditures and military power, which "far exceed reasonable security needs."

The perpetuation of American military superiority, he insisted, "would be an insurmountable obstacle to ridding the world of nuclear weapons. . . . Unless we discuss demilitarization of international politics [and] the reduction of military budgets . . . talking about a nuclear-free world will be just rhetorical."[42]

Gorbachev is right, of course, that America's present military superiority over Russia (and everyone else) would increase if everyone in the world got rid of nuclear weapons. But will that country's own national security be enhanced if it insists instead on keeping them indefinitely? Let us, again, consider two alternative futures. In one, Russia walks with us down the road toward abolition. In a post-abolition world, its leaders face many tricky policy choices as they square off politically with the greatest military power on the planet, the United States. They try to persuade Washington, on an ongoing basis, that although the United States could lick them in a direct military showdown, the costs for America of pulling the trigger—even after inevitable victory—would far exceed the benefits. After all, most of the states in the world today are non-nuclear weapon states, and they find a way to live with their conventional military inferiority to Washington. Similarly, Moscow does its best to avoid ever engaging in a direct military confrontation with the United States, taking it day by day.

In the other, Russia insists that it must hold on to nuclear weapons forever because it cannot risk confronting the United States with its inferior conventional forces alone. Before long, many other states decide that they, too, must hang on to nuclear weapons—or soon get some of their own. Thus, by the middle of the century, we have not nine, but nineteen nuclear weapon states on the planet. So the risk of accidental nuclear launches increases exponentially. So does the risk that a hot political crisis will degenerate into a nuclear war. So does the risk that some sober national leader will conclude that a nuclear first strike is the optimal policy option for addressing some geostrategic dilemma. And so does the risk that a couple of nuclear warheads will find their way into the hands of non-state actors, such as the grandsons of the men who took a Moscow theater hostage a few years ago. Or perhaps they might be the grandsons of the defenseless Georgians who were brutally slaughtered by the mighty Russian military in the summer of 2008. "I promise you today that I'll remind them of everything they have done," said

Georgian president Mikheil Saakashvili on the day he accepted Russia's humiliating ceasefire, "and one day we will win."[43]

So which alternative future, on balance, will best serve the long-term interests of the people of Russia?

ABOLITION: IN THE INTEREST OF ALL

The great insight that Mikhail Gorbachev and Eduard Shevardnadze used to break up the logjam of the cold war was the concept of mutual security. If you threaten your adversaries, they will threaten you right back. But if you make your neighbors more secure, you make yourself more secure. The basis of peace is to understand the insecurities, the vulnerabilities, and the fears of the other side.

The same holds true for all the countries in the world today. Consider this three-part strategy for persuading all states to abjure the nuclear choice and join us on the road to abolition. First, the United States needs to stop threatening other states. We cannot persuade others to eliminate or forego nuclear deterrents unless our foreign policy becomes vastly less menacing than it was during the Bush administration's tenure. States such as Russia will be much more likely to choose the first of the two alternative futures I have posited if we do not endeavor to expand NATO into Georgia, Ukraine, and presumably thereafter the suburbs of Moscow. States such as Iran will agree to remain non-nuclear indefinitely only if we can convince them that we will not launch preemptive, unilateral, illegal wars of aggression against them, or establish a permanent military encirclement around them, or endeavor, overtly or covertly, to overthrow their regimes. We must renew America's traditional commitment to building enduring world peace through the world rule of law. We might consider whether we really need to maintain overseas bases in nearly three-fourths of all the countries in the world, and whether our overwhelming conventional military superiority really enhances our own national security. We need to persuade other countries that they do not need a nuclear arsenal to deter us, because they have nothing to fear from us.

Few have made this case more plainly than Republican senator Chuck Hagel, who said in November 2007, "Now is the time for the United States to actively pursue an offer of direct, unconditional, and comprehensive talks with Iran." Then, turning the language of the Bush administration on its head, he added, "We should make clear that everything is on the table. . . . We must be clear that the United States does not . . . seek regime change in Iran. There can be no ambiguity on this point."[44] Writer Conn Hallinan has also argued for this conciliatory strategy:

> Any successful movement to abolish nuclear weapons will not only have to see that Article VI of the NPT is carried out, it will also have to address the Treaty's preamble: ' . . . in accordance with the Charter of the United Nations, States must refrain in their international relations from the threat or use of force. . . . ' As long as the great powers maintain the ability to invade countries, overthrow regimes, and bomb nations into subservience, weaker countries will inevitably try to offset those advantages. The quickest and cheapest way to do that is to develop nuclear weapons."

Hallinan reminds us that perpetual U.S. belligerence, combined with America's conventional military dominance, is incompatible with both the text and the spirit of both the NPT and the U.N. charter. He makes the point, however, that if such a world order appears to be in the cards, it will become infinitely more difficult to persuade other states to proceed with us toward abolition. They will do so, he says, only if we can convince them that "the weak need no longer fear the strong."[45]

Second, just as I argued above regarding America and Russia, we must work to convince all states that their long-term national interests will best be served by a world of zero nuclear weapon states rather than by a world of two or three dozen nuclear weapon states—even if they are among the two or three dozen. Too many things can go wrong in that future world. When it does, it will generate a cascading catastrophe—not only for the immediate victims, but also for the whole of the human community. Including those among the two or three dozen.

Finally, we must confront the towering hypocrisy of the nuclear double standard directly: first in words, then in deeds. We must call upon all the non-nuclear weapon states to resist the Faustian temptation to acquire nuclear arms, and call upon all the nuclear weapons states, including ourselves, to resist the Faustian temptation to keep them. Imagine how both the Iranian nuclear standoff and the global nuclear policy debate would have been transformed, in a stroke, if President Bush, at some point in his tenure, had simply said something like this:

> Iran, we expect you to abide by your NPT obligation not to produce or acquire nuclear weapons. In return, you can expect us to abide by our NPT obligation to get serious about eliminating our nuclear weapons. We do not expect you to endure the nuclear double standard forever until the end of time. We understand that you—and many other countries—will not forever forego nuclear weapons if we insist on forever retaining nuclear weapons. We understand that in the long term humanity must choose between dozens of nuclear weapon states or zero nuclear weapon states. We know that ultimately, the human race must abolish these abominations, or they will abolish us.

President Bush, of course, was very unlikely ever to have uttered such sentiments. But President Obama, admirably, has begun to recast America's nuclear rhetoric in just such a fashion. Perhaps he will continue to talk the talk. And perhaps, too, he will begin to walk the walk, in a serious and urgent way, toward a nuclear weapon–free world.

If it's not too late by then.

CHAPTER 9

The Architecture of a Nuclear Weapon–Free World

MY CHILDHOOD PASTOR at St. Edna's Catholic Church in Arlington Heights, Illinois, the Reverend James Doherty, an irascible and intimidating old Irishman, liked to tell a story about something that happened across the water from his beloved homeland many centuries ago. It was right around the turn of the thirteenth century, and a traveler was venturing across medieval France, when he stumbled upon the very beginnings of Chartres cathedral. It took a full sixty-six years to construct, from 1194 to 1260, and here it was, in its very earliest stages. The traveler approached the workers and asked, "What are you doing?"

"Me?" said the first. "I'm carving stone. That's what I do. I'm a stone carver."

"Me?" said the second. "I'm cutting glass. That's what I do. I'm a glasscutter."

"Me?" said the third. "I'm hammering nails. That's what I do. I'm a carpenter."

Then the traveler saw an old, old woman, tiny, hunched over, sweeping dust and debris, her hands wrapped around an ancient broom that looked like it had seen every bit as much of the hard life of medieval Europe as she had. The traveler asked, "What are you doing?"

The old lady paused, and then stood up straight, all four feet, eleven inches of her, and answered, "Me? What am I doing? What does it look like I'm doing? I'm building a cathedral! A cathedral that will soar to the heavens. A cathedral that will stand for a thousand years. A cathedral that will give everlasting glory to the spirit of the divine. Come back in a couple of centuries, traveler, and see what I have wrought!"

We might take any number of lessons from this tale. One is that, in many endeavors, we are engaged on undertakings that may take many years to construct, and may endure far longer still. A second is that every person has a role to play, none is a spectator, every one of us can be a part of some great collaborative undertaking. Perhaps the most crucial lesson here, however, is the importance of articulating a clear vision of what one is trying to create. You hike to the summit of a mountain step by step, but you also have a final goal. You build a house board by board, nail by nail, but you also have a blueprint. An image of the finished product. An architecture.

The same is true of our strivings toward a nuclear weapon–free world. We cannot construct our cathedral, after all, unless we know what we are setting out to build.

INSPECTIONS THERE AND HERE

Perhaps the single most important element of any architecture of abolition, especially for Americans, needs to be put front and center at the outset. It is a point that has not occurred to 99 percent of even the informed public who think about these issues. It is a consequence of nuclear disarmament that will astound many Americans and infuriate many others. Nevertheless, incontrovertibly, it is a key aspect of abolition, and the one that offers the only possible long-range solution to the great problem of the nuclear age.

If we expect other states—Iran, North Korea, any other state—to submit to intrusive inspections by international authorities, then we ourselves have to submit to intrusive inspections by international authorities. If we demand that other nations allow the outside world to show up, unannounced, at their front door, demanding to examine their most sensitive national security secrets, then we must be willing to do the same. The kind of unprecedented intrusions on sovereignty to which Iraq was forced to subject itself between 1991 and 2003 (and which, as will be discussed below, succeeded to a significant extent) are the same kind of intrusions on sovereignty to which we must eventually subject ourselves.

Indeed, this point was made vividly just days before the inauguration of President Obama. On January 17, 2009, journalist Selig Harrison appeared in Beijing after one of his frequent visits to North Korea.

He has visited there since 1972, and is one of the very few western journalists who was ever permitted to interview the state's founder, the late Kim Il Sung. Pyongyang often uses Harrison as conduit for messages to Washington. Now, in Beijing, he reported that North Korea was demanding a brand-new concession in the interminable negotiations over the fate of its nuclear program: the country would allow international inspections inside its borders, but only if its own officials were permitted to inspect U.S. military bases inside South Korea.[1]

On this point, a post-abolitionist world will differ fundamentally from the present nuclear status quo under the NPT (see Chapter 7). Recall that article 3, which requires states to open themselves to IAEA inspections, applies only to non–nuclear weapon states. In 1968, these states ceded a significant portion of sovereignty, over their own activities on their own soil, by agreeing to permit external agents, beyond state authority or control, to come into their countries, poke around, ask delicate questions, and examine their most sensitive national security assets. No such requirement is laid on the nuclear weapon state parties to the NPT. They are not expected to allow any external examination of their nuclear facilities at all.

They will be, however, in a post-abolitionist world. A rigorous, elaborate, widespread, unannounced, intrusive inspection system must be universal. In the end, it will not work for any unless it applies to all. And if Americans don't like the idea of that? Tough. Our only choice is between outside interference in the affairs of Chicago, Trenton, and Norfolk or losing Chicago, Trenton, or Norfolk. There can no longer be any question of fiercely guarding our sovereignty, as rightwing demagogues chronically demand. Yes, international inspections here would intrude upon our sovereignty. But detonations of atom bombs here would also intrude upon our sovereignty. The only question is, which of those two intrusions do we find least excruciating?

"Complete nuclear disarmament implies not just a significant evolution in verification, but an evolution of the international system," says Trevor Findlay, executive director of the Verification Research, Training, and Information Centre (VERTIC) in London. "States will have to change their attitudes towards the limits of sovereignty, the rule of international law and governance of the international system . . . if nuclear disarmament is ever to be negotiated."[2] Robert Wright made

these same points more graphically in a *New York Times* op-ed shortly
after 9/11: "Would you rather that your office building face a remote
risk of being searched by international inspectors, or the risk of being
blown up?"[3] The unfortunate reality is that, today, America directly
confronts that choice. Facing that choice, and making it, is the price we
must pay if we are ever to exorcize our nuclear demons for good.

AT THE DAWN: NUCLEAR PROBLEMS AND
NUCLEAR SOLUTIONS

On June 13, 1946, Bernard Baruch spoke on behalf of the American
government before the first meeting of the new U.N. Atomic Energy
Commission (AEC). He not only put forth a number of concrete
proposals for nuclear disarmament and international nuclear control
(known as the Baruch Plan) but also captured the enormity of the
historical stakes:

> My fellow-citizens of the world. We are here to make a choice
> between the quick and the dead. . . . If we fail, then we have
> damned every man to be the slave of Fear. Let us not deceive
> ourselves: We must elect World Peace or World Destruction. . . .
> Science has torn from nature a secret so vast in its potentialities that
> our minds cower from the terror it creates. Yet terror created by
> weapons has never stopped man from employing them. . . . It will
> not be an easy job. The way is long and thorny, but supremely
> worth travelling. All of us want to stand erect, with our faces to the
> sun, instead of being forced to burrow into the earth like rats. The
> pattern of salvation must be worked out by all for all.[4]

It turns out that the solutions proposed by the first generation of
nuclear thinkers, in the first two years after Alamogordo and Hiroshima
and Nagasaki, remain the best solutions to our enduring nuclear predica-
ment. They still offer the optimal answers for banishing that nuclear
genie right back into its bottle and corking it up for good.

On January 24, 1946, at its first meeting, in its first resolution, the
brand-new U.N. General Assembly set up the AEC to confront the
terrifying new nuclear problem. The resolution's text contained three
important components: international control of all things nuclear,

abolition of nuclear weapons, and international inspection to see that abolition had been carried out and maintained. "The Commission shall proceed with the utmost dispatch and inquire into all phases of the problem. In particular, the Commission shall make specific proposals . . . for control of atomic energy to the extent necessary to insure its use only for peaceful purposes . . . for the elimination from national armaments of atomic weapons . . . [and] for effective safeguards by way of inspection and other means to protect complying States against the hazards of violation and evasion."[5]

Two months later, the U.S. State Department issued the Acheson-Lilienthal Report, so named because David E. Lilienthal, chair of the Tennessee Valley Authority, had served as chair of the board of consultants who drafted the report, while Dean Acheson, undersecretary of state, had served as chair of the committee that had reviewed and then presented it publicly. Like the U.N. resolution, the report emphasized three components, similar to but distinct from those put forth by the General Assembly. First, no state could have a permanent monopoly on the atomic bomb; the spread of nuclear secrets and capabilities among nations was only a matter of time. Second, no state could aspire to any defense against the atomic bomb. Planes might be shot down and missiles intercepted, but eventually atomic offenses would beat all conceivable defenses. Finally, the roads to atomic power and atomic weaponry were, by the nature of the technology, largely parallel. Permitting the first would make controlling the second almost insurmountably difficult.

Today the central solution proposed by the Acheson-Lilienthal Report appears to be anachronistic, quaint, or at least hopelessly beyond the bounds of any political possibility. The report declared that international ownership of all things atomic was the best hope for allowing humankind to harness the potential of atomic power while preventing a worldwide race to acquire atomic weapons. It proposed the creation of an international Atomic Development Authority, which would own and operate all mines, plants, and materials that could be used for the production of either atomic power or atomic weapons. But the report failed to adequately address the question that Plato had raised more than two millennia earlier: who would guard the guardians? It did put forth a vague notion of transnational civil servants—scientists and administrators whose loyalties would attach to something larger than the country where they happened to have been born. But who would appoint or select them? In practice, the answer would have to be national governments; and it is difficult to imagine that, in a world of power politics, they would appoint anyone not fully committed to serving as instruments of national power.

On December 31, 1946, the AEC issued its own first report. It elaborated extensively on both the Acheson-Lilienthal Report and the Baruch Plan, and endeavored to articulate how the principles contained in those plans might be put into practice. It rejected, however, the Acheson-Lilienthal idea of international ownership, opting instead for rigorous external inspections of nationally or privately owned nuclear assets. Following are the AEC report's unambiguous conclusions and provisions:

- "The development and use of atomic energy are not essentially matters of domestic concern of the individual nations but rather have predominantly international implications and repercussions."
- "Whether the ultimate nuclear fuels be destined for peaceful or destructive uses, the productive processes are identical and inseparable."
- "The control of atomic energy to ensure its use for peaceful purposes, the elimination of atomic weapons from national armaments, and the provision of effective safeguards . . . must be accomplished through a single unified international system of control and inspection."
- "An effective system for the control of atomic energy . . . must be established by an enforceable multilateral treaty or convention . . . possessing adequate powers."
- "The treaty or convention should include, among others, provisions for:
  - "Affording the duly accredited representatives of the international control agency unimpeded rights of ingress, egress, and access . . . within the territory of every participating nation, unhindered by national or local authorities.
  - "Prohibiting the manufacture, possession, and use of atomic weapons by all nations. . . .

- "Specifying the means and methods of determining violations of its terms, setting forth such violations as shall constitute international crimes, and establishing the nature of the measures of enforcement and punishment."
- "Once the violations constituting international crimes have been defined and the measures of enforcement and punishment therefore agreed to . . . there shall be no legal right, by 'veto' or otherwise, whereby a willful violator . . . shall be protected from the consequences of violation of its terms. The enforcement and punishment provisions . . . would be ineffectual if, in any such situations, they could be rendered nugatory by the 'veto' of a State which had voluntarily signed the treaty."[6]

Most members of the press enthusiastically embraced the AEC's first report, as did many mainstream members of the foreign policy establishment and all the main bodies of organized atomic scientists, including the American Federation of Atomic Scientists and the British Association of Atomic Scientists. It was attacked in the United States, however, by conservative voices who called it naïve and idealistic. These opponents were already pushing to expand and exploit the American nuclear monopoly, and aspired to a permanent nuclear superiority even if that monopoly eventually disappeared. Of course, those voices carried the day. The elimination of atomic weapons, and rigorous international control over all atomic matters, was not to be. The nuclear genie was out of the bottle, and the nuclear arms race was on.

The Model Nuclear Weapons Convention

In the mid-1990s, shortly after the cold war's abrupt and unexpected demise, a large group of scientists, lawyers, nuclear policy experts, and civil society representatives began to hammer out a draft treaty to eliminate all nuclear weapons from the face of the earth. The work was coordinated by four venerable nuclear disarmament advocacy organizations: the Lawyers' Committee on Nuclear Policy (LCNP), the International Association of Lawyers against Nuclear Arms (IALANA), the International Network of Scientists and Engineers against Proliferation (INESAP), and the Nobel Peace laureate group International Physicians for the Prevention of Nuclear War (IPPNW). In 1999, they published a monograph called *Security and Survival: The Case for a Nuclear Weapons Convention*, which contained the entire text of what they called the Model Nuclear Weapons Convention (MNWC) and extensive commentary on its provisions. The monograph was updated and reissued in 2007, this time under the title *Securing Our Survival.*[7]

The MNWC is an effort to describe and define virtually all the elements of a scheme to abolish nuclear weapons—and ensure that they stay abolished. But it will come as little surprise that its content bears a remarkable similarity to those first structures of global atomic governance proposed by Acheson, Lilienthal, Baruch, and the AEC. Why?

Because those are the only answers there are to the enduring dilemmas of the nuclear age.

The MNWC is, indeed, a model of a universal, verifiable, and enforceable treaty to eliminate nuclear weapons permanently. Such a convention would require the phased dismantling and destruction, by a deadline, of every nuclear weapon on earth, and would prohibit thereafter the development, production, testing, deployment, stockpiling, transfer, threat, or use of nuclear weapons. (Recall from Chapter 7 the similar language that the U.N. General Assembly has employed every year since 1996.) It would also impose strict worldwide controls with rigorous inspection provisions over all nuclear fuels, technologies, and activities.

The MNWC contains several key components:

- It would require not just the destruction of nuclear weapons but also the destruction or conversion of all vehicles capable of delivering nuclear weapons.
- It would prohibit thereafter not just the production of nuclear weapons but also the production of all weapons-usable nuclear materials.
- It would include numerous provisions for verification of compliance with its requirements, both technical and political.
- It would create legal obligations for both states and individuals. All citizens of the human community would be personally prohibited from participating in any of the activities banned by the convention, would be responsible for reporting violations

coming to their attention, and would receive protection for doing so.

- It would require all state parties to enact their own national legislation to provide for the prosecution of individuals who violate provisions of the convention and to protect individuals who report violations.

- It would create a new body called the Agency for the Prohibition of Nuclear Weapons, that would oversee both the process of abolition and compliance with the convention in the post-abolition world. Unlike the present IAEA, the agency would not promote nuclear energy. Its exclusive raison d'être would be to monitor all peaceful nuclear energy activities on the planet, and to ensure that none was diverted toward nuclear weapons development. In addition, it would not be an unaccountable international bureaucracy, but would be governed by a conference of state parties to the convention, including an executive council composed of forty-four state party members elected by the conference as a whole.

- It would legally replace the NPT. All the existing international legal obligations now contained in the NPT would be superseded by the new convention.

- It would be both universal and nonwithdrawable—unlike the NPT and most other international treaties in effect today. It would be more like the American Constitution as confirmed by the American Civil War. If it were legally possible under the convention for one state to reequip itself with nuclear arms, all states would feel compelled to maintain the capability to do so in short order. Indeed, under those terms, probably no state would be willing to enter such a convention in the first place.

I differ on one minor but crucial point with the authors of the MNWC. It is not a substantive policy point, but a public relations point. Just as I believe the NPT might have been more successful had it been given a name that more accurately described its true purposes, I think the authors of the MNWC gave their model treaty the wrong name. To attract attention and immediate enthusiasm from the broad public, it should be called the Model Nuclear Weapons Elimination Convention.

A hypothetical Nuclear Weapons Convention might contain any kind of content about nuclear weapons policies, agreements, and international understandings. It could recognize a permanent group of nuclear haves and another of nuclear have-nots (which, as I've discussed, the NPT does not do even though many people believe it does). It could allow, invite, encourage, and legally authorize all states to develop nuclear weapons. In this age of short attention spans, in a time when so many other important political causes are competing for finite activist energies, in this post–cold war era when the nuclear peril, however inappropriately, has faded from public consciousness, we need to grab people's attention rapidly and directly. Calling the hypothetical treaty we desire a *Model Nuclear Weapons Elimination Convention* would leave no confusion. It would make crystal clear what that treaty is about: not, just, a treaty about nuclear weapons, but a treaty about nuclear weapons abolition.

The authors of the MNWC, of course, do not expect international leaders to enact their draft treaty in every particular. Rather, the purpose of the exercise is to demonstrate that a convention to eliminate nuclear weapons can be conceived, that the hard and thorny issues can be confronted, and that we can envision the specific architecture of a nuclear weapon–free world. So in this book I will continue to refer to the existing draft as the MNWC, but will henceforth refer to a hypothetical future treaty, not yet fully defined, to be someday actually enacted in the world, as a Nuclear Weapons Elimination Convention (NWEC).

IS IT POSSIBLE BOTH TO RETAIN NUCLEAR ENERGY AND TO ABOLISH NUCLEAR WEAPONS?

Although the MNWC would not prohibit nuclear energy, it would express a strong preference against it, and would promote alternative sources such as wind, solar, tidal, geothermal, and hydroelectric energy. Moreover, in an optional protocol, it would provide incentives and assistance to develop renewable energy technologies to states that chose to forego nuclear energy or phase out existing programs.

Like the MNWC, I do not insist on the abolition of nuclear energy. As it has for the MNWC, this position will likely generate intense opposition from those who believe, with substantial and credible grounds, that the risks of nuclear energy far outweigh the benefits, that preservation of the planet requires the abolition of both nuclear weapons and nuclear power, and that the world's future energy needs can be fulfilled through substantial investments in renewable energy. These arguments gained considerable momentum in January 2009, when Germany, in conjunction with more than seventy other countries, launched an initiative to create an International Renewable Energy Agency to be funded largely by the 250 billion dollars in annual government subsidies that now go to supporting nuclear and fossil-fuel technologies.[8]

Many people, including a number with impeccable green credentials such as James Lovelock, Stewart Brand, and the Right Reverend Hugh Montefiore, take the opposite stance, and insist that nuclear energy must play a crucial role in humanity's efforts to confront the challenge of climate change. Again, I, like the MNWC, do not advocate nuclear energy either. Perhaps we might call this an agnostic position on the nuclear energy question. The focus here is on figuring out how, if the human race substantially expands its use of nuclear energy in the decades to come, we still can manage to abolish nuclear weapons, and ensure that the one will not inevitably lead to the other.

Most of the world's nuclear reactors are fueled by uranium enriched to less than 5-percent U-235 (with the remaining 95 percent or more the less dangerous isotope U-238). But the same equipment and facilities used to enrich uranium to the 5-percent level can, with a bit of adjustment, be used to enrich uranium to the 20-percent level, where a nuclear detonation becomes possible, or even up to the 90-percent level, where a nuclear detonation becomes much more efficient and destructive.

The obvious solution, in today's pre-abolition world, is for non-nuclear weapon states to continue to be allowed to build nuclear reactors (as the NPT permits), but for them to obtain the necessary fuel from an outside source. That way, these states can procure nuclear fuel for their reactors, but not the technologies to transform those fuels into material suitable for nuclear weapons. That way, these states can generate nuclear energy without obtaining the capacity to build nuclear bombs.

President Bush's proposed solution, however, is not the answer. On February 11, 2004, he suggested, "The world's leading nuclear exporters should ensure that states have reliable access at reasonable cost to fuel for civilian reactors, so long as those states renounce enrichment."[9] In

Bush's vision, nuclear fuel–producing facilities would be limited to just a few states—those who already have them—which, in our present pre-abolition world, would further entrench the two-tier system. The nuclear haves would possess both nuclear weapons and the technologies to create the fuels for those weapons, while the nuclear have-nots would be denied either. It is hard to resist identifying any such scheme as a double double standard.

The have-nots are very unlikely to accept such an arrangement as part of a pre-abolition nuclear status quo. Indeed, during the Bush era, the Non-Aligned Movement, whose members include far more than half the states in the world, repeatedly dismissed the idea.[10] But the scheme would probably be unacceptable in a post-abolition world as well. It is difficult to believe that the longstanding non-nuclear weapon states would react with equanimity if told that the double standard for nuclear weapons was henceforth eliminated but would now immediately be replaced with a new nuclear double standard, this time for nuclear enrichment capabilities. Once again, they would have ended up on the wrong side of the divide.

Mohammed El-Baradei of the IAEA has put forth a different and better idea that might be acceptable to non-nuclear weapon states—both today and tomorrow. Not surprisingly, it evokes the answers advanced by that first-generation of thinkers who grappled with the nuclear question. In El-Baradei's view, all nuclear fuel production technologies and facilities, anywhere in the world, ought to be placed under the strict control of an impartial international agency, which would then oversee and supervise the supply of nuclear fuels to all states.[11] On its very first day in office, the new Obama administration expressed its support for the concept, saying it intended "to establish a new international nuclear energy architecture—including an international nuclear fuel bank, international nuclear fuel cycle centers, and reliable fuel supply assurances—to meet growing demands for nuclear power without contributing to proliferation."[12]

The venerable American diplomat Thomas Pickering emphasizes that such an international regime could not convey legitimacy and credibility unless the availability of fuel to purchasers was clearly based only on whether a state was in conformity with its legal obligations on non-proliferation and disarmament, and not tied to political horse trading. In today's pre-abolition world, he says, the international community would need to "put aside a certain amount of fuel in a truly neutral country and allow the IAEA to sell that fuel on the basis that it hadn't found the purchaser in violation of its non-proliferation obligations. That would be a method of assuring countries that fuel sales wouldn't be used to extract political concessions."[13]

The best answers proposed for non-nuclear weapon states in a pre-abolition world provide the basis of the best answers to keep all states from reacquiring nuclear weapons in a post-abolition world. These proposals form the essence of how a hypothetical NWEC could allow nuclear energy to persist on our planet indefinitely, without the risk that the capability to generate nuclear power would lead inevitably to the capability to build nuclear weapons. No state would ever be allowed, under such a treaty, to enrich uranium to a level suitable to fuel nuclear bombs. (Indeed, under the MNWC, it would become illegal, anywhere on earth, to enrich uranium to a level above 20 percent.) All nuclear fuel production facilities would be controlled by something like El-Baradei's impartial international agency, or the MNWC agency, or the Atomic Development Authority proposed so very long ago in the Acheson-Lilienthal Report. That agency would take charge of both the distribution of nuclear fuels for nuclear power and the disposition of spent fuels, and ensure that none of them are converted into fuels suitable for nuclear weapons.

In a speech before the United Nations in December 1953, the new American president, Dwight D. Eisenhower, proposed that Washington and Moscow simultaneously remove significant quantities of fissile material from their growing nuclear weapons stockpiles and provide it to other states to generate nuclear energy. These states would formally agree to use it exclusively for peaceful purposes and to have such uses verified by international controls. Eisenhower's plan, known as Atoms for Peace, contained three of the foundational ideas for addressing the problem of nuclear fuel. First, states that wanted to pursue nuclear energy would have fuel provided from the outside. Second, to obtain such fuels, states would have to agree to international inspections. Third, and arguably most important, as the non-nuclear weapon states obtained fuel for nuclear energy and agreed not to develop nuclear weapons, the nuclear weapons states would engage in nuclear disarmament.

Unfortunately, this last component fell by the wayside. Instead, the United States and the USSR simply produced more and more nuclear fuel, plenty both to sell to other states for nuclear energy and to retain for themselves for nuclear weapons. Yet the third component of Atoms for Peace could serve as a crucial element of a post-abolition architecture. Nuclear fuels for nuclear energy could be supplied not just from internationally supervised fuel production facilities, but also from dismantled nuclear weapons themselves.

A hypothetical NWEC would need to institute strict controls at both ends of the nuclear fuel cycle. When the fuel rods in a nuclear reactor become "spent," a plutonium reprocessing plant can, through chemical separation processes, remove from them a quantity of weapons-grade plutonium, suitable for use in an atom bomb. (The remainder can then be used to fuel a nuclear reactor again.) To allow states to generate nuclear power without developing the reprocessing capabilities to separate out weapons-grade plutonium, the world community should simply ban such reprocessing altogether, and empower an impartial international agency to take custody of, secure, and dispose of the spent fuel from all nuclear power plants. The MNWC agrees, saying that "all plutonium reprocessing facilities shall cease operations and be permanently closed."[14] This means that, even if we are going to permit nuclear power to continue indefinitely, nuclear power in the future must be fueled exclusively by uranium. Reprocessing of spent nuclear fuel, even if it can produce additional fuels for additional nuclear power generation, is simply too dangerous to be permitted anymore. Even if it can be used for nuclear energy, it is not essential to nuclear energy. And it poses to great a risk for utilization in something other than nuclear energy.

Such an approach makes sense from both an international security and an economic perspective. In an effort to seriously confront global climate change, a 2003 MIT study calculated several of the requirements and consequences of an expansion of nuclear power—from the roughly 360 gigawatts generated today to about 1,000 gigawatts by the middle of the twenty-first century. The study concluded that when one considers both the high cost of building and operating spent fuel reprocessing plants and the continued availability of relatively cheap uranium (and anticipated technological advances to improve uranium extraction and recovery techniques), the most economically advantageous course will be to fuel nuclear reactors with uranium rather than resort to reprocessing spent fuel.[15]

The ultimate goal, says Michael Spies, should be "to end the spread of new national nuclear fuel production facilities, and to phase out existing non-international facilities, including in the weapon-possessing states."[16] In a world without nuclear weapons but with nuclear power remaining, the only solution is for all nuclear fuel production facilities and spent fuel processing services to be operated under strict international control.

DISMANTLING NUCLEAR WEAPONS AND DISPOSING OF NUCLEAR MATERIALS

The dawn of the nuclear age has presented us with challenges of time scale so vast as to be beyond human comprehension. As George F. Kennan said late in life, those who have so vigorously pursued nuclear weapons and nuclear energy for more than half a century have burdened us "with huge stockpiles of poisonous nuclear wastes that they . . . still do not how to dispose of safely. This situation is to be dumped upon our descendants, who will curse us for saddling them with so dangerous and almost insoluble a problem."[17] Today, still, no one really knows what to do with either the radioactive waste that nuclear reactors generate, or the radioactive materials that might be extracted from dismantled nuclear weapons. Plutonium remains toxic for a quarter of a million years, and some nuclear materials can remain dangerously radioactive for as long as 3.8 million years.[18] No one has yet come up with a foolproof solution that guarantees that these materials will not drastically harm human health, other living creatures, and our planetary environment over the very long term.

Options currently include down-blending highly enriched uranium into low-enriched uranium that can be used only in nuclear reactors for power generation, converting plutonium and uranium into mixed-oxide fuel for the same purpose, dispatching dangerous materials to a deep geologic excavation such as Yucca Mountain in Nevada, destroying the nuclear elements in underground nuclear explosions, and even launching nuclear materials on spacecraft and directing them into the sun. But all of these solutions are imperfect and have their risks, both obvious and otherwise. For example, the MIT study just mentioned also forecasts that, to permanently store the nuclear waste that would be generated under its 1,000-gigawatt scenario, "new repository storage capacity equal to the currently planned capacity of the Yucca Mountain facility would have to be created somewhere in the world roughly every three or four years."[19] In any case, President Obama essentially killed the existing Yucca Mountain project in his first budget, as he had promised to do during his campaign.

Longtime nuclear weapons and nuclear energy abolitionist Alice Slater of the Nuclear Age Peace Foundation argues persuasively that part of the reason we have not yet obtained adequate solutions to the disposal problem is that much of the technical research has been conducted by the nuclear weapons labs themselves, which obviously have a vested interest in maintaining the nuclear status quo: "The best, cheapest, and quickest way to secure the material from theft is to put it behind gates with guns and guards . . . until a new generation of scientists, untainted by weapons work and ecological unconsciousness, has addressed the disposition conundrum. With adequate resources and new thinking, we may discover new properties of nuclear materials, which will enable us to render them inert over a shorter period of time."[20]

The MNWC acknowledges that current disposition solutions are inadequate to the task. Therefore, it says simply, "All existing stocks of special nuclear material shall be placed under preventive controls and storage, until a safe method of final disposal is found and approved by the Agency."[21] But not knowing what to do with the stuff inside a nuclear weapon over the very long term is hardly an argument for keeping nuclear weapons intact. A couple of dozen kilograms of highly radioactive plutonium sitting in a box is incredibly dangerous, and will be for generations to come. Yet a couple of dozen kilograms of plutonium shaped into the cores of nuclear weapons is surely more dangerous still. Surely we should not wait for a "safe method of final disposal" to emerge before addressing the immediate nuclear weapons peril. If we do not, the human race may not have to worry about the dangers that highly radioactive nuclear materials might pose decades, or centuries, or millennia down the road. Because there may be no human race to worry about them.

VERIFYING IRAQ'S NUCLEAR DISARMAMENT

The world has already seen a successful case of verifying compliance with legally mandated disarmament. Where? In Iraq. From 1991 to 2003. On August 2, 1990, the state of Iraq invaded, conquered, and occupied its neighbor Kuwait, an act universally condemned by the international community. During the following January and February, Iraq was forced out militarily by what the first Bush administration called Operation Desert Storm, a U.S.-led coalition authorized by the U.N. Security Council. Soon thereafter, the Security Council authorized unprecedented intrusions on Iraqi sovereignty, to ensure that the government of Saddam Hussein could not develop chemical, biological, or nuclear weapons of mass destruction. Traditional IAEA inspectors were supplemented by a new body that the Security Council created especially for the purpose: the U.N. Special Commission (UNSCOM), which later became the U.N. Monitoring, Verification, and Inspection Commission (UNMOVIC). The Security Council insisted to a prostrate Iraq, which had virtually no bargaining power to object, that international inspectors must be allowed to talk to anyone, unannounced, and to go anywhere, unannounced.

Journalist Mark Hibbs, who writes for the technical industry publications *Nuclear Fuel* and *Nucleonics Week*, concluded that, before Desert Storm, Iraq may have been three years away from producing enough highly enriched uranium to make an atomic bomb.[22] The Saddam Hussein regime also maintained substantial chemical and biological weapons programs in various stages of development. Nevertheless, during several hundred inspections in the dozen years between the end of the Gulf War in 1991 and the beginning of the U.S. invasion in 2003, UNSCOM, UNMOVIC, and IAEA inspectors revealed, identified, and dismantled the complete Iraqi stockpile of WMDs and their long-range delivery missiles, even though the Iraqis made considerable efforts to obstruct their efforts.[23] And, of course, as is well-known, when the United States invaded and occupied the country in 2003 (this time, of course, without U.N. authorization), it was not able to find any WMDs at all.

The case of Iraq before 1991 demonstrates that merely allowing states to declare which nuclear facilities they possess and then opening only these to IAEA inspection is not sufficient to verify compliance with nuclear prohibitions. Iraq had allowed inspections of its declared nuclear facilities many times before August 2, 1990. But only the inspection regime imposed after the first Gulf War—that enabled inspectors to go where they wanted to go rather than only where Baghdad said they could go—could reveal that Iraq had come close to constructing its own nuclear weapons at secret facilities unknown to the outside world. Previously those facilities had been inaccessible to the IAEA, simply because they had been undeclared.

Iraq's verification precedent is unique: the international community has never legally required any other country to open itself so completely to external investigation. Former vice president Dick Cheney referred to the inspection system as "the most intrusive system of arms control in history."[24] Once Iraq agreed, under great duress, to cede some of its national sovereignty to an international authority, Saddam Hussein's regime was unable to hide or preserve any substantial nuclear weapons programs or other WMD pursuits. Despite the obstacles that Saddam Hussein constructed and his protests about his state's inequitable treatment, despite the fact that international inspectors had to make up the rules as they went along since no one had ever tried "anywhere, anytime" inspections before, the inspections in Iraq were a spectacular success.

The key difference between the verification record in Iraq and the verification provisions under a hypothetical NWEC becomes immediately apparent. With regard to intrusions on its national sovereignty, Iraq was treated differently from every country in the world. Under an NWEC, all states, universally and equally, would be expected to bear such intrusions—and unlike Iraq, would have volitionally agreed to them.

If the world succeeded in the particular case of Iraq, despite all the obstacles that Saddam Hussein constructed, then it seems reasonable to suppose that the world can succeed in the general case as well. It is to that general case–the verification of a prohibition on nuclear weapons not just in one state, but in every state—that we now turn.

VERIFYING UNIVERSAL
NUCLEAR DISARMAMENT

In December 1987, at the third summit meeting in Washington, D.C., between President Ronald Reagan and Soviet General Secretary

Mikhail Gorbachev, Reagan stretched his Russian language skills to their limit, proclaiming, "*Dovorey no provorey*. Trust but verify."

"You repeat that at every meeting," said Gorbachev.

"I like it," Reagan replied. The United States and the USSR had just concluded an agreement to dismantle all the intermediate-range nuclear missiles that both sides held in Europe. Before long Soviet officials were observing the physical destruction of American Pershing II nuclear missiles, while Americans were watching the simultaneous dismantlement of Soviet SS-20 missiles.[25]

Although nuclear disarmament advocates may disagree with much of Ronald Reagan's legacy, today, we should like *dovorey no provorey* too. No aspect of a hypothetical NWEC will be more important than the question of whether compliance with its provisions can be credibly verified. Nothing would cause such a convention to unravel more quickly than a suspicion that other states were cheating—and getting away with it. Indeed, nothing would more surely convince states not to enter into an NWEC in the first place.

Fortunately, the technologies and techniques available for monitoring compliance with nuclear disarmament agreements have advanced a great deal since the Soviet-American arms control agreements of the cold war. The inspections in Iraq pioneered several new avenues for verification, including radioisotope monitoring, portal control systems, environmental sampling analysis, wide area surveillance, real time surveillance, on-site sensors, and remote sensors in faraway ground facilities. Overhead photography from satellites and aircraft can now quickly provide high-resolution images over large areas (and the American program to develop giant spy dirigibles could enhance these capabilities). The concentration of krypton-85 in the atmosphere can be gauged to detect clandestine plutonium separation activities. Advances continue in seismological, radionuclide, hydroacoustic, and infrasound monitoring technologies.

A nongovernmental organization called the Verification Research, Training, and Information Centre (VERTIC) was founded in the United Kingdom in 1986, to develop and promote "effective and efficient verification as a means of ensuring confidence in the implementation of international agreements." The center maintains elaborate programs on the verification of agreements pertaining to war and peace, the environment, and disarmament. VERTIC is probably the leading source today for the latest developments on both the technologies and techniques of verification, which will only continue to improve.[26] But even today, if most contemporary verification methods were implemented under the terms of an NWEC, it would be virtually impossible to hide a program to develop and construct nuclear weapons.

But who would carry out such verification under a hypothetical NWEC? The IAEA today has no independent intelligence capability but must go hat in hand to national governments to request even rudimentary intelligence assistance. Because it is so dependent on these governments, the IAEA naturally finds it difficult to criticize them. In fact, IAEA officials told reporters that U.S. government intelligence sharing diminished substantially after Director General El-Baradei contradicted Bush administration statements on weapons of mass destruction in Iraq. Obviously, the verification agency created in an NWEC will need capabilities both more robust and more independent than the IAEA presently possesses. Yet ideally, international authorities will also receive help from the state parties themselves, who will possess an enormous interest in ensuring that other states continuously comply with an abolition agreement. It will do the cause of abolition no good at all if the Americans develop giant dirigibles, and then refuse to share either the technologies or the products with anyone else.

Many states, of course, already maintain well-established and -funded intelligence organizations and operations, which they could employ under an NWEC to verify compliance for themselves. The MNWC would explicitly encourage state parties to do so, and in fact would require states to report any violations they might uncover or suspect directly to the MNWC agency.

In addition, the MNWC also places that same requirement upon individuals. An NWEC should also provide substantial protections, perhaps even monetary rewards, for those with the courage to reveal secret nuclear programs. "A million dollars to any citizen who provides information that leads to proof that any state, or entity, or individual, is engaged in activities that violate the requirements of the NWEC." Such whistleblower safeguards and inducements could be a great deterrent to potential violators. Any state leadership that even thinks about embarking on a surreptitious nuclear path will never be sure that its efforts, if pursued, will not be disclosed by one of the participants, perhaps for a price. That possibility would weigh heavily in a state's benefit-cost calculations about whether to take a stab at cheating—and might well serve as the decisive discouragement.

According to the late Joseph Rotblat, a Manhattan project physicist turned abolition advocate and 1995 Nobel Peace laureate, the whistle-blowing element is a crucial aspect of any proposed abolition regime: "Citizens—including, especially, scientists—[would] acquire a legal obligation to report on any efforts to build weapons of mass destruction. If violations are occurring, scientists will realize that something is going on. With this societal system of verification in place in addition to all the technical means, the chances of any nation building up a nuclear arsenal in a completely clandestine way, without its being detected, is extremely small."[27]

The dismantling of nuclear weapons complexes around the world will, of course, end the employment of thousands of technical nuclear weapons professionals. Few priorities for any abolition regime could be higher than ensuring that these individuals, unemployed and idle, do not go to work for hypothetical violators of a hypothetical NWEC. Yet paradoxically these same individuals could provide a crucial tool for verification. The MNWC recommends that they be offered key roles in the process of nuclear weapons dismantlement, destruction, and verification. Who better to render a verdict on whether nuclear weapons development activities are taking place in a post-abolition world than former professionals in nuclear weapons development?

Perhaps it is not too much to claim that, for many, it would give their post–nuclear weapons complex lives some meaning and purpose. Surely some designers already have mixed feelings about the nature of their profession, even if they are able to convince themselves that, through deterrence, the most destructive implements ever invented can lead to an enduring world peace. To turn their technical skills to the cause of nuclear disarmament—for example, generating new technologies and techniques for verification or disposal—would let them become prime players in one of the greatest achievements in human history.

Yet no matter how many razzle-dazzle technologies might emerge, no matter how effective societal verification might prove to be, the most important technique for verifying compliance with an NWEC will be good old-fashioned on-the-ground inspections: of sensitive national facilities, conducted by international authorities, anywhere, anytime.

As the Iraqi case makes clear, the "anywhere, anytime" proviso is crucial. The crucial difference between the period before Baghdad's invasion of Kuwait in August 1990 and the period after its eviction in 1991 wasn't something technological, it was something political. But the problem endures. In October 2008, the United States and North Korea struck a deal that allowed the interminable disarmament process on the Korean peninsula to resume. International inspectors, however, were granted access only to nuclear sites that the North Korean government had declared to exist. If inspectors sought access to other suspicious sites, they would be granted access only by "mutual consent."[28] In other words, the North Korean government retained the power to say no.

North Korea's position is understandable. Like Iraq between 1991 and 2003, it is being asked to subject itself to a level of intrusion far greater than that presently required of most other states. Nevertheless, the power to say no cannot be permitted to anyone under any hypothetical universal nuclear disarmament regime. The MNWC authorizes both systematic inspections (regularly scheduled with notice) and challenge inspections (anytime, any place, without notice). These challenge inspections could be initiated by the MNWC agency, or requested by any state party that might suspect prohibited activities. International inspectors could request as much information as they deem necessary, including visual inspections; radiological measurement with portable detectors; full access to rooms, locked filing cabinets, and computer codes; and interviews with state personnel—or even their neighbors.[29]

So if international inspectors would possess such unlimited authority to intrude upon the sovereignty of any country in the world, how would we ensure that they possess reasonable grounds for doing so? Perhaps the best approach might be to create a structure analogous to the U.S. procedure for obtaining domestic search warrants for a suspected crime. For instance, the Los Angeles Police Department possesses the right within city limits to go almost anywhere, anytime, without notice. Officers can show up on my doorstep, demand entry, and open every closet, drawer, and cabinet in my home. But they must possess some reasonable grounds for doing so. And before showing up on my doorstep, they must demonstrate, to an impartial judge, that that they have "probable cause" for doing so. That judge will grant that search warrant only if the police can prove that they are likely to find evidence of some crime inside my house.

The analogy seems obvious. In a hypothetical post-abolition world, international inspectors would have the right to go anywhere, anytime, without notice, in any country in the world. But only if they first go before an impartial judicial body to demonstrate that they have probable cause to suspect they will find evidence of some violation.

The MNWC recognizes that a verification regime might be abused, perhaps to place excessive burdens on a state for politically motivated reasons, perhaps for reasons of espionage. Consequently, the convention directly prohibits both signatories and international verification authorities from engaging in such activities: "Verification . . . shall be based on objective information, shall be limited to the subject matter of this Convention, and shall be carried out on the basis of full respect for the sovereignty of States Parties and in the least intrusive manner possible."[30] Moreover, it designates a body for rendering such judgments: the convention's executive council, comprised of elected representatives from forty-four rotating states. The council would be charged with determining whether a particular challenge inspection request is "frivolous, abusive, or clearly beyond the scope of this Convention."

Clearly, there needs to be a fine balance between an inspection regime's level of intrusiveness and a state's assurance that, in opening itself to such intrusion, it will not sacrifice its most sensitive national security secrets. (This was always a central issue in Soviet-American arms control negotiations.) That will especially be the case if suspicion emerges that those requesting or performing such intrusions possess nefarious motives, moved less by a quest for verification than by efforts at harassment or espionage. Or if some states find themselves subjected to deeper and more frequent intrusions than others. The MNWC takes a stab at striking that balance. However, it will be up to the drafters of our hypothetical NWEC, and then to those who implement it and bring it into being, to address and maintain that tension with equilibrium, poise, and diplomatic finesse.

ADJUDICATING AND ENFORCING UNIVERSAL
NUCLEAR DISARMAMENT

Of course, it may turn out that as a post-abolition regime unfolds, razzle-dazzle technologies, on-the-ground inspections, or societal verification may raise suspicions that some state is, in fact, violating the provisions of the NWEC. What then? Today the U.N. Security Council is the ultimate international legal arbiter over matters of war and peace. Cognizant of and limited by this reality, the MNWC therefore leaves the matter of enforcement essentially in the Security Council's hands. Suspected violations of the MNWC will be deemed "a threat to the peace" (the U.N. Charter's trigger phrase for enforcement action), and then be referred by the MNWC's executive council or conference of state parties to the Security Council, which could then proceed as it would against any other such threat.

Unfortunately, the Security Council's track record of responding in concert to violators of the international laws pertaining to war and peace is, to say the least, inconsistent. John Burroughs of the Lawyers' Committee on Nuclear Policy is one of the world's leading authorities on the various international legal regimes that govern nuclear armaments, both present and prospective. In 2007, he critiqued the shortcomings of the Security Council regarding enforcement of contemporary nuclear arms control agreements.[31] But under any such future agreement, the Security Council—under the rules hammered out in San Francisco in 1945 and still prevailing—would face much the same enforcement difficulties.

Burroughs starts by pointing out the most obvious fact regarding the present regime: the NPT simply contains no provisions for enforcement when states do not comply with the treaty—neither for non-nuclear weapon states that violate their obligation to forego nuclear weapons, nor for nuclear weapon states that violate their obligation to eliminate nuclear weapons. That would obviously have to be different in any kind of an NWEC.

Yet if that NWEC simply declared that violations would be referred to the U.N. Security Council, the most obvious contradiction immediately presents itself. The five permanent members of the Security Council, who can veto any proposed council action, are all nuclear weapon states. If, under an NWEC, one of these states was accused of violating its NWEC obligations and the violation was referred to the Security

Council, that state could formally prevent the council from taking any action at all.

Burroughs emphasizes that, under the present regime, decisions made on nuclear questions by states that are both permanent Security Council members and nuclear weapon states are, in the eyes of the rest of the world, "automatically suspect."[32] It is bad enough that under the NPT an entirely different set of rules applies to the nuclear weapon states. But consider how it appears to have those states serving as judge, jury, and enforcer on all questions of whether non-nuclear weapon states are complying with the NPT. This is precisely the situation that has prevailed between the Security Council and Iran since 2003. And, as the rules of the United Nations presently stand, it is precisely the situation that would prevail under a hypothetical NWEC. Any perceived disparity in enforcement deliberations between, say, China and India, would be automatically suspect in the eyes of the rest of the world. It is difficult to comprehend how other states might ever view such an arrangement as fair or, indeed, why they would ever sign on to such an arrangement in the first place.

In addition, says Burroughs, the present Security Council is "conspicuously not representative" of the power realities of today's world.[33] The five winners of a war that ended during the first half of the last century are indisputably not the five most significant actors in contemporary international politics. (Leave aside for the moment the question of whether the world ought to be governed by a small group of "great powers," or whether instead our sociopolitical imaginations might someday invent better mechanisms of global governance, and begin to move toward creating something on the world level resembling a parliament of humankind.) For years, U.N. restructuring advocates have pushed for modernization of the council's permanent membership and for many other modifications in the structures of the San Francisco charter, so far, without success. This stagnation in the power realities of an earlier era clouds the legitimacy of virtually every decision the council undertakes today. Without change, it would certainly cloud the legitimacy of any decision it might undertake tomorrow regarding the enforcement of an NWEC.

Finally, Burroughs points out a crucial fact that is almost never discussed: the Security Council "is a political body that acts on an ad hoc basis to maintain peace and security, not a technical or judicial body charged with making determinations in accordance with general principles. . . . the Council is not bound, and does not attempt, to address all cases in a given category or to ensure consistency in treatment of similar situations, a requisite of law."[34] His insight raises the crucial distinction between adjudication (determining whether a violation of a law or an agreement has occurred) and enforcement (responding to such a violation). Today, despite Burroughs's concern, the Security Council both judges whether a state threatens international peace and security, and decides what kind of response to pursue.

The MNWC recognizes this flaw in our contemporary system of global governance. The solution it offers is that, while the Security Council would still ultimately decide how the international community would respond to a violation, the entire conference of state parties to the MNWC would determine whether a party was in violation of the convention. This proposal strikes me as one of the MNWC's few defects. A universal assembly of states, though it may not possess all the flaws that Burroughs identifies in the Security Council, is still more like a legislative body than a judicial body. To render a legal judgment as to whether a violation of a treaty has occurred, some kind of judicial body is a far better alternative. Perhaps the present World Court could perform such a role under an NWEC. Or perhaps a new body might be created, composed of judges and staff members with technical expertise in the nuclear field. Only after such a judicial body rendered a verdict on whether a violation had actually occurred would a case be referred to the Security Council for enforcement.

That would certainly be an improvement over the present system. Nevertheless, the many other imperfections of the U.N. Security Council as the mechanism for enforcing violations of an NWEC would remain. In the end, one can envision only one real solution to the problem of enforcing an NWEC under the present U.N. Charter. Not surprisingly, it is the solution advanced only months after the birth of both that Charter and the bomb itself.

It should be recalled that the U.N. Charter is a pre-nuclear document, signed in San Francisco on June 26, 1945, three weeks before the detonation of the first atomic bomb. Indeed, President Eisenhower's secretary of state, John Foster Dulles, a participant in the original charter deliberations and no starry-eyed internationalist, later said, "As one who was at San Francisco, I can say with confidence that if the delegates there had known that the mysterious and immeasurable power of the atom would be available as a means of mass destruction, the provisions of the Charter dealing with disarmament . . . would have been far more emphatic and realistic."[35]

Almost immediately after that power was revealed, Bernard Baruch indicated just what those alternative charter provisions ought to be. The single most important feature of the Baruch Plan was its insistence that the international response to violations of any hypothetical future nuclear disarmament agreement must be freed from the requirement of U.N. Security Council unanimity: the veto. "U.S. Will Tell Atom Secret, Destroy Bombs, if UN Establishes Controls without a Veto," read the headline of the *New York Times* on June 15, 1946. Thirteen years later, philosopher Bertrand Russell described the essence of the problem: "So long as the Veto exists, [the United Nations] lacks an essential characteristic of any Government . . . that it can enforce decisions upon recalcitrant members of the State which it represents. What should we think of a national State in which any burglar could veto laws against theft?"[36]

One way to prevent a hypothetical nuclear burglar from taking such an action might be for the NWEC to include a provision that modifies the veto over nuclear disarmament matters. Perhaps enforcement might be authorized only with the assent of both four-fifths of the council's fifteen members and four-fifths of its five permanent members. Thus, if one of the permanent five wanted to block an action, it would have to enlist the support of at least one other permanent member or of at least three other members altogether. Or a simpler solution might be for the NWEC to require that a party may not veto any action in the Security Council directed against itself.

Numerous similar schemes might be devised. Without similar amendments to the U.N. Charter itself, their standing under international law would remain unclear. Nevertheless, any NWEC would have to put forth the principle, unambiguously, that no state can violate the convention and then veto actions that might be undertaken by the international community to respond to the noncompliance. Several years ago the *Economist* said, "The vetoers would veto a veto of the veto" since, under articles 108 and 109, the charter cannot be amended without the assent of all five permanent members. It is admittedly difficult in the present historical moment to envision abolishing or even modifying the veto. But we must put the idea squarely on the table if we are to talk about an enduring architecture for a nuclear weapon–free world. If we cannot foresee how exactly we might get rid of the veto, one thing we can know for sure is that we will never get rid of the veto if no one says that we ought to get rid of the veto. And to enforce the abolition of nuclear weapons—and, arguably, for many other twenty-first century global governance challenges as well—we ought to get rid of the veto.

The MNWC contains specific provisions that make it a crime for any citizen of the world to participate in work directed at reintroducing nuclear weapons, and also obligates every state party to make such activities a national crime as well. Such crimes would be indictable and prosecutable before either national courts or the new International Criminal Court (ICC). The ICC was created in 1998 to prosecute (and, we hope, to deter) genocide and other crimes against humanity when national legal mechanisms are inadequate to the task. Because endeavoring to renuclearize the world ought to be considered a crime comparable to genocide, the drafters of the MNWC felt that the ICC would be a natural and critically useful tool for enforcing the convention.

But in the end, perhaps the most important initiative toward the enforcement of an NWEC would be to prevent the problem ever from arising. Both the MNWC and the elaborate commentaries presented in *Securing Our Survival* emphasize the importance of providing incentives for compliance rather than threats of punishment. After all, it has been known since long before the nuclear age began that you catch more flies with honey than with vinegar. If an NWEC makes clear that a state's interests will be considerably enhanced if it adheres to the prohibition on nuclear weapons in a post-abolition world, most states will choose to do so.

If that strikes some as hopelessly naïve or idealistic or "soft," consider that most states today already choose not to pursue activities prohibited under international law, despite the absence of effective enforcement measures. The best example, perhaps, is slavery. Currently, there are various international legal conventions against slavery and a widespread moral norm adjudging that it violates the collective conscience of a civilized human community. Although it unfortunately persists in many parts of the world, virtually no one on the planet openly advocates its legalization or legitimization.

But the limitations that Burroughs describes on U.N. Security Council enforcement actions apply to slavery just as much as they do to the NPT. So why don't veto-holding members of the Security Council openly advocate international trafficking in slavery? The answer is not because they fear enforcement action from the Security Council. If Russia, for instance, openly instituted slavery, and a council member put forth a resolution condemning its action and authorizing a collective response, Russia could veto the resolution. No, states forego instituting slavery and engaging in international slave trafficking because their assessment of the likely benefits and costs leads them to conclude that it would not be in their interest to do so. The international furor, and the quite tangible accompanying consequences, would be the overriding variable in the cost column.

The analogy to a hypothetical future ban on nuclear weapons seems quite precise. Just as abolition of slavery in the nineteenth century was followed by virtually universal condemnation of the practice, so, too, will the abolition of nuclear weapons be followed by a similar rejection of the institution. Enough so to make it virtually inconceivable that any state in a post-abolition world might consider re-entering the nuclear game, assess the likely benefits and costs, and conclude that it could possibly be in its interest to do so.

HOBBES, LOCKE, AND THE APOCALYPSE: CAN WE ENFORCE UNIVERSAL NUCLEAR DISARMAMENT WITHOUT WORLD GOVERNMENT?

What has variously been called a world state, world federation, or world government is one of the great ideas in the heritage of humanity, dating back at least to St. Augustine's *City of God* more than 1,500 years ago. World government enthusiasts argue that a single universal sovereign is the only plausible idea ever advanced to abolish war itself. They insist that adequate governance at the global level now requires what everyone already seems to agree is required at every other level: a legislative, an executive, and a judicial branch, and police to enforce the law. They contend that the division of the human race into some two hundred sovereign states, each with its own army, navy, and air force, engaged in endless arms races with the latest in military technology, perpetually seeking to strike a "balance of power" (and succeeding only most of the time), does not need to be the end of history. They envision instead a next step in the social evolution of our species: a single, politically unified human community, a divided earth after countless generations becoming a united earth, an enduring world peace through enforceable world law, a Federal Republic of the World. They claim that this probably ought to be considered what Unitarian/Universalist minister Mark Gallagher calls no less than the "the biggest idea in the history of history."[37]

In the centuries since Augustine, the idea of a world state has been articulated and advanced in works such as Dante Alighieri's *De Monarchia* (circa 1310), Jean-Jacques Rousseau's *Lasting Peace through the Federation of Europe* (1756), Immanuel Kant's *Perpetual Peace* (1795), Alfred Lord Tennyson's *Locksley Hall* (1842), H. G. Wells's *The Open Conspiracy* (1928), Mortimer J. Adler's *How to Think about War and Peace* (1944), Emery Reves's *The Anatomy of Peace* (1946), and Grenville Clark and Louis Sohn's *World Peace through World Law* (1958). (Mr. Clark was Alan Cranston's first mentor.) It was the central idea behind the 1947 *Preliminary Draft of a World Constitution*, the product of a group of leading postwar intellectuals assembled by University of Chicago president Robert Maynard Hutchins. It continues to be promoted today, albeit obscurely, by nongovernmental advocacy groups and initiatives such as the Democratic World Federalists (www.dwfed.org), World beyond Borders (www.worldbeyondborders.org), the World Federalist Movement (www.wfm.org), and Citizens for Global Solutions, descendant organization of the United World Federalists (www.globalsolutions.org), which Alan Cranston served as president between 1949 and 1952.

Nevertheless, might not there be a possible architecture of global governance in between unrestricted national sovereignty and world government? And—whether or not world government might be desirable or achievable for a host of other aspirations—might not such an in-between destination be adequate for the aspiration of enforcing universal nuclear disarmament? To grapple with this question, it is useful to recall an essential distinction between the political philosophies of Thomas Hobbes and John Locke.

If states do choose to accept the limitations on their sovereignty described in this chapter, that voluntary choice will not be so different from the social contract that Thomas Hobbes wrote about in his masterpiece, *Leviathan*, in 1651. In Hobbes's prepolitical state of nature, where "the life of man [is] solitary, poore, nasty, brutish, and short," all individuals lived in a state of perpetual insecurity, and perpetual fear that others would inflict harm upon them.[38] Hobbes was not claiming that this was the reality of the prehistoric human condition. Rather, it was a continuous danger, the chaos to which human affairs always held the potential to descend. (And yet, as suggested in Chapter 5, Nicholas Wade's 2006 book *Before the Dawn* suggests that the "Hobbesian state of nature" does, in fact, provide a pretty accurate description of prehistoric human life.) Hobbes's answer was for rational individuals to forge among themselves a social contract, by which, acting in their own self-interest, they relinquish some of the absolute freedoms they possess in the state of nature—most especially the freedom to inflict violence upon others, even in response to violence inflicted upon themselves. In return, they gain a new freedom, from endless cycles of violence and vengeance, and from the perpetual fear of mutual annihilation. For Hobbes, the enforcement of such a contract requires an absolute monarchy, which Hobbes likened to the Leviathan, the great sea monster from the biblical Book of Job.

But later political philosophers, such as John Locke, argued that societies could successfully forge such social contracts without such an absolute power for enforcement. An impartial adjudicator was necessary, yes, but the power of that adjudicator could be limited and, for Locke, must be founded on the consent of those over whom it was exercised. The same holds true today regarding the possibility that states could forge what we might call a "nuclear social contract." It is often said that states today live in a Hobbesian global state of nature—because we have nothing like a world government, either absolute or limited, that has anything like a real power of enforcement over those states. This is why the Bush administration, for example, was able to forego Security Council approval and invade Iraq anyway, even after it became clear in the early months of 2003 that the United States could not garner

U.N. support for such an invasion. Almost all international legal scholars agreed that the invasion was illegal under international law. But in the Hobbesian global state of nature, there are no tangible international consequences for illegal international acts.

Humanity may not ultimately solve the problem of war with anything less than a true world government. Yet before that day dawns, states might conclude that, as regards the nuclear question, it is in their interest to cede some of their freedom, and allow the kinds of limited intrusions on sovereignty that this book advocates. In return, they will gain a new freedom—freedom from the perpetual fear of mutual nuclear annihilation. And as Locke might have argued, perhaps such a nuclear social contract might succeed without the necessity of an absolute power for enforcement.

Indeed, to assume otherwise seems to be the epitome of "letting the perfect act as the enemy of the good." Why? Because a world government is not likely to come into being in the next decade or two. Yet the dangers posed by the nuclear status quo are quite immediate, and quite likely soon to come to pass. To insist that the enforcement problem is insoluble without a world government would be essentially to give up on trying to forestall the many nuclear perils this book has endeavored to illuminate.

An enlightened public policy debate certainly ought to grapple with the questions of whether a world state is desirable, whether it is achievable, and whether any other alternative might be envisioned to free ourselves forever from the scourge of war. Such a debate about the merits of and prospects for the idea of world government is almost wholly nonexistent in today's public policy arena. H. G. Wells insisted that "a federation of all humanity, together with a sufficient measure of social justice to ensure health, education, and a rough equality of opportunity [might well] mean such a release and increase of human energy as to open a new phase in human history."[39] And such a federation of all humanity may indeed come to pass tomorrow.

But we need to stave off the apocalypse today.

THE EDIFICE OF ABOLITION
The human community has already established international conventions that outlaw the development, production, and use of biological

and chemical weapons: the Biological Weapons Convention (BWC) of 1972 and the Chemical Weapons Convention (CWC) of 1992. The verification provisions of the CWC are much more intrusive than they would probably have to be in an NWEC, simply because nuclear weapons are more complex. It would be much easier to conceal a chemical weapons program (perhaps within existing agricultural or pharmaceutical facilities) than it would be to conceal a nuclear weapons program. Under the CWC, any member state can demand an international inspection of any designated building in any other state. Although the treaty does contain legal loopholes that allow that second state to stall, it is still the closest thing to a robust and verifiable disarmament agreement, with teeth, that the human race has achieved thus far.

Just weeks before 9/11, the world was also on the verge of enacting a strong protocol to the BWC, which would have incorporated inspection provisions comparable to those of the CWC. But the second Bush administration, new in office, with John Bolton serving as point man, rejected the protocol that had been years in the making. Apparently, pharmaceutical companies successfully lobbied the administration toward that end because they were concerned that their trade secrets might be revealed.

Virtually all the states in the world, including the United States, have committed themselves to these agreements and (in the case of the CWC) to accept the severe intrusions on sovereignty contained therein. Clearly, they concluded that the national security benefits that might be obtained from chemical or biological weapons would be far outweighed by the national security costs of the open and unregulated pursuit of chemical and biological weapons around the world (and an open bazaar in which non-state actors might obtain such weapons).

Regarding nuclear weapons, I believe that states will similarly cede a measured portion of their sovereignty to an international authority if they conclude that the benefits of their own possession of nuclear weapons are outweighed by the dangers of the possession of nuclear weapons by others. Put another way, they will do so if they can be persuaded that whatever benefits nuclear weapons might provide for them are outweighed by the risks that nuclear weapons bring to them.

This chapter can hardly claim to have sketched the architecture of a nuclear weapon–free world in every detail. It has scarcely begun to describe the edifice of abolition. However, perhaps it is not too much to claim that it has demonstrated that it is possible to envision constructing such a cathedral. With the rigorous and detailed work, in the months and years to come, of a great many stone carvers, and a great many glass-cutters, and a great many broom pushers, ours can become a cathedral that will soar to the heavens. Ours can become a cathedral that will stand for a thousand years. If we can eliminate forever the possibility of bringing about our own demise by our own hands—at least with nuclear weapons—then ours can become a cathedral that will give everlasting glory to the spirit of the divine.

Come back in a couple of centuries, travelers, and see what we have wrought.

CHAPTER 10

Breakout

COULD SOMEONE CHEAT AND RULE THE WORLD?

MANY YEARS AGO, I earned a master's degree in international studies from the University of Southampton in England, after being named a Rotary Foundation Ambassadorial Scholar. It's a marvelous program that dispatches students from all over the world to all over the world—to study, mingle, and break bread in an effort to cultivate world citizenship and transnational understanding. Recipients are often chosen less for their academic achievement than for their loud personalities.

Most every weekend I would jump on a train into London, ninety-nine minutes from Southampton Central to Waterloo Station, and then explore the city via the marvelous subway system, known to all as the tube. One Saturday afternoon, I noticed an advertising banner board in one tube station—a huge drawing of a hideous and decidedly evil extraterrestrial, with the huge caption "Ruler of All the Universe." I strolled over to take a closer look and found, at the bottom of the banner, in very small letters, the words "Find Your Future Job in the *Sunday Times of London*."

It has often been claimed, almost as if it were self-evident, that if a state in a post-abolition world were suddenly to reveal a few nuclear warheads—that it had either previously squirreled away or constructed after disarmament—that state would immediately and irresistibly become a hideous and decidedly evil "Ruler of All the World." Among those who argue against nuclear weapons abolition, this is known as the breakout scenario. But in truth, the breakout scenario is a hopelessly flawed canard. As this chapter will demonstrate, if a state in a post-abolition world suddenly revealed a few or even a great many nuclear warheads, it would not be able to do much of anything with them at all.

SO WHAT IF YOU'VE GOT
A FEW NUCLEAR WEAPONS?

Over the years, the breakout scenario has been the most oft-repeated objection to nuclear weapons abolition. Despite the wealth of potential verification measures described in Chapter 9, something quite fundamental must be admitted. We will never be sure, 100 percent sure, that during the process of universal nuclear weapons dismantlement, someone didn't hide a few bombs in the basement. And we will never be sure, 100 percent sure, that after the completion of universal nuclear weapons dismantlement, someone isn't building a few atom bombs in some hidden weapons lab or warehouse or garage. The fear is that some state will whip back the curtain and suddenly announce, "We fooled you all! Accede to our demands by Tuesday, you pathetic weaklings, or a nuclear rain of ruin will descend upon your puny and defenseless nations." Then the world will live unhappily ever after under their less-than-benevolent global dictatorship.

But would revealing a few nuclear warheads really enable the possessor to impose its will on all non-nuclear actors? Could such a cheater indeed "rule the world?" The contention here is that a hypothetical breakout state, a sole nuclear weapon state on the planet, would be utterly unable to impose its will on anyone else by threatening a nuclear strike. Yes, nuclear weapons might provide the possessor with a nuclear deterrent—against conventional attack—as I argued in Chapter 8 regarding North Korea and Iran today. But although that might admittedly enhance the incentives for a state to attempt such breakout, it would not mean that by doing so they could force other states to do their bidding. And it is the latter, not the former, that has always been advanced as the definitive reason why the world cannot risk nuclear weapons abolition.

Any state in a nuclear weapon–free world that contemplated not just nuclear deterrence, but nuclear coercion would confront two powerful disincentives. First, the United States can today promise a devastating retaliatory strike on any country in the world with its conventional capabilities alone (see Chapter 8). If a breakout state actually pulled the trigger on a nuclear first strike, the conventional response from the United States would be every bit as devastating as if the United States still possessed thousands of nuclear weapons. If such a cheater endeavored to deliver a nuclear rain of ruin upon others, it would be inviting a conventional rain of ruin upon itself.

Chapter 8 focused on the overwhelmingly superior conventional military capabilities of the United States today. However, in the breakout scenario, that superiority would be even more pronounced. Because the breakout state, in most any imaginable circumstance, would likely face not just the conventional military power of the United States, but that instead of all states. The outrage, both that the breakout state had cheated on the nuclear abolition treaty and that it was now rattling its newly disclosed nuclear saber to extort some kind of concessions from someone, would almost certainly be universal. And it would generate not only universal condemnation, but also a universal response. In the words of Joseph Rotblat, a breakout state would find itself confronted by "the combined conventional military might of the whole world."[1] Good old tried-and-true traditional deterrence, it seems, would operate just as effectively in a post-abolition world as it did during both the cold war and post–cold war eras. Any leaders choosing to roll the breakout dice would be inviting both national and personal suicide. And it really will not matter to them whether that fate is delivered by nuclear or conventional means.

Second, the breakout state would also come under enormous political, economic, and moral pressure from the rest of the world. In a world of ever-increasing globalization, where "soft power" is frequently more decisive than hard power, there is a great deal to be said for considerations of international stature, world opinion, and moral revulsion. Any state in a post-abolition world that tried to bully its way to some geostrategic objective with a nuclear club would instantly be labeled as the planet's greatest pariah. And if it were actually to fire a nuclear weapon in pursuit of such a goal, and thus commit the largest instantaneous mass murder in history, the state would be seen as the greatest moral outlaw in history. How could any state conclude that such a course of action could possibly serve its own national interests?

Those who consider themselves hardheaded realists, steeped in the perspectives of realpolitik, will dismiss this second disincentive, and contend that, in a hypothetical nuclear moment of truth, it will count for little, and hardly prove decisive.

Yet history is not on their side. Because it turns out that a number of the military conflicts that took place during the nuclear age, upon consideration, appear to be quite analogous to the breakout scenario. And it turns out, too, that the decisive factor during these analogous situations was almost never the first disincentive, and almost always the second.

THE HISTORICAL POWER OF
THE SECOND DISINCENTIVE

Senator Alan Cranston was fond of pointing out one of the more remarkable ironies of the nuclear age: each of the original five nuclear weapon states has lost a war to a non-nuclear weapon state.[2] In 1956, Britain lost a war against Egypt and lost the Suez Canal in the process. In 1962, France lost a war against Algerian freedom fighters and was forced to grant the country independence. In the 1960s and 1970s, the United States lost a war against North Vietnam and the Viet Cong insurgency. In 1979, China lost a war against Vietnam. And in the 1980s, the USSR lost a war against the *mujahedin* insurgency in Afghanistan. The analogy between these historical episodes and the breakout scenario seems clear: states with nuclear weapons tried to force certain behaviors from states or forces without nuclear weapons. Yet their nuclear monopoly in relation to the other party did not enable them to achieve their objectives.

There is, however, a crucial distinction between a hypothetical breakout state and these historical cases. I've argued that a breakout state could not successfully carry out nuclear coercion because of both the worldwide ostracism and the catastrophic (even if conventional) military retaliation that would inevitably ensue. But if the nuclear states in these past cases had used or threatened to use nuclear weapons to forestall their eventual defeat, it is inconceivable that anyone would have launched a catastrophic military retaliation (nuclear or conventional) against them.

If the USSR, for example, had employed a nuclear weapon in Afghanistan, it is inconceivable that the United States would have retaliated with a nuclear strike against the Soviet Union. Why not? Because it would have been met with a nuclear reply against the United

States. So why didn't Moscow ever employ or even threaten to employ nuclear weapons against the mujahedin?

Similarly, if the United States had employed a nuclear weapon in Vietnam, China or Russia would not have retaliated with a nuclear strike against the American homeland because that country would, in turn, have met a U.S. nuclear reply against its own homeland. For Hanoi, the United States might as well have been the only nuclear weapon state in the world. No other actor anywhere could credibly threaten a nuclear strike on the United States in retaliation for an American nuclear strike on Hanoi. Yet even though the U.S. strategic position seemed to mirror that of our hypothetical breakout state, America still could not rule the day in Vietnam.

The Nixon administration did exert pressure on Hanoi during its first year in office, with its famous 1969 "November ultimatum," threatening catastrophic attacks on North Vietnam if its government would not bargain in good faith to end the war. It is unknown for certain whether explicit nuclear threats were included in an effort to frighten Hanoi's leadership into complete capitulation. But if they were, what is known for certain is that any such threats did not work. North Vietnam was not cowed into submission by the United States. North Vietnam defeated the United States

The same kind of analysis can be applied to the other cases. No one would have launched an attack on China, nuclear or conventional, if it had used nuclear weapons against Vietnam in 1979. No one would have launched an attack on France, nuclear or conventional, if it had somehow endeavored to hold on to Algeria with nuclear arms. If London, in an effort to forestall its humiliating withdrawal from Suez in 1956, had said, "Immediately return the Suez Canal to our control or we will drop an atom bomb on Cairo," would the USSR, or anyone else, have launched a massive military attack, nuclear or conventional, on the United Kingdom? Of course not. Yet the United Kingdom did not attempt to make any such nuclear threat . . . and lost the canal it had expended such toil and treasure to build almost a century prior.

The conclusion seems unavoidable. In these past five cases, these nuclear weapon states did not use or threaten to use their nuclear arms. Instead, they accepted defeat at the hands of states or forces that possessed no nuclear arms—even though it seems clear that if they had employed their nuclear weapons it would not have resulted in any kind of massive retaliation against them. So they must have been dissuaded from using nuclear weapons by something else.

Indeed, the same kind of analysis can be applied to many contemporary international political tangles as well. Consider, for example, Cuba, with which the United States has been at loggerheads for more than a half century now. Why doesn't Washington say to Havana, "Bring an end to the Castro regime and Communist rule, open yourselves to American commerce, and institute a puppet regime closely tied to us—or nuclear-armed B-52s will soon be heading from Barksdale Air Force Base in Lousiana southward over the Gulf of Mexico?" After all, Cuba could not retaliate with conventional weapons in any meaningful way. Moreover, no one in the world would retaliate with nuclear weapons. Therefore, if it is not the prospect of anyone imposing "unacceptable damage" upon the United States that stops the United States from making such a nuclear threat, it must be something else.

What geopolitical variables have kept these nuclear weapon states from employing nuclear weapons, even though they were failing to achieve their military and political goals in any other way? Why do nuclear monopolies not enable states to impose their wills upon non-nuclear opponents? If our possession of thousands of nuclear weapons provided us with no advantage in confrontations with states possessing no nuclear weapons, why do so many people assume that a hypothetical breakout state in a post-abolition world could wield any leverage in confrontations with states possessing no nuclear weapons?

As Sherlock Holmes famously said, "it is an old maxim of mine that when you have excluded the impossible, whatever remains, however improbable, must be the truth."[3] It appears that in each of the historic cases I've mentioned, the tangible possibility of massive retaliatory damage did not loom large in decisionmakers' calculations. So the only explanation left is the intangible: international stature, world opinion, universal moral revulsion. Hardheaded realists may scoff at such a claim. But however improbable it seems, it appears to be the truth.

ONCE THERE WAS A LONE BREAKOUT STATE—THE UNITED STATES

The five cases above appear to show the predominance of that second intangible disincentive in preventing a nuclear-armed actor from imposing its will on non-nuclear-armed adversaries. Let us now turn to another historical case, this time one where the first, hard, tangible variable of military deterrence seemed to carry the day.

Those who suggest that, if a single state suddenly became the only nuclear-weapon state on the planet it would inexorably rule the world seem to forget that once, there was only a single nuclear weapon state on the planet: the United States. Between July 16, 1945, and August 29, 1949, when the Soviet Union successfully tested its first atomic bomb, our nation was the sole nuclear nation. So why, during the historical crucible that was the first four years of the cold war, did we not employ our nuclear monopoly to "rule the world"? Why didn't Washington rattle its bright, shiny, and terribly large nuclear saber to coerce the Soviet Union into submission on questions such as the governance of Berlin or the occupation of Eastern Europe?

In fact, several conservative American commentators argued for just such a course during that fleeting period.[4] Among the most influential was James Burnham, who for many years wrote a column for the *National Review* called "The Third World War." He and other critics believed that the struggle with the communists was America's epic confrontation: if we did not decisively defeat them, they would cataclysmically defeat us.

The American nuclear monopoly was crucial to commentators such as Burnham. It was, however, unclear whether they advocated simply using our nuclear capability to bully Moscow, or instead crossing the Elbe and launching a preventive war of "rollback" into Eastern Europe with conventional forces alone (with the bomb in the background as bargaining chip), or instead actually launching a nuclear first strike against the Soviet heartland, without immediate provocation or pretext, putting an end to communism—and likely much else.

Even Winston Churchill, no longer British prime minister, apparently suggested during this time that the West issue a direct ultimatum to Stalin: abandon East Berlin, evacuate East Germany, and retreat to the Polish frontier—or American atomic bombers would pulverize Soviet cities. That is about as direct an example of nuclear coercion as one could construct.

Yet there is no evidence that such a dare was ever in fact issued to Moscow. Even if it was, it certainly didn't work. Between 1945 and 1949, the United States did not employ its nuclear weapons militarily or wield them politically in any meaningful way. Yet we were the breakout state with an absolute nuclear monopoly. Why did it not enable us to get our way on virtually every international question of the hour?

In answer, some might claim that we were a rational, sober, benevolent, non-imperialistic state with no interest in swaying the behavior of others. But the United States was a powerful international player, engaged in high-stakes power politics in the postwar global arena. Surely we used every gadget in our political toolbox to maximize our national interests in the international sphere. If we could have achieved tangible political gains through nuclear coercion, we would have.

Perhaps a better answer comes straight from the world of realpolitik. Because the Soviet Union, while lacking the nuclear deterrent for the moment, still possessed a powerful military hammer of its own. It was the same hammer it had used to crush Nazi Germany, less than four years after it had been invaded and nearly crushed itself in Hitler's Operation Barbarossa, launched on June 22, 1941. And it was a hammer that probably served in large measure to deter the United States from attempting to wield its nuclear monopoly.

When the Second World War ended, the United States rapidly demobilized its forces, and millions of seasoned American soldiers returned home to farms, factories, offices, and classrooms. The USSR, however, retained its mighty land army, 4 million strong, deployed immediately adjacent to Western Europe. In addition, because of the intensity of the war on Germany's eastern front, these soldiers were, if anything, far more seasoned than the American soldiers, who were now in any case mostly gone. The Red Army, between 1945 and 1949, almost certainly possessed the capacity to overrun Western Europe, and institute complete Soviet control of northern Eurasia from the Pacific to the Atlantic.

Therefore, it seems that even though the USSR did not yet have the bomb, a rough and ready mutual deterrence (if not yet mutually assured destruction) had already emerged. Why didn't Moscow choose to invade and conquer Western Europe? At least in part, because it was deterred by the threat of retaliation from the American atomic arsenal. (Also, too, because it had its hands quite full recovering from the devastation wrought by the Second World War, and because such an invasion could not possibly have served its own national interests, and hence was probably never seriously considered or even coveted in Moscow.) And why didn't the United States attempt forcibly to impose its will on the Soviet Union through overt nuclear coercion? At least in part, because it was deterred from doing so by the threat of retaliation from the Red Army, poised in eastern Germany across the Elbe River, the English Channel practically in its sights, capable not so much of imposing "unacceptable damage" on the American homeland but of seizing what was then surely America's most vital international interest—a free and democratic Western Europe allied not with the USSR, but with us.

There is some evidence that Washington did rattle its nuclear saber in 1946 to "encourage" Moscow to withdraw its forces from northern Iran—which it did. President Truman made this assertion in his memoirs; subsequent research in Soviet archives suggests that Stalin was not moved by the apparent threats. Yet even if he was, this episode seems to be the exception that proves the rule. At the very beginning of the cold war, northern Iran was largely insignificant. As a political concern, it could not remotely compare to the Soviet presence in East Berlin in the heart of western Germany, let alone the occupation and communization of all of Eastern Europe—and the threat it posed to the West. During the period of our nuclear monopoly, when we ourselves were indeed the "breakout" state, we did not achieve any of the big geopolitical things we might have desired through nuclear coercion. Indeed, for the most part, it appears that we did not even try.

Probably, primarily, because the mighty Red Army deterred us from doing so.

So What If Iran Acquires Nuclear Weapons?

Few international political issues received more attention during George W. Bush's second term than the possibility that Iran might acquire nuclear weapons. Today it still stands high on Secretary of State Hillary Clinton's foreign policy agenda. Yet a very simple question has rarely been asked: If Iran did acquire nuclear weapons, what could it do with them?

Indeed, Senator Clinton answered that question herself, most directly, during her 2008 presidential campaign. Asked by an *ABC News* reporter in April how she would respond to an Iranian nuclear attack on Israel, she replied, "I want the Iranians to know that if I'm the president, we will attack Iran. . . . In the next 10 years, during which they might foolishly consider launching an attack on Israel, we would be able to totally obliterate them."[5]

However indelicate and unsubtle Clinton's speculations might have been, it is difficult to dispute their validity. If Tehran does in fact become a nuclear weapon state in the next few years, the "policy option" of launching a sudden and unprovoked nuclear first strike, on Israel or anyone else, would result in certain and immediate destruction for the Iranian nation—and in certain and immediate death for the leaders who had initiated such a strike as well.

Sometimes the question of what Iran might actually do with nuclear weapons was expressed in a single word. "If the Iranians were to have a nuclear weapon," said President Bush in 2006, "they could blackmail the world."[6] He offered no explanation, however, of exactly what *nuclear blackmail* might mean. My *American Heritage Dictionary* defines *blackmail* as "extortion by the threat of exposure of something criminal or discreditable." In other words, "Pay me money, or I'll reveal that you embezzled the community chest, or dispatched the leaky ferryboat, or seduced the farmer's daughter." What that has to do with the political utility of nuclear weapons is difficult to discern.

Does it mean that a state might try to coerce another state by threatening a nuclear first strike? ("Evacuate the entire Israeli presence in the West Bank and East Jerusalem by next Thursday, or else.") But all existing nuclear weapon states already possess the capability to make such coercive threats. And yet, as this chapter has indicated, it is difficult to identify significant historical instances where, when the heat was on, any of them have actually done so. Does it mean that such a state might use its nuclear capability to persuade someone else *not* to do something? ("Don't send tanks across the Elbe, or else." "Don't try to pull a regime change on us, or else.") But that's the traditional meaning of nuclear deterrence. Why is it legitimate geopolitical behavior in the one case, but nuclear blackmail in the other?

In her April 2008 remarks, Senator Clinton did not say that if Iran used nuclear weapons, the United States would necessarily employ its nuclear arsenal "to totally obliterate them." As Chapter 8 made clear, she didn't need to: we could do so with our conventional capabilities alone. Add the undeniable reality that if Iran were even to acquire nuclear weapons—let alone threaten to use them, let alone actually use them—it would result in immediate pariah status as well, and we see therefore that the similarities between a hypothetical nuclear-armed Iran and a hypothetical nuclear-armed breakout state appear once again quite precise.

If Iran obtains a nuclear arsenal, it could not use it to coerce concessions out of some other state—because of both the enormous intangible political costs and the certainty of devastating retaliation. If a breakout state revealed a nuclear arsenal, it could not use it to coerce concessions out of some other state—because of both the enormous intangible political costs and the certainty of devastating retaliation. A hypothetical nuclear-armed breakout state in a post-abolition world would have no more ability to "rule the world," or rule anything, than would a hypothetical nuclear-armed Iran in a pre-abolition world.

So What If Israel Possesses Nuclear Weapons?

The case of Israel, which today possesses a nuclear monopoly over its many hostile adversaries, seems also analogous to the breakout scenario. I argued in Chapter 2 that if any state can credibly claim that a nuclear deterrent is essential to its security, it is Israel. Moreover, since 1973, that nuclear deterrent has likely been one of the factors that dissuaded other states in the Middle East from launching an overt conventional military assault on Israel (though it did not dissuade Egypt from launching the 1973 Yom Kippur War). But in considering the breakout scenario, the question is not whether Israel's nuclear arsenal has deterred external aggression, but whether its nuclear monopoly has enabled it to dominate its adversaries, dictate its terms, and impose its will upon its enemies.

In 1989, writer Mark Gaffney reported that Israeli statesman Shimon Peres had said, "Acquiring a superior weapons system would mean the possibility of using it for compellant purposes—that is, forcing the other side to accept Israeli political demands, which presumably include a demand that the traditional status quo be accepted and a peace treaty signed."[7] The historical record offers little evidence that Israel has endeavored to employ its nuclear arsenal to achieve such a political end. Nevertheless, even if it has tried, few things could be clearer than that it has failed in every respect. What exactly has the Israeli nuclear arsenal persuaded other Middle Eastern states to do? Has such a peace treaty been signed? Has a nuclear monopoly enabled Israel to rule the region, or compel its enemies to do its bidding?

In addition, although Israel's nuclear weapons undoubtedly have played a role in deterring invasion, they have not deterred uprisings in the West Bank, rocket attacks from Gaza and Lebanon, or suicide bombings within Israel itself. Israel's nuclear monopoly has not enabled it to impose its will upon its adversaries, and hasn't even prevented the murder of its own citizens in the heart of its own cities. Any more than a breakout state's nuclear monopoly would enable it to impose its will upon any of its adversaries at all.

COST-BENEFIT ANALYSIS

If one examines the breakout dilemma from the perspective of a simple cost-benefit analysis, it is difficult to imagine why any state, in our hypothetical post-abolition world, would even think about giving it a go. The costs would be enormous and the benefits would be non-existent. That reality would appear to be even more apparent for the leaders of such states themselves. The most certain of the external responses to an attempt to engage in breakout would be directed at the individuals in charge of the perpetrating state themselves.

Imagine, for example, that Syria has whipped back the curtain and revealed a dozen nuclear warheads. It makes demands on Israel and, after noncompliance, launches a nuclear-tipped missile at Tel Aviv. It's possible, I suppose, that the international community would not call forth a massive and comprehensively devastating conventional military retaliation to destroy every bit of infrastructure in the country and kill millions of Syria's citizens. What does seem certain, however, is that external military forces, in short order, would immediately attack all of Syria's leadership centers, kill all its leaders, and eliminate and replace the regime.

Retired Air Force general George Lee Butler, who led the U.S. Strategic Command in the early 1990s and then made a splash by coming out unambiguously for abolition soon after his retirement, laid out this case in a 1998 interview with Jonathan Schell. Let us imagine, he said, not only that a hypothetical breakout state reveals a hidden nuclear weapons cache but that it actually launches one. "[The response] would be an immediate and unconditional intervention, which, if necessary, goes in and physically removes the leadership of the state, puts the country under occupation subject to a global mandate, for whatever period of time is deemed necessary, just as we did at the end of World War II with Japan and Germany. It would be done according to a law which was put in place . . . to authorize just that"—presumably as part of the nuclear weapons abolition treaty itself.[8] How could any leaders believe they could advance not just their state's interests, but their own personal interests, by giving a roll to those dice?

But what if they are irrational individuals, not concerned about optimizing their own national or personal interests but longing to martyr themselves in service to a glorious greater goal? For Israel, this has been the great existential fear regarding a nuclear Iran, especially in light of Mahmoud Ahmadinejad's many reprehensible remarks about both the Jewish past and the Israeli future. Nonetheless, the answer remains "extremely unlikely." It is hard to identify any episode in history where the leaders of a state initiated such a suicidal undertaking. We have seen plenty of individuals who are willing individually to martyr themselves, from suicide bombers at Israeli bat mitzvahs to the odious 9/11 hijackers. But collective martyrdom—an act that sacrifices not just one's own life but the lives of thousands of one's fellow citizens—is both more difficult to identify in the past, and more difficult to envision in the future. "They're crazy," said science fiction author and former Newt Gingrich advisor Jerry Pournelle, when asked whether the leaders of Iran might pull such a collective suicide switch, "but they're not that crazy."[9]

Still, nothing can preclude the possibility, in a nuclear-armed world, that some future Ahmadinejad may wake up one morning and decide to spin the nuclear wheel of fortune. But that leads to the most crucial point. Because if the leaders of a nuclear-armed state decide they want to pull the trigger on such an undertaking today, there is nothing we can do currently to prevent it. Our nuclear weapons cannot stop them from doing that today. Our only hope for dodging this particular nuclear bullet is to keep such leaders from getting their hands on nuclear weapons in the first place. Moreover—since Chapter 2 revealed the futility of trying to solve this and all other nuclear dilemmas by trying to keep nuclear weapons out of the hands of, only, the irrational—our only hope is to begin to move expeditiously toward nuclear weapons abolition.

Chapter 8 made the case that nuclear weapons are not only militarily unnecessary for the United States, but politically useless as well. This chapter elaborates upon that point—but prospectively rather than retrospectively. Because just as nuclear weapons have been useless for purposes of coercion throughout the nuclear age, it appears that they would be just as useless for purposes of coercion in a post-nuclear age as well. A breakout state could not and would not rule the world. The nuclear weapon's greatest irony, it would appear, is that it is both inconceivably powerful and astonishingly powerless. Yesterday. Today. And tomorrow.

CHAPTER 11

How It Might Happen

TRANSFORMING ABOLITION FROM
A UTOPIAN FANTASY INTO A
CONCRETE POLITICAL GOAL

"THOSE WHO PROFESS to favor freedom and yet depreciate agitation are men who want crops without plowing up the ground. They want rain without thunder and lightning. They want the ocean without the awful roar of its many waters. Power concedes nothing without demand."[1]

That statement, actually, was not uttered by a nuclear weapons abolitionist. It was by another kind of abolitionist: Frederick Douglass, in 1849.

There has long been about nuclear matters, said Canadian philosopher Michael Allen Fox a quarter-century ago, "a sense in which we are already experiencing a kind of . . . 'psychological fallout.' I am referring here to fear, gloom, despair, cynicism, fatalism, meaninglessness, apathy, and related psychological aberrations and mental paralyses by means of which the arms race holds us hostage . . . [and] which takes its daily toll quite apart from the actual use of nuclear weapons."[2]

Today we might posit a different kind of psychological fallout. Whereas during the east-west nuclear standoff it was fear and despair, now it is too often indifference or obliviousness. What remains, instead of gloom and cynicism, is an intuitive—but deeply mistaken—assumption that the demise of the cold war also ended the possibility of nuclear war. Or, alternatively, many people believe that we do not control our technologies but that they control us, that nuclear weapons must now dwell permanently on the stage of human history, that for those of us living after the dawn of the nuclear age, we have little choice but to resign ourselves to our eventual nuclear fate. Day after day, as nuclear disarmament advocates endeavor to articulate the goal of a nuclear weapon–free world, they hear comments such as "you can't put the nuclear genie back into the bottle," "nuclear weapons cannot be uninvented," and "it's a nice idea, but it will never happen."

But as Geoffrey Blainey writes in the last line of his splendid 2002 *Short History of the World,* "in human history, almost nothing is preordained."[3] Nuclear abolition may be a distant dream, or hidden just around the next corner. Anyone who witnessed the fall of the Berlin Wall—or lived through 1989, 1990, and 1991 when the Soviet empire, the communist system, and the USSR itself simply vanished overnight—can never again say, "That will never happen." At the time of those events, I was a graduate student at the RAND/UCLA Center for Soviet Studies, and I can attest that none of the world's leading Sovietologists remotely saw them coming.

For that matter, who among us in, say, January 2004 believed that a black man would move into the White House a mere half-decade down the road?

"Not one of us," said George Bernard Shaw, "has enough knowledge to be a pessimist."[4] The rubbish heap of history is piled high with forecasts—of events or developments or movements—which the wisest figures of the day were quite certain would "never happen." Except they did. In 1519, Ferdinand Magellan set sail in five ships, with 270 men, to the west. Three years later, under the leadership of the late Magellan's first mate, Juan Sebastian Elcano, eighteen bedraggled men returned in a single leaking vessel—from the east. In December 1903, Wilbur and Orville Wright put human beings aloft, an entire three meters into the air, for twelve long seconds. Less than two-thirds of a century later, in a craft directly descended from the one launched by the brothers at Kitty Hawk, Michael Collins, Buzz Aldrin, and Neil Armstrong departed from the surface of the earth, and set down a spacecraft on the surface of the moon.

"Of all the sins and sinners in the world," said Dante, "the hottest rings of fire in Hell are reserved for those who, on matters of great and crucial controversy, maintain their neutrality." For things that may seem remote in the present political moment, we must say that we will never get there unless someone says that we ought to get there. We will never reach any goal, however outlandish, unless someone is brave enough to aspire to that goal. We must contend that the abolition of nuclear weapons is not only the sole solution to the threat of nuclear annihilation, but something we can transform from a utopian fantasy into a concrete political goal.

Especially because civil society movements, mighty mobilized citizen forces—when they have acted in such a way—have repeatedly transformed the forces of history. Human rights, civil rights, women's rights, labor rights, the peace movement, environmental activism, humanizing economic globalization: in each arena, coalitions have been built, legislators and diplomats have been annoyed, momentum has snowballed, and ideas have been transformed into action. It does not always happen overnight. The women's suffrage movement took much of a century to come to fruition in the United States—from the meeting of a few brave souls in Seneca Falls, New York, in 1848, to the passage of the nineteenth amendment in 1920. Indeed, the abolition of slavery, perhaps the single best example of a successful civil society campaign, took a great deal longer than that. Nevertheless, it eventually unfolded into the greatest political and social achievement in American history.

The movement to abolish nuclear weapons shares much with the movement to abolish slavery some two and three centuries ago. Activists, even while making pragmatic political arguments and compromises, are driven by profound moral convictions about the utter unacceptability of the thing itself. They have toiled in the trenches for many decades without success. Their goal is complete elimination of the institution, relegating it to an embarrassing feature of our past rather than a permanent part of our future.

But there is, of course, a crucial difference between the two. Millions of slaves sweated, bled, and perished on this continent for two-and-a-half centuries, and the anti-slavery movement sweated and bled against it for nearly as long. In the case of nuclear weapons, we surely do not have 250 years to spare. If we cannot manage to get rid of nuclear weapons in less than two and a half centuries, nuclear weapons, in all likelihood, will manage to get rid of us.

SELF-FULFILLING PROPHECY

"Nothing can doom man," said philosopher and theologian Martin Buber, "but the belief in doom."[5] If people believe that nuclear weapons elimination is a fantasy, they will be sullen and cynical and will refuse to invest their blood, toil, tears, and sweat in the enterprise. George F. Kennan wrote incisively about this phenomenon in 1982, when cold war tensions were high and fears about a nuclear conflict between the United States and the USSR intense: "To millions of people on both sides . . . [nuclear war] is something inevitable. This is a frame of mind that, once adopted by influential people, does more than anything else to make war inevitable . . . because whoever views war as inevitable tends to neglect the things that might have been done to prevent it."[6]

But if people believe that elimination of nuclear weapons is possible, they will actively work to bring it about. If real political progress toward nuclear weapons abolition is not terribly "politically realistic" today, then building a civil society movement to shift the terms of the nuclear policy debate can perhaps make it more realistic tomorrow. If, as every freshman learns in Political Science 101, politics is "the art of the possible," then our work, as abolitionists, is about expanding the parameters of political possibility.

"The best lack all conviction," said William Butler Yeats, "while the worst are full of passionate intensity."[7] Perhaps we might tremulously tinker with the genius of Yeats, and suggest that the crux of the matter here is not so much whether the best and the worst among us choose to engage in the public square, but whether the best or the worst within us drives our political convictions and actions. If the nuclear danger causes us to succumb to hopelessness, fear, and hate—the worst within us—then we will succumb to our desires to safeguard ourselves only with escalation and force. But if we can aspire instead to genuine security for both ourselves and our adversaries, to hope for a better day tomorrow, perhaps even to love our enemies—the best within us—then we can overcome our fears, and devote ourselves to nuclear weapons abolition, enduring world peace, and a just and sustainable future for the community of humankind.

Perhaps the reader will indulge the author to confess that this point, possibly, is no less than the point of this book itself.

Procedural Mechanisms

Members of the disarmament community have posited a number of plausible real-world scenarios regarding how a formal international process directed at eliminating nuclear weapons might be launched and pursued:

- A route could be developed through the ongoing U.N. Conference on Disarmament (CD). This body, located in Geneva, was created by the United Nations in 1978 as a way of consolidating several predecessors. It was intended to serve as the sole international forum for multilateral negotiations on arms control and disarmament. Its predecessors negotiated both the NPT and the Comprehensive Test Ban Treaty (CTBT), and the consolidated body negotiated the chemical and biological weapons conventions. The CD can, however, be hamstrung by the rule of consensus: one party can effectively stall proceedings indefinitely. In fact, the CTBT talks had to shift to the U.N. General Assembly when India did just that. In recent years the fundamental disputes at the heart of the nuclear status quo had prevented the CD from even agreeing on an agenda, let alone commencing negotiations on abolition. In an encouraging sign, however, in May 2009 the CD approved a working group to begin negotiations on a treaty banning the production of any fissionable material suitable for nuclear warheads.
- The General Assembly could initiate a special multilateral negotiating conference, separate from the CD, to overcome existing obstacles.
- An Ottawa-style process might prove promising. In the 1990s, Canada brought together representatives from most other countries to negotiate a ban on anti-personnel landmines. Although the ban is still not universal, it continues to generate enormous moral pressure on the few holdouts (including the United States) and has largely eliminated new deployments of these hideous weapons, which can inflict horrific injuries on innocent civilians many years after a conflict has ended.
- Certain key states could lead the process:
  - Great Britain, which has repeatedly indicated its support for abolition, which has reduced the operational readiness of its atomic arsenal, which—through both governmental initiatives and organizations such as VERTIC—has undertaken

quite detailed studies on nuclear disarmament verification measures, and whose citizenry has long maintained one of the world's most intelligent and enduring antinuclear movements. This scenario could become more plausible now that the cozy relationship between former president George W. Bush and ex–prime minister Tony Blair has passed from the scene. In 2007, Britain decided to replace its aging fleet of Trident submarines, which contains the nation's entire nuclear arsenal, at a cost well over 100 billion dollars—more than chump change in a country with less than one-fifth of America's gross domestic product. Nevertheless, few think the decision is final, and an extended debate about whether to reverse it could well evolve into proposals for Great Britain to take the lead in launching a multilateral negotiating process directed toward abolition.

- India has always insisted that its decision not to join the NPT and to conduct nuclear weapons tests in 1998 was driven in large part by the refusal of the nuclear weapon states to take their disarmament obligations seriously. Nuclear politics are a big deal in India, the country that coined the term *nuclear apartheid*. Many Indians are quite proud that their country defied the West, refused to succumb to the nuclear double standard, and joined the nuclear club. Yet the government has repeatedly stated that it is willing to get rid of all its nuclear weapons when the other nuclear states get serious about getting rid of theirs.

- Japan holds a unique place in atomic history, and brings a unique moral voice to the table. An anti-nuclear sentiment, both broad and deep, has prevailed consistently in the country since 1945. Yet after the North Korean nuclear test in the fall of 2006, nuclear politics emerged front and center—with some Japanese arguing that their country must now build its own nuclear deterrent, while millions of others remain determined to resist that step. The mayor of Hiroshima, Tadatoshi Akiba, has proposed that states send representatives to his city to commence negotiations on a nuclear weapons elimination treaty. More than 1,000 other "mayors for peace" around the world have endorsed his plan, with its goal of completing abolition by August 6, 2020, the seventy-fifth anniversary of the day his city was catapulted from obscurity into eternal remembrance.

- A conference of state parties to the NPT could work to transform the treaty into something like the NWEC described in Chapter 9. In fact, article 8 of the NPT specifically provides for such a conference. This scenario appears to be a most promising mechanism to generate broad support for and participation in a nuclear weapons elimination initiative. It is worth a closer look.[8]

Transforming the NPT from Nonproliferation to Elimination

Article 8 of the NPT contains provisions not just for amending the treaty, but for convening a conference to review its entire framework. As it happens, these provisions are remarkably like those in the U.N. Charter's article 109 for calling a world summit to review its entire framework.

Section 1 of article 109 provides for convening a comprehensive conference "for the purpose of reviewing the present Charter" upon a vote of two-thirds of the members of the General Assembly and any nine of the fifteen members of the Security Council. Section 2, however, provides that any amendments that might come out of such a conference must first be approved by two-thirds of the members of the General Assembly, including all five permanent members of the Security Council. So while the Security Council's permanent members can exercise the long-lamented great power veto over any actual amendments, they cannot veto the convening of a formal summit to review the charter itself.

Many who advocate a wholesale redesign of the U.N. system suggest that article 109 is a promising vehicle for generating both governmental and public support for the concept. I myself spearheaded a 1995 initiative called the Campaign for a New U.N. Charter, which, rather than advocating any particular kind of U.N. Charter revisions, pushed to activate article 109, to convene a comprehensive charter review conference to consider the most appropriate revisions for the challenges of the twenty-first century. Why does article 109 hold such promise?

First, it is in the charter itself. The framers of the charter, including Franklin D. Roosevelt and Winston Churchill, apparently believed that their successors might in future consider a reinvention of the entire U.N. system. If not, why would they have included article 109 at all? In fact, section 3 of article 109 proposed to call such a conference during "the tenth annual session of the General Assembly"—1955—and reduced the requirement for convening it to a simple majority. Unfortunately, by then the cold war had largely frozen out any such bold international political innovations. The section's language is vague as to whether the lowered threshold applies just to that tenth session or perpetually thereafter, and no one since has put it to the test.

Second, the call to convene such a comprehensive U.N. Charter review conference would not necessarily have to get everyone to agree on the precise outcomes in advance, but simply to come together behind a formal process to consider the most optimal structures of global governance for today and tomorrow. That combination of both a specific call to action and open possible outcomes could mobilize a broad coalition of actors, with a wide variety of alternative world-order visions, to come together behind a specific action agenda.

Finally, even if one or all of the veto-wielding powers resisted, such a review conference could still be legally convened and held. In that event, the political and moral pressure on those who resisted would become immense. At a minimum, they would be pressed to engage in a full, formal, expansive debate about the great global governance questions of the age.

Today, after nearly two-thirds of a century, the world has seen neither a single substantive revision to the U.N. Charter, nor the convening of an article 109 charter review conference. It still might. One small but hopeful sign of change took place in the spring of 2008, when nearly five hundred students from around the world gathered in Monterrey, Mexico, to conduct a Model Article 109 U.N. Charter Review Conference, which simulated not the United Nations of today—like the venerable Model U.N. program—but rather a redesign of today's United Nations for tomorrow's needs.[9] Surely, the human race will not govern itself in 2045 with international institutions invented in 1945. Surely someone, somewhere, sometime will move to seriously confront the question, "What kind of U.N. system would we create if we were designing it from scratch today?"

Before that happens, however, we have a more urgent agenda—the abolition of nuclear weapons. And article 8 of the NPT, it turns out, contains much the same promise as article 109 of the U.N. Charter. Section 1 reads: "Any Party to the Treaty may propose amendments to this Treaty . . . [and] if requested to do so by one-third or more of the Parties to the Treaty, the Depositary Governments shall convene a conference . . . to consider such an amendment." Section 2 declares: "Any amendment to this Treaty must be approved by a majority of the votes of all the Parties to the Treaty, including the votes of all nuclear-weapon States Party to the Treaty." An amendment, of course, could be just a few words to update some minor point in the NPT. It could also be a proposal to scrap the treaty altogether, and replace it with a universal, verifiable, and enforceable NWEC. Moreover, although the five nuclear weapon state parties to the NPT can veto any amendment to the treaty, they cannot veto the convening of a conference to consider such amendments.

"I am certainly not an advocate for frequent changes in laws and constitutions," said Thomas Jefferson in 1816, only forty years after he authored the American Declaration of Independence. "But institutions must advance also to keep pace with the times. We might as well require a man to wear still the coat which fitted him when a boy as civilized society to remain ever under the regimen of their barbarous ancestors."[10]

The parallel possibilities for change that lie within article 109 and article 8—as a vehicle for generating both governmental and civil society support—could hardly be more exact. First, article 8 would be undertaken formally and legally under the provisions of the NPT itself, thus conveying great legitimacy. Recall that the World Court has already concluded that the NPT creates "an obligation to pursue in good faith and bring to a conclusion negotiations leading to nuclear disarmament in all its aspects." What better way to fulfill that obligation than to convene a formal conference authorized by the provisions of the NPT itself?

Second, as with article 109, the call to convene such a conference wouldn't necessarily require everyone to agree in advance on the precise provisions that would emerge in the outcome, but simply agree to activate article 8 so that governmental representatives can start negotiating those provisions. Presumably, though, there would be more advance agreement here than there would be regarding the U.N. Charter—because the NPT already states that its central goal is a nuclear weapon–free world.

Finally, and most importantly, even if one or indeed all of the NPT's nuclear weapon states resisted, a review conference still might legally be convened and held. In such a case, the political and moral pressures on the holdout states, both from other states and from civil society forces within those states, would steadily gain steam, more and more, like a teakettle coming to a boil. The nuclear weapon states would be forced to confront questions such as "Do you intend for the nuclear double standard to persist indefinitely? Do you believe the human race can both retain nuclear weapons and avoid nuclear catastrophe forever? Or do you intend to get serious about complying with your article 6 obligation, undertaken more than four decades ago, to give us a nuclear weapon–free world?"

The call to convene an article 8 NPT review conference by civil society, and the promise (or threat?) to convene such a conference by a critical mass (approaching one-third) of state party governments would serve as an enormous encouragement to the nuclear weapon states—to move the issue to the top of their agendas, to recognize that they cannot achieve nuclear nonproliferation unless they are willing to get serious about nuclear disarmament, and to get busy making the abolition of nuclear weapons happen.

Now all we need to do is build a civil society movement demanding that states "Activate Article 8," to deliver a call to the ramparts so loud, so annoying, and so insistent, that governments will find us impossible to ignore.

ONE SUCCESSFUL ANTINUCLEAR MOVEMENT

"The future is unknowable," said Churchill, wrapping up his masterful *History of the English Speaking Peoples,* "but the past should give us hope."[11] I've already discussed several arenas in which civil society movements have successfully altered the course of history. But it so happens that the nuclear arena itself offers more than one example of similar success.[12] In the 1950s and early 1960s, for instance, an antinuclear movement took aim at a tangible and precise goal—and achieved it. The movement focused its fire not only on forestalling a hypothetical future global thermonuclear war, but also on bringing a halt to an immediate, actual nuclear harm: radioactive fallout from nuclear tests. At the time the United States, the USSR, and later, to a much smaller extent, China, the United Kingdom, and France, were carrying out hundreds of nuclear test detonations in the air. Most of the Soviet tests took place in remote parts of Kazakhstan, most of the American tests in the remote desert of Nevada or remote parts of the Pacific. But the detonations blew radioactive fallout high into the sky, and wind carried it for thousands of miles in all directions. A 1991 study estimated that the global radioactive fallout from the era will eventually result in more than 2 million cancer fatalities, and inflict many other health and environmental impacts as well.[13] Tiny radioactive particles, invisible to our eyes but insidiously deadly nonetheless, rained down upon us all, everyone, everywhere in the world, infiltrating the planet's air, water, soil, plants, animals, and people.

The movement that arose to end these nuclear tests consisted of hundreds of nongovernmental organizations (NGOs) and thousands of passionate and committed citizens around the world. A ban on nuclear testing was a central plank of the 1956 presidential campaign of the Democratic party's nominee, Adlai Stevenson. Some of the greatest moral giants of the twentieth century—Albert Einstein, Pablo Casals, Norman Cousins, Linus Pauling, Bertrand Russell, Albert Schweitzer—lent their reputations to the cause. Lord Russell, a mathematician and philosopher who had won the Nobel Prize for Literature in 1950, served as the founding president of the British Campaign for Nuclear Disarmament (CND), and was arrested for taking part in a sit-down protest outside the Ministry of Defense at Whitehall—when he was eighty-nine years old.

In 1957 antinuclear advocates in the United States launched the National Committee for a Sane Nuclear Policy, which mobilized 25,000 members within a year.[14] In 1958, the CND launched its annual Aldermaston March, always beginning at noon on Good Friday, where thousands of citizens walked the fifty miles between the Berkshire town of Aldermaston (site of the U.K.'s Atomic Weapons Research

Establishment) and Hyde Park in London. They carried banners: "Activity with Us Today or Radioactivity Tomorrow!" and "We Don't Dig Doom." The pilgrimage was eventually duplicated in more than thirty countries.[15] "Whenever I talk to people about disarmament, it's always the test ban treaty they bring me around to," said Joseph B. Godber, Great Britain's minister of state, in 1962. "It has to do with the here and now, and they want an end to this fouling of the air they breathe."[16]

Writing from his hospital at Lambaréné, Schweitzer described the big picture: "The continuation of the perfecting of weapons necessarily entails the resumption of nuclear tests. These tests are necessary for the creation of arms superior to those in existence. It is deplorable, it is terrible, it is agonizing. . . . For thousands of men are condemned to suffer and die from nuclear radiation, and generations of newborn children will continue in increasing numbers to be deformed, incapable of living." Then the good doctor zeroed in on the importance of pushing governments through public pressure—and revealed how governments often pushed back:

> All this is happening because public opinion the world over has treated lightly the dangers of nuclear radiation. It let the military and the diplomats be, as if it were a question of ordinary politics. . . . All negotiations regarding the abolition of atomic weapons remain without success because no international public opinion exists which demands this abolition! . . . The big obstacle to forming this public opinion in the West is that governments want to prevent the development of this opinion, and use as a weapon to call those who support this opinion as being suspect of being communists. This defamation is the most horrible weapon all [peace advocates] have to fear.[17]

Just substitute the word *unpatriotic* for the word *communists* in that passage, or perhaps the words *on the side of the terrorists* or *soft on Ahmadinejad,* and you have a most precise contemporary analogy.

Some of the NGOs engaged in excruciatingly detailed research and advocacy. Physicians for Social Responsibility, instigated by a brilliant young pathologist named Walter Bauer, collected the baby teeth of children and scientifically demonstrated that the calcium normally present in them was being systematically replaced by radioactive strontium-90.[18]

Few studies, however, had more impact than the words of those who had been catastrophically affected by the detonation of atmospheric nuclear tests in close proximity to them. Lijon Eknilang, of the Marshall Islands, recounted her experiences years later:

> I was eight years old at the time of the Bravo test on Bikini in 1954. I woke up with a bright light in my eyes. There was a huge brilliant light that consumed the sky. Soon after we heard a big loud noise and the earth started to sway and sink. . . . A little later . . . it began to "snow" in Rongelap. We had heard about snow from the missionaries, but this was the first time we saw white particles fall from the sky. We kids were playing in the powder, but later everyone was sick and we couldn't do anything. . . . My own health has suffered as a result of radiation poisoning. I cannot have children. I have had seven miscarriages. One was severely deformed—it had only one eye. Many of my friends keep quiet about the strange births they had. They gave birth, not to children as we like to think of them, but to things we could only describe as "octopuses," "apples," "turtles," and other things in our experience. . . . The most common have been "jellyfish" babies. These babies are born with no bones in their bodies and with transparent skin. We can see their brains and hearts beating. There are no legs, no arms, no heads, no nothing.[19]

The civil society movement for banning such tests eventually triumphed. Thanks to a combination of influential statements from revered figures such as Schweitzer, the agonizing testimonies of victims, and incessant public pressure, the United States, the USSR, and Great Britain signed the Limited Test Ban Treaty (LTBT) on August 5, 1963, just hours before the eighteenth anniversary of Hiroshima. Though this treaty fell short of banning nuclear tests altogether, it did ban them underwater, in the atmosphere, and in space; and it did eventually halt the widespread radioactive contamination that we had been inflicting upon ourselves since July 16, 1945—indirectly upon virtually everyone on the planet, and quite directly on such unwitting individuals as Ms. Eknilang. "Our problems are manmade—therefore they can be solved by Man," said President John F. Kennedy, who presided over the signing of the treaty. "No problem of human destiny is beyond human beings."[20]

Unfortunately, however, this antinuclear movement soon largely disappeared. And therein lies a sharp and poignant irony. The antinuclear movement of the 1950s and early 1960s was focused on both the actual harm being inflicted by nuclear testing and the potential harm of nuclear war. The LTBT did bring an end to the testing (above ground at least). Yet it did little to diminish the prospect of nuclear war itself. The absolute numbers of nuclear weapons continued to rise, and the east-west stalemate dragged on, along with the possibility that a hot political confrontation could descend into nuclear darkness. It would remain for another, later antinuclear movement to take on not just nuclear testing, but the nuclear arms race itself.

ANOTHER SUCCESSFUL
ANTINUCLEAR MOVEMENT

A couple of decades later, another surging antinuclear movement grappled again with the nuclear question. In the early 1980s, millions of people around the world, frightened out of their homes and onto their streets by President Reagan's nuclear saber rattling, mobilized a vast new civil society movement calling for a nuclear freeze.

Who of a certain age does not remember sentences like these: "Three years ago we could blow up the world 77 times over. Now we can blow up the world 177 times over"? It all had a Strangelovian madness apparent to even the most casual observer. President Reagan had dramatically increased the American military budget, was seeking to add new kinds of nuclear missiles to the American arsenal, had deployed new intermediate-range nuclear missiles in Europe, and had appointed officials to high-ranking posts who spoke, without a trace of irony, about waging and winning a "limited nuclear war" (see Chapter 6).

In response to all this, the forces of peace said simply, "Stop building more and ever more nuclear bombs! No More! Just stop!" The movement, which asked American and Soviet leaders to freeze a nuclear arms race that was spiraling out of control, grew exponentially throughout 1981 and 1982, both inside and outside the United States. After several large antinuclear demonstrations in Western Europe, a wide coalition of peace, antinuclear, environmental, and religious forces began planning a gathering and a statement of unprecedented magnitude. The specific action agenda was the *Call to Halt the Arms Race,* written by intrepid organizer Randall Caroline Forsberg, which detailed a proposed U.S. and Soviet freeze on the production, testing, and deployment of nuclear weapons and delivery vehicles. Forsberg had initially floated the proposal in 1979, but Reagan's election in November 1980 gave her efforts an enormous impetus.

The wave reached its zenith on June 12, 1982, when perhaps as many as 1 million people gathered in New York's Central Park, demanding that the arms race be halted at once. Companion rallies were held both at the Rose Bowl in Pasadena (90,000 in attendance) and in San Francisco (with 50,000 participants). By the day of the rallies, nearly 200 city councils along with 40 county councils, 150 organizations, 169 members of the U.S. House of Representatives, and 25 U.S. senators had endorsed nuclear freeze resolutions. In addition, demonstration organizers in New York had assembled a nuclear freeze petition containing no less than 2.3 million signatures (this in the days before the Internet), which they presented to the American and Soviet missions at the United Nations.[21]

Forsberg, who received a MacArthur genius award for her efforts, died in October 2007—with exquisite irony, just a few days after the death of Colonel Paul Tibbets, commander of the USAAF B-29 *Enola Gay* that dropped the atomic bomb on Hiroshima. In her obituary, the *New York Times* called the June 12 rally the largest political demonstration in American history.[22]

At first, President Reagan dismissed the nuclear freeze movement, labeling it "a dangerous fraud" and asserting that its leaders were those "who want the weakening of America."[23] Yet during his second term, the administration did not just halt the nuclear arms race but actually began to reverse it. It negotiated and enacted arms control treaties that, for the first time, actually committed Moscow and Washington to reduce their aggregate quantities of nuclear weapons in one case, and eliminate an entire category of nuclear weapons in another. The Strategic Arms Reduction Treaties (START), which commenced negotiations under Reagan but were signed by the first President Bush, contained provisions for actually reducing the size of each side's respective arsenals. Compare that name with the Strategic Arms Limitation Treaties (SALT) of an earlier era, which had merely limited the size of various components of each side's nuclear arsenal.

In addition, in 1987, Moscow and Washington negotiated and signed the Intermediate Range Nuclear Forces Treaty (INF), which for the first time abolished an entire category of nuclear weaponry: intermediate-range nuclear-tipped ballistic missiles designed to be launched from Western Europe and land onto Soviet territory, or vice versa. Moreover, during the second Reagan administration, government officials ceased all talk of waging and winning a limited nuclear war. Instead, the president himself made a joint statement with Mikhail Gorbachev at their first summit in Geneva in 1985, declaring, "A nuclear war cannot be won and should never be fought."[24] And at Reykjavik in 1986, the president and the general secretary came achingly close, at least in principle, to striking a deal for abolition, and committing to go all the way to zero.[25]

"First they ignore you. Then they laugh at you. Then they fight you," said Gandhi. "Then you win."[26] The nuclear freeze movement won substantial victories, playing an enormous role in both reversing the nuclear arms race and ending the nuclear brinksmanship so evident in the first half of the 1980s. Neither the actual nuclear disarmament nor the change in nuclear rhetoric during Reagan's second term would likely have happened without the insistent, powerful, and impassioned nuclear freeze movement during the president's first term. Yet this very success, along with the 1985 accession of the charismatic Gorbachev as leader of the USSR, led the freeze movement largely to fade away by the second half of the 1980s. American citizens began to perceive that the cold war was winding down, and began to believe that nuclear cataclysm was a fate we had successfully avoided.

The cold war, of course, did come to an end, only a few short years after that. However, the vast nuclear arsenals remain to this day. And, as this book has elaborately maintained, a whole host of nuclear perils, some old and some new, still threaten the future of the human race.

ANOTHER SUCCESSFUL
ANTINUCLEAR INITIATIVE

Although perhaps not quite as well known, another successful and far more recent antinuclear movement is worth our consideration. As I discussed in Chapter 6, the Bush administration, early in its tenure, announced plans for a nuclear weapon called the robust nuclear earth penetrator (RNEP) or nuclear bunker buster. Because its underground detonation would have launched vast quantities of lethally radioactive dirt into the sky, some estimated that a single RNEP attack could kill more than a million people.[27] Although the peace movement as a whole, agitated by the invasion of Iraq, seemed almost completely oblivious to this possibility, a robust coalition of nuclear disarmament advocacy organizations mobilized an intense campaign to stop the creation of this new nuclear weapon. Opposition was spearheaded by Peace Action, the Los Alamos Study Group, and the Friends Committee on National Legislation (an arm of the Society of Friends, or Quakers). Demonstrating great inside-the-beltway sophistication, they focused on generating citizen action among the constituents of key congressional members involved in nuclear weapons budget requests.

Senator Pete Domenici, Republican of New Mexico, was a crucial target, both because he chaired the Senate Energy and Water Appropriations Subcommittee and because New Mexico is a center of nuclear weapons design and development. So volunteer citizen activists outside New Mexico began contacting voters inside New Mexico, urging them to press Domenici and their other representatives to stop these perilous new nuclear plans. The process was similar to telephone campaigning before a November presidential election, when voters from solid blue or red states reach out to voters in swing states.

Before long, staff members in Senator Domenici's Albuquerque office were forwarding nine hundred letters a day to his Washington office, all from New Mexicans opposing the bunker buster. Soon Domenici announced that, although he continued to support the overall nuclear weapons complex, he would not endorse the Bush administration's funding request for the RNEP. As a direct consequence, the administration did not seek any money for the bunker buster in fiscal year 2007—a tangible victory that would never have happened without a precisely focused flood of outrage from ordinary citizens.[28]

THE NEXT SUCCESSFUL
ANTINUCLEAR MOVEMENT

It is probably fair to say that—in addition to the three tangible successes chronicled above—the forces of peace activism and antinuclear advocacy have also played a large role in preventing nuclear weapons from actually being used since August 9, 1945. Surely the great taboo that has arisen against nuclear use during the past two-thirds of a century evolved in large measure because of public outrage against the possibility of nuclear war. Recall Seymour Hersh's conclusion that the nuclear option against Iran was put on ice by President Bush because administration officials concluded that such an attack would be "politically unacceptable." What is that, if not us?

So what will it take, now, to build another successful antinuclear movement? This time not for an end to nuclear testing, nor for a nuclear freeze, nor for preventing the development of some particular new nuclear weapon. What will it take, now, to mobilize a civil society political force that will move political leaders to eradicate nuclear weapons from the face of the earth forever?

Perhaps the most striking sign that abolition has become a respectable topic among members of the foreign policy establishment is that opponents have begun pushing back. In the past, mainstream foreign policy professionals did not bother to denounce the idea of nuclear weapons elimination because it was too far off the radar screen. No more: as with any revolution, the forces of reaction have begun to emerge. President Carter's secretary of defense, Harold Brown, and President Clinton's CIA director, John Deutsch, wrote an op-ed in the November 19, 2007, *Wall Street Journal* denouncing the first *Wall Street Journal* op-ed by the Gang of Four (discussed in this book's opening chapter) as "The Nuclear Disarmament Fantasy." Since President Obama announced his vision of a nuclear weapon–free world, figures as diverse as James Schlesinger, Jonathan Tepperman, Fred Iklé, and Amitai Etzioni have come out unambiguously against the idea of abolition.

And in November 2008, during the Bush-Obama transition, Air Force chief of staff Norton A. Schwartz traveled to Barksdale Air Force Base in Louisiana, home to much of the American B-52 nuclear-capable bomber force. Although his ostensible purpose was to inspect nuclear security procedures (in the wake of some of the nuclear mishaps I've discussed), he felt compelled to speak to the assembled aviators about the value of American nuclear weapons themselves: "I think we have not yet arrived at the moment where going to zero will make sense. And to those who have argued deterrence is a fading phenomenon, something from the Cold War that is no longer applicable, they are full of [it]."[29]

Looks like the debate is on.

Many different constituencies might come together today to form a mighty new movement for nuclear weapons abolition. Each contains millions of potential citizen activists. Just in the United States, for example:

- Millions worry that Mohammed Atta's cousin will show up in an American city with an atomic bomb in his suitcase. Polls indicate that 40 percent of Americans "often worry about the chances of a nuclear attack by terrorists."[30]
- Millions follow the news, on front pages nearly every day, about the nuclear quests of Iran and North Korea. And, as Chapter 2 maintained, before long likely many others who will follow their lead.
- Millions marched in the spring of 2003 to prevent the preemptive, illegal, and unwise U.S. invasion of Iraq, showing the contemporary potential for substantial peace organizing.
- Millions constitute the liberal, progressive, Democratic party base. They came out enthusiastically behind the presidential candidacy of Barack Obama, and are now insistently demanding that he become the liberal, progressive, visionary president they yearn for him to be.
- Millions of high school and college students and young adults were politically engaged for the first time by the Obama candidacy, and could now be drawn to a grand, sweeping, idealistic vision—like a nuclear weapon–free world brought about by, and for, their generation.

The past decade has seen a resurgence in student peace organizing, arguably more vibrant than at any time since the 1960s. The army of the young has often been a key component of political movements, most particularly in American history in bringing an end to the war in Vietnam. "The young do not know enough to be prudent," said novelist Pearl Buck, "and therefore they attempt the impossible, and achieve it, generation after generation."[31] One idea for igniting their enthusiasm and participation in the abolitionist cause might be to imitate the Model

Article 109 Charter Review Conferences described above, and organize on college campuses a series of Model Article 8 NPT Review Conferences—albeit perhaps with a sexier name, such as a Model World Summit to Eliminate Nuclear Weapons Forever. This approach could not only enlist young people to support abolition, but could engage them in figuring out how to get from here to there. Such model review conferences could probably even generate substantial new funding. Potential megadonors like to be asked to fund specific projects, especially when they are new and innovative, and especially when they are about motivating a new generation of participants.

Most importantly, a campaign focused exclusively upon abolition could capture the public imagination as nothing else in the nuclear realm ever has. While most citizens supported treaties such as SALT, START, and INF, none generated a great deal of public interest or enthusiasm. Likewise, calling today for "securing nuclear weapons and materials," or "nuclear stability," or "reducing the numbers of nuclear warheads" would not likely excite many ordinary people. In contrast, the two great, successful antinuclear movements described above were each about a big, straightforward, simple idea: "ban all nuclear tests forever" in the 1950s and 1960s, and "stop building ever more nuclear weapons" in the 1980s. "Political power," says science fiction author Kim Stanley Robinson, "comes out of the look in people's eyes."[32]

The authors of *Securing Our Survival* argue that this approach is precisely what transformed the landmine campaign from obscure wonkery to public cause and success. For several years in the 1980s, negotiations about landmines had been bogged down in technical disputes over obscure questions such as how to define the difference between smart mines and dumb mines. (No such disputes, presumably, were in evidence about the leaders who chose to deploy them.) When the focus shifted to a comprehensive approach—universal prohibition—the Mine Ban Treaty followed in short order. "A key to the success of the landmines campaign," say the authors of *Securing Our Survival*, "was that the focus on a complete ban, not just on control of landmines or a ban on certain types . . . captured public attention as a meaningful and visionary measure."[33]

In an insightful November 2008 article in the *Nonproliferation Review,* Nathan Pyles argues that the nuclear disarmament movement can be successful only if it boils down its message to something simple, clear, and compelling. He emphasizes the importance of setting a deadline for the completion of abolition, citing the success of President Kennedy's directive in May 1961 not just to send human beings to the moon and back, but to do so "before this decade is out."[34] Like Mayor Akiba, Pyles also suggests the seventy-fifth anniversary of the atomic devastation of Hiroshima: "At 8:15 A.M., on the morning of August 6th, [2020,] the last remaining nuclear warheads around the world could be simultaneously and publicly disarmed. This date carries the emotional reminder of the tremendous and tragic human cost of nuclear war. It provides a fateful image that should never befall another generation."[35]

Perhaps it is not too much to claim that this book has endeavored to offer a big idea, boiled down to a mere seven components, that civil society might now articulate and rally around and promote. It is a big idea that both could capture the public imagination in much the same way that other big ideas have in the past, and provide a very precise policy prescription to demand that governments pursue:

1. Humanity's only long-term choice is between a world of dozens of nuclear weapon states or zero nuclear weapon states.
2. Because a world of dozens of nuclear weapon states—and thousands of nuclear weapons available to non-state actors—will inevitably bring one of many possible nuclear catastrophes tomorrow, our only alternative is to move to abolish nuclear weapons today.
3. The human race committed to abolish nuclear weapons in the NPT more than forty years ago.
4. The United States can protect its national security without nuclear weapons, and enlightened foreign policies by the strong can convince the less strong to live without them as well.
5. Much of the hard conceptual work on the global governance architecture of a nuclear weapon–free world is already underway (and on the consequences if someone finds a way from within that architecture to "break out").
6. The way to create that architecture, the way to get from here to there, is to activate article 8 of the NPT, and launch a formal multilateral negotiating process to transform the Nuclear

Nonproliferation Treaty into a Nuclear Weapons Elimination Convention.

7. The provisions of that convention should ensure that we get the job of abolition done, completely done, by August 6, 2020.

HOW IT MIGHT HAPPEN

One never can tell what might be the effect of a single lonely act of courage and conviction, by a single individual, as it ripples outward over the lake of time. Take the case of Gordon Zahn, American Catholic pacifist, who died in 2007 at the age of eighty-nine.[36] In 1943, at the age of twenty-five, Zahn refused to fight in the Second World War, regardless of whether "our side" was in the right. He chose instead the path of conscientious objection, and was immediately dispatched to a Civilian Public Service facility known as Camp Simon, located near Warner, New Hampshire.

In 1967 and 2003, it might have been relatively easy for an American to proclaim oneself a pacifist, even to officially declare oneself a conscientious objector, because the United States was fighting extremely unpopular wars. But it must have been excruciatingly difficult to choose that course in 1943, when the United States was fighting wars in Europe and the Pacific that were supported by virtually every citizen in the land. Zahn's politics were not particularly complicated: he simply believed, quietly but insistently, that he could not call himself both a soldier and a Christian. But as a consequence, he was ostracized not only by most Americans he encountered, but even by leading officials of the Catholic Church. He wrote to the archbishop of Milwaukee seeking a blessing for his decision, but never received any reply. After the war, he enrolled with fellow conscientious objector Dick Leonard at St. John's University in Collegeville, Minnesota, where both students faced unremitting hostility from both returned veterans and several Benedictine priests on the faculty who had served as chaplains during the war. After a year, the men were told they were no longer welcome on campus.

Mr. Zahn and Mr. Leonard eventually went on to graduate from the College of St. Thomas in St. Paul, Minnesota. One of their professors there was Eugene McCarthy, who went on, of course, to win a seat in the U.S. House, then to win a seat in the U.S. Senate, and then, in

1968, to wage one of the most consequential antiwar presidential candidacies in American history. Though usually one assumes that it is the teacher who influences the student, and not vice versa, perhaps it is not too much to speculate that Mr. McCarthy's subsequent role in history may have been shaped, in some small measure, by the presence in his classroom a couple of decades earlier of a couple of rare World War II conscientious objectors.

Zahn wrote several books about the act of conscientious objection. *Another Part of the War: The Camp Simon Story* was about his own experiences, while *In Solitary Witness: The Life and Death of Franz Jagerstatter* focused on an Austrian farmer, husband, and father of four who refused duty in the German *Wehrmacht,* and was thus beheaded by the Nazis on August 9, 1943. On August 9, 1995, at Nagasaki's fiftieth-anniversary commemoration of its atomic bombing, Daniel Ellsberg, whose decision to illegally release thousands of pages of classified documents about Vietnam (known as the Pentagon Papers) was also one of the most consequential antiwar acts in American political history, told the audience that the writings of Gordon Zahn had helped to stiffen his spine as he deliberated about whether to go forth. (His son, Robert Ellsberg, had served as an editor at the *Catholic Worker* newspaper, and had recommended the admittedly obscure books to his father.)

In 1977, Zahn wrote about choosing the conscientious objector route and anticipating its possible consequences:

> If the Warner experience accomplished nothing else, it did give tangible evidence of Catholic resistance, weak and flawed though it most certainly was, to a war effort that claimed almost unanimous support. It represented a rejection of the dreadful excesses that marked that war and established a precedent for the more widespread opposition to war. . . . Opposition to World War II prepared the ground for what was to come. . . . And if this is too much to claim, the seventy-five men assigned to Warner can take satisfaction in knowing that, despite all the frustrations and hardships, the experience made it possible for them to avoid participation in the organized and planned mass destruction of human beings that was to find its logical culmination in the twin horrors of Auschwitz and Hiroshima. That ought to count for something.[37]

During his own 1968 campaign for the presidency, Robert F. Kennedy liked to quote George Bernard Shaw, who said, "You see things and you say, 'Why?' But I dream things that never were, and I say, 'Why not?' "[38] Imagine early in this decade an enormous growth of citizen pressure within the United States for nuclear weapons abolition—incited by a surging new civil society movement with a focused agenda not unlike the seven points offered above. Imagine, too, a similar growth of citizen demands in other countries, pressing both their own governments and the U.S. government to pursue abolition—again incited by burgeoning civil society pressure. In addition, imagine that many of those other governments actually respond positively to their own citizens, and promise them that they will act to eliminate their own nuclear arsenals if they have them, and that they will pressure all states with nuclear arsenals to get serious about eliminating theirs.

Imagine then that President Barack Obama—who has repeatedly stated that he shares the goal of a nuclear weapon–free world—finds himself facing millions of Americans and other citizens around the world demanding nuclear abolition. Dozens of other governments, too, are pressing the United States to pursue abolition (and are perhaps threatening their own nuclear proliferation, implicitly or otherwise). With these kinds of shifts in the political winds, perhaps it won't have to be Great Britain or India or Japan or some other state, but the United States, that will actually take the lead and initiate a process directed at negotiating a Nuclear Weapons Elimination Convention. Airplanes, missiles, and submarines have traditionally been called America's "nuclear triad," so perhaps we might identify a new "antinuclear triad"—American citizens, other world citizens, and other world governments—that can move the most crucial government in the world, the government of the United States. But that will only happen if thousands and thousands of individuals each now decides to undertake, like Gordon Zahn, their own single, lonely, individual acts of conscience.

There's a story, possibly apocryphal, that early during FDR's first term, labor representative Sidney Hillman scored a meeting with the president and eloquently and insistently laid out the case for comprehensive legislation that would guarantee American workers the right to organize. "I agree with everything you've said," FDR replied. "Now go out and make me do it." Two years later, after intensive efforts by a mobilized and impassioned labor movement built from the individual acts of thousands of laborers, the Wagner Act became law.

How might abolition happen? It might happen if enough people commit to transform it from laudable intention to concrete political action. It might happen if enough people work to ban the damned things, to prohibit them, to establish a universal, verifiable, and enforceable convention to get rid of them, and to ensure that they can never reenter the history of the human race. It might happen if enough people believe that it can happen, and roll up their sleeves to make it happen, and commit to toil, for the long haul, until the job is done, to put the nuclear genie back into its bottle for good.

After all, said Victor Hugo, a contemporary of Frederick Douglass, "No army can withstand the strength of an idea whose time has come."

CHAPTER 12

Apocalypse Never

IN 1971, WHEN Henry Kissinger went to China on behalf of President Nixon in a secret effort to reestablish diplomatic relations between our two great nations, he had much to discuss with his interlocutors in Beijing. There had been, after all, no official contact between the estranged adversaries since the founding of the People's Republic in 1949. In the course of their conversations, and in the spirit of good-natured ideological sparring, Kissinger asked Mao's longtime associate Zhou En-Lai if he cared to share an opinion about the historical impact of the French Revolution. Zhou considered the question for a moment and then replied, "I think it is too soon to tell."

If this book has tried to make anything clear, it is that, regarding the ultimate role of nuclear weapons in human history, it is, indeed, too soon to tell.

As the 1986 Reykjavik summit wound to a close, and it became apparent that the deal to abolish nuclear weapons that the American and Soviet leaders had so very nearly agreed upon would not be reached, Soviet foreign minister Eduard Shevardnadze put the magnitude of the lost opportunity into perspective: "Let me speak very emotionally, because we have come very close to accomplishing this historic task. And when future generations read the record of our talks, they will not forgive us if we let this opportunity slip by."[1] In one sense, Shevardnadze seems to have overstated the case. Except among a few academics, international policy wonks, and NUTS, the train we missed at Reykjavik does not generate a great deal of outrage or lamentation. No one on talk radio, in the blogosphere, or on the nation's op-ed pages lambastes Reagan, Gorbachev, or Shevardnadze for that which might have been.

But imagine if we blow it. Imagine if, in the next couple of decades or so, we find ourselves in a world of not nine, but nineteen or twenty-nine nuclear weapon states. And imagine that the human race is forced to absorb a nuclear terror attack, or an accidental nuclear launch, or the unfolding of a political crisis into a nuclear war, or the intentional initiation of a nuclear first strike. Moreover, imagine then all the adverse consequences that might well cascade from that initial crossing of the nuclear Rubicon.

One supposes, then, that Shevardnadze's prognostication will be vindicated. Future generations will not forgive those three individuals for coming so heartbreakingly close to abolition in 1986, only to "let this opportunity slip by." However, it seems likely that Mr. Reagan, Mr. Gorbachev, and Mr. Shevardnadze will not be the only ones they will blame.

They also will not forgive us.

"If you are religious," said novelist Arundhati Roy shortly after India conducted its nuclear weapons tests in 1998, "then remember that this bomb is Man's challenge to God. It's worded quite simply: We have the power to destroy everything that You have created."[2] Ms. Roy is a wonderful writer, but one might suggest that on this point she has it precisely backwards, and that "this bomb" should be seen instead as God's challenge to man. Can our social imagination, our governing institutions, and our political courage catch up with our ever-accelerating scientific and technological prowess? Nowhere is that challenge presented more starkly, nowhere are the stakes conceivably higher, than in the challenge of abolishing nuclear weapons, and saving ourselves from nuclear apocalypse.

Jonathan Schell, in his eloquent book *The Unfinished Twentieth Century*, published in 2001 at the dawn of our new millennium, reminds us that the ancient Greeks bequeathed to us the insight that no one should be called happy before one's demise, because a stroke of ill fate at the end can undo everything that one has lived for, aspired to, and achieved.[3] The meaning of any individual life can hinge on its closing chapter. So just as the historical story of Lenin, Stalin, and communism will be defined forever by its sudden collapse between 1989 and 1991, observes Schell, so too might the historical meaning of the nuclear age depend on its ending.

If one or more of the many possible nuclear calamities that this book has described do come to pass, future generations—if any—will likely view the invention of the atomic bomb as the single greatest catastrophe ever to befall the human race. And they will view the widespread disinterest and indifference to nuclear matters among both policymakers and the public, at least since the end of the cold war, as perhaps the most shocking complacence in all of history.

But if things go in a different direction, something like the one advocated in Chapter 11, future generations could consider the story of the nuclear age, as a whole, among the greatest of all humanity's triumphs. They will know that, in the course of a vicious and devastating war in the first half of the twentieth century, we created for the first time the means to bring about the extinction of our own species, even the extinction of all species, by our own hands. Yet they will see that some two-thirds of a century or so later, somehow, we managed to find a way to eradicate our weapons rather than ourselves. And just as we look back at our ancestors who brought us out of the caves and into the light of possibility, our descendants will look back at us, their ancestors, the generation that made the abolition of nuclear weapons happen, with a measureless gratitude. And perhaps even with wonder, and admiration, and awe.

GLOBAL CITIZENSHIP, PLANETARY PATRIOTISM, AND ALLEGIANCE TO HUMANITY

Perhaps the most important element that could enable us to leave that legacy, for our descendants, could be our definition of the challenge itself. One of the central points of this book is that abolishing nuclear weapons will serve not only the national interests of the United States and other individual states, but the common human interest as well. The famous Einstein-Russell Manifesto of 1955 made this point, when its signatories claimed to speak "on this occasion, not as members of this or that nation, continent, or creed, but as human beings, members of the species Man, whose continued existence is in doubt." They continued: "We want you, if you can . . . to consider yourselves only as members of a biological species which has had a remarkable history, and whose disappearance none of us can desire. . . . If you can do so, the way lies open to a new Paradise; if you cannot, there lies before you the risk of universal death."[4]

Many Americans possess a profound sense of human solidarity, an ethic of shared destiny, an intuition that, as Dr. King liked to observe, we may have come over on different ships but we're all in the same boat now. Consider, for example, the many people who, in the first weeks after 9/11, displayed not an American flag but the increasingly popular Flag of Earth—a dazzling artistic rendition of our sun, our moon, and our increasingly fragile home. In a rapidly globalizing world, we feel that our greatest connections are not necessarily with other Americans, but with people everywhere who hold similar beliefs, values, and larger perspectives. We demand that cold calculations of American national security be accompanied by some consideration of common human security, the welfare of the whole, the global public good. We insist that our deepest loyalties are not necessarily to the country where we happen to have been born, but instead to the planet where all of us were born. We believe that the whole earth—first seen by the Apollo 8 astronauts on December 24, 1968, and captured in their breathtaking and immortal photograph—is something greater than the sum of its parts.

Those ventures into outer space have already served as one of the greatest cultivators of this idea of human unity. On July 20, 1979, the tenth anniversary of humanity's first footsteps on the moon, Apollo 11 commander Neil Armstrong was asked how he felt as he saluted the flag up there. "I suppose you're thinking about pride and patriotism," he told the reporter. "But we didn't have a strong nationalistic feeling at that time. We felt more that it was a venture of all mankind."[5]

Many other astronauts have expressed similar sentiments about the sensation of looking back at the planet of our birth. "The Earth was small, light blue, and so touchingly alone," said Russian Aleksei Leonov, "our home that must be defended like a holy relic." "The first day or so we all pointed to our countries," said Saudi Sultan bin Salman Al-Saud. "The third or fourth day we were pointing to our continents. By the fifth day, we were aware of only one Earth."[6] "From out there on the moon, international politics look so petty," said Edgar Mitchell, one of only twelve humans to have walked on the surface of another world. "You want to grab a politician by the scruff of the neck and drag him a quarter million miles out and say, 'Look at that, you son of a bitch.'"[7]

This is why the late Carl Sagan claimed that spaceflight might be considered subversive. Although governments have ventured into space largely for nationalistic reasons, "it was a small irony that almost everyone who entered space received a startling glimpse of a transnational perspective, of the Earth as one world."[8] Seeing our planet as a whole, apparently, enables one to see our planet as a whole.

Such sentiments, of course, are hardly limited to astronauts. The idea that planetary patriotism can serve as a key engine of human progress has a long and distinguished lineage. As Nobel economics laureate John Kenneth Galbraith once said, "the greatest political conflict of our time [is] that of national interest as opposed to international, transnational concern and responsibility."[9] We stand in the tradition of what psychologist Erik Erikson called an "all-human solidarity." We seek to cultivate what Sovietologist Robert C. Tucker called "an ethic of specieshood."[10] We serve as the vanguard of what Voltaire called "the party of humanity." We endorse the declaration, regardless of our faith traditions, of Baha'allah, founder of the Bahai faith, who said, "The Earth is but one country, and mankind its citizens."[11] We embrace the task assigned us by science fiction author Spider Robinson, who, while eulogizing fellow writer Robert A. Heinlein, said, "I think he would be pleased if we dispensed with the illusion that there are any passengers on Spaceship Earth, and took up our responsibilities as crew members."[12]

American politicians often appear behind the curve regarding such sentiments. Even the inspirational and visionary Barack Obama concluded his inaugural address on January 20, 2009, with the same ritualistic phrase, "Thank you, God bless you, and God bless the United States of America." Perhaps it is not too much to hope that someday an American political figure might utter those exact same words, but then add one additional phrase: "And God bless, too, the whole of the family of humankind." Perhaps we can dream that someday American schoolchildren will begin their school day by standing up, hands over hearts, and saying together: "We are citizens of the United States and citizens of Planet Earth. We are national patriots and planetary patriots. We pledge allegiance to the flag of the United States of America. And we also pledge our allegiance to humanity." And perhaps we can aspire for these visions of Einstein's and Russell's "new Paradise," these yearnings for One World, to serve as perhaps our most crucial impetus—as we endeavor to build a movement to ensure that we don't blow it up first.

The Chronological Stakes

During the darkest hours of the Cuban missile crisis, President Kennedy went swimming in the White House pool with an old friend from his first congressional campaign, David Powers. After a few laps, Kennedy stopped, turned to Powers, and said, "If it weren't for these people that haven't lived yet, it would be easy to make decisions of this sort."[13] Today there are more than 6.8 billion living human beings. An extinction-producing nuclear war, therefore, would arguably be 6.8 billion times worse than killing one person. But such an act would entail even more: killing 6.8 billion people would forestall the possibility that an infinite number of their descendants will ever get the chance to be born, a crime of infinite magnitude.

However, these calculations might hold a more visceral meaning if we endeavor to make them, somehow, finite. Carl Sagan, it turns out, performed just such an exercise. In the early 1980s, the public imagination became captivated by the hypothesis of nuclear winter. Armchair strategists had long played the gruesome game of calculating the likely human deaths that would result from a full-scale east-west nuclear exchange. Certainly many millions would die, likely hundreds of millions, possibly more than a billion—perhaps amounting to half of the 3 or 4 billion people alive then on earth. One might have thought that would have been bad enough.

But the nuclear winter research that emerged in the 1980s told a worse story. The conclusion was that such a nuclear exchange would hurl so much soot into the sky (from both the nuclear detonations themselves and from the vast infernos that would follow) that average global temperatures would plummet, produce months of blackened skies, and possibly bring about the extinction of our species, along with thousands of others. One might have thought there were no numbers to calculate after that, other than the human population itself at the hour of our doom.

But Carl Sagan went a step further. He tried to calculate the number of future human lives that, after our collective suicide, would forever remain unlived. He started with the fact that the mean lifespan of a successful species, in the 3.5-billion-year record of life, has been about 10 million years. At about 100,000 years old, then, *Homo sapiens* is now only 1 percent of the way to being able to call itself "average."

According to Sagan, if we make it the other 99 percent of the way, some 500 trillion human babies will be born during the next 9.9 million years.[14] Or they won't, if we don't. (The total number of humans who have ever lived, since the emergence of our species, is probably less than 100 billion.)

Sagan's estimate, however, may turn out to be a stingy one if the human race begins to expand beyond its original planetary home. Isaac Asimov's *Foundation* novels, widely considered the greatest science fiction series ever constructed, are set not 10 million, but a mere 25,000 years or so down the road. But Asimov's work envisions several million star systems colonized by the human race, and several quadrillion human beings alive in just one generation. Humans have become so numerous and so widely dispersed, in fact, that fictional future anthropologists debate which among those several million stars was humanity's original sun.

But our potentially infinite future is about more than just the sheer numbers of unborn humans; it is also about our infinite potential. Few have spoken as vividly about the vista of human possibility than H. G. Wells. "We look back through countless millions of years and see the great will to live struggling out of the intertidal slime," he said in his famous 1902 lecture called "The Discovery of the Future" before the Royal Institution in London.

> We see it turn upon itself in rage and hunger and reshape itself, pursuing its relentless inconceivable purpose, until at last it reaches us and its being beats through our brains and arteries. . . . It is possible to believe that all that the human mind has ever accomplished is but the dream before the awakening. . . . Out of our lineage, minds will spring, that will reach back to us in our littleness . . . [and] beings who are now latent in our thoughts and hidden in our loins, shall stand upon this earth as one stands upon a footstool, and shall laugh and reach out their hands amidst the stars.[15]

"The greatest good for the greatest number," said Wells's contemporary and friend, President Theodore Roosevelt, "applies to the number within the womb of time, compared to which those now alive form but an insignificant fraction."[16] Today's decisions about nuclear weapons will affect not only the human beings of 2010, but also those of 2110, of 22,110, of 802,701. Who are we to put their very chance to exist at risk? It is in our hands to give the possibility of life to all of our potential descendants, or to strip them of it before they ever have the chance. Our species may have a virtually infinite future—in time, in space, in both the sheer numbers of humans and their potential achievements.

But only if we can manage, now, to dodge the bullet in the chamber in the gun in our own hands.

THE COSMOLOGICAL STAKES

In 2003, Martin Rees published an extraordinary book. Sir Martin is the Royal Society Professor at Cambridge University, and England's astronomer royal. The book carried the terrifying title, *Our Final Hour*. In it, he surveyed the universe of awful things that could go terribly wrong for the human race during the next hundred years or so (nuclear dangers prominent among them, but hardly alone), estimated their probabilities, then delivered this astonishing verdict: "I think the odds are no better than fifty-fifty that our present civilization on Earth will survive to the end of the present century."[17] (One wonders how two entire American presidential campaigns can go by since then without a single candidate even addressing such a dire judgment, however valid it may be.)

The book jacket, at least on the American edition, ratcheted up the rhetoric further still. It claimed that Rees would argue inside that it was largely a tossup whether "the human race" would survive until 2099— a forecast somewhat more dire than what the author actually delivered. Still, leaving aside the probability assessment delivered by Rees for the moment, it is fair to say that, in the case of nuclear weapons, uniquely, the book-jacket characterization was the more accurate one.

Jonathan Schell has written often about the ascending gradation of the crimes of extermination that human beings might commit.[18] Genocide, he explains, is an act aimed at exterminating all members of a particular human group, defined by ethnicity, race, religion, or some other collective hatred. Specicide would exterminate all members of all human groups, while ecocide, or perhaps biocide, would exterminate the whole circle of life on our planet. The complete sterilization of planet Earth itself.

An asteroid impact, certain solar disruptions, or perhaps other cosmological cataclysms could deliver such an ecocide without breaking a sweat. Today, however, although biotech or nanotech may reach it someday, nuclear weapons are the only creation of the human mind with the capacity to bring that about. On any given Thursday morning. Before lunch.

"I propose a new word to replace the misleading term nuclear war," said philosopher John Somerville in 1982:

> Since we already have a series of nouns which denote successively wider ranges of killing—suicide for killing oneself, infanticide for killing infants, genocide for killing national or ethnic groups—and since nuclear weapons can now kill all human beings and obliterate [all life] in one relatively brief conflict, it seems appropriate to call such a conflict *omnicide*. . . . The supremely ironic fact is that today we live in fear and in possible sight of the human committing this crime so unspeakable that it does not even have a name, this crime so enormous it can be committed only once.[19]

This possibility of extinction, whether delivered by our own hands or from the cosmological beyond, surely stands as the ultimate rationale for why humanity should venture into space and reach for the stars. Abolishing nuclear weapons, absolutely as soon as possible, is probably the single most important task the human race can pursue right now to ensure our long-range survival. Yet even people who eat right, exercise every day, and look both ways before crossing Fifth Avenue still take out life insurance policies. Our current historical moment—a period in which we might say we have the capability to destroy ourselves yet have not yet found a way to save ourselves—is the human race's ultimate window of vulnerability. But we also have a window of opportunity, to endeavor, over the next few centuries or so, to establish humankind permanently beyond the cradle of our birth—first perhaps on our own moon; then on Mars, in the asteroid belt, and on some of the moons of Jupiter and Saturn; and eventually beyond the bounds of our solar system. If we can venture slowly but inexorably outward, in tiny lifeboats afloat on an infinite sea, eventually to live among the stars, then it becomes difficult to envision any catastrophe that could comprehensively wipe out the progeny of Mother Earth. Then, we would be as close to immortality as the universe itself.

"Even a few pioneering groups," says Rees, "living independently of Earth, would offer a safeguard against the worst possible disaster—the foreclosure of intelligent life's future through the extinction of all humankind."[20] Similarly, physicist Stephen Hawking, in remarks just before boarding his widely publicized zero gravity airplane flight in April 2007, said, "Life on Earth is at risk of being wiped out by a disaster, such as sudden global warming, nuclear war, a genetically engineered virus. . . . I think the human race has no future if it doesn't go into space."[21] "I am a short-time pessimist," said Robert A. Heinlein, "but a long-time optimist."[22] The actions of the astronauts who went to the moon, he continued, and of the thousands more on the ground who helped to make those voyages happen "tend toward the survival of the entire race of mankind. The door they opened leads to hope that h. sapiens will survive indefinitely long, even longer than this solid planet on which we stand tonight. As a direct result of what they did, it is now possible that the human race will never die."[23]

But not if we kill ourselves off before we have scarcely even gotten started.

If we do, the consequences might be even worse than one might initially suppose. Simply by virtue of its sheer extent in both space and time, our galaxy and our universe may well be teeming with life, some of it complex and sentient and with an intelligence approaching (or far exceeding) our own. If this is the case, it is difficult to suppose that our fate on earth could have much of an overall cosmic significance. In 1690, Dutch mathematician and astronomer Christiaan Huygens famously articulated this view, in a work he dramatically titled *New Conjectures Concerning the Planetary Worlds, Their Inhabitants and Productions:* "How vast those Orbs must be, and how inconsiderable this Earth, the Theatre upon which all our mighty Designs, all our Navigations, and all our Wars are transacted. . . . A very fit consideration, and matter of Reflection, for those Kings and Princes who sacrifice the Lives of so many People, only to flatter their Ambition in being Masters of some pitiful corner of this small Spot."[24]

If we are in fact just a single grain of sand among a vast cosmic seashore of life, the stakes are still, of course, infinitely high for us.

However, they may be even higher. There is another, more portentous alternative. Senator Alan Cranston, when he had exhausted all of the policy arguments for abolition at his disposal, often asked quite simply, "What if we are alone?" It is far from impossible that an almost infinitely intricate set of conditions was necessary first for life spontaneously to arise out of base matter, and then for that life to evolve over billions of years into creatures capable of inventing mathematics, art, music, literature, and cosmology. The emergence of life itself may be exceedingly rare. Alternatively, life itself may be not uncommon, but the development of that life into something complex, something aware of itself, something like us, may be exceedingly rare. Possibly even unique.

After all, on the one data point that we presently possess, it appears that simple organisms emerged about 100 million years after the cooling of the earth's crust roughly 4 billion years ago. But 3 billion more years had to pass before those simple forms evolved into even basic multicellular organisms. And nearly 1 billion more years had to pass after that—only 100,000 years or so ago—before that multicellular life evolved into human-level intelligence. For most of the history of life on earth, that life was nothing but individual cells of blue-green algae—your grandparents, floating on the surface of the primordial seas, infinitely patient, their future destiny latent within. Yet if that destiny remained latent first for a full three billion years just to move past single cells, and then for another 0.9999 billion years after that to move from the first multicellular creatures to something approaching our own level of intelligence, it certainly suggests that the emergence of beings with minds like ours was not inevitable. It could have been, to the contrary, an exceedingly remote possibility, that just happened to have taken place here. And only here.

"So long as we know about only one biosphere, our own," says Rees, "we cannot exclude its being unique: complex life could be the outcome of a chain of events so unlikely that it happened only once within the observable universe. . . . The emergence of intelligence may require such an improbable chain of events that it is unique to our Earth. It may simply not have occurred anywhere else, not around even one of the trillion billion other stars."[25] We may be the only ones, ever. We may be utterly alone. We may be the singular point, anytime and anywhere, at which the universe became aware of itself. And we, ourselves, may present the singular chance for life to evolve and develop and grow and travel and fill the universe with an infinity of possibility.

And so, says Martin Rees, "we live at what could be a defining moment for the cosmos, not just for our Earth. . . . It may not be absurd hyperbole—indeed, it may not even be an overstatement—to assert that the most crucial location in space and time (apart from the big bang itself) could be here and now. The choice may depend on us, this century."[26]

Got that, policymakers, activists, philanthropists, citizens, and presidents? Does that seem just possibly as important as whatever other matters you devoted your attention to last week? Rees contends, astoundingly but not implausibly, that in all of space and time, in the entire universe, in the 13.7 billion years that have transpired since it all began, it is possible that no being could engage in a more consequential task for the fate of creation than to work, here and now, for the abolition of nuclear weapons (or the few other causes with implications for the survival of the human race). If that does not persuade you that the nuclear question is worth perhaps just a bit of your blood, toil, tears, and treasure, what will?

KOKURA FOREVER

In the Fukuoka Prefecture in southwestern Japan lies a medium-sized city named Kitakyushu with a population of about 1 million people. It was founded in 1963 as the amalgamation of five smaller cities in the area, the largest of which was called Kokura. Kitakyushu is a lovely modern city with a well-preserved ancient castle inside its limits. Yet it is also a somewhat nondescript city, with nothing in particular to distinguish it from many other cities in Japan and around the world. Except for one unique characteristic, one episode, one distinction that is possessed by no other city in the world. On the morning of August 9, 1945, for the American B-29 Superfortress called *Bockscar*, carrying the world's third atomic bomb called Fat Man, Kokura was the target.

The mission was bedeviled by problems from the moment the plane took to the air. *Bockscar* and an accompanying B-29 laden with instruments arrived at an assembly point off the coast of Japan, intending to meet a third photographic plane, but it was not there. The two aircraft circled fruitlessly for forty minutes until, behind schedule, *Bockscar*'s commander, Major Charles W. Sweeney, decided to proceed.

When the two aircraft arrived above Kokura, they found that on this day it was shrouded in clouds and haze, and the smoke still churning from nearby American firebombing raids several days earlier. The twin Superfortresses made three long passes over the city, in an effort to confirm visually that it was in fact Kokura below. If the obscurity had cleared even for a moment, that would have become the moment of Kokura's doom. But it did not. Fuel was running low, both because of the delays and because a transfer pump on *Bockscar* had failed immediately after takeoff. So Major Sweeney decided to divert his mission to the designated secondary target, the city of Nagasaki.

The atomic weaponeer, Navy commander Frederick Ashworth, decided that if Nagasaki were similarly obscured, they would abort the mission and ditch the atom bomb off the coast of American-occupied Okinawa. Indeed, when they arrived above Nagasaki, the city was also shrouded. But at 11:01 A.M., a brief break in the cloud cover allowed *Bockscar's* bombardier, Captain Kermit Behan, visually to confirm the target. Fat Man was released. Forty-three seconds later, 469 meters above Nagasaki, it detonated.

The Japanese now employ a phrase, "Kokura luck" to connote circumstances where individuals escape some great misfortune, without even knowing that it was heading their way. Kokura, it turns out, by luck, by the most capricious whim of the gods, was spared from its atomic destiny. Just as every other city on earth, for nearly two-thirds of a century now, has been spared from nuclear devastation also by luck, also by the most capricious whim of the gods. In this sense, we might say that Kokura can be taken to represent every other city in the world.

Nevertheless, Kokura's fate has not yet been sealed. It managed to elude the atomic bomb on August 9, 1945, and ever since. So, too, has every other city in the world. But that does not mean that any of them have permanently escaped the nuclear peril. Kokura, and all other cities, still live under John F. Kennedy's nuclear sword of Damocles, "hanging by the slenderest of threads," suspended above the heads of every one of their citizens. In this sense, too, we might say that Kokura can be taken to represent every other city in the world.

Including yours. There it is. Can you see it? The atomic sword, hanging, so precariously, over your very head, and those of your family, and those of your neighbors, and those of each and every member of the family of humankind.

Unless and until each and every one of us, together, decides now to snatch that foil away, to cut that perilous thread, and to turn every single nuclear sword, everywhere on earth, into the ploughshares of peace that the prophet Isaiah envisioned, for us, so many long centuries ago. The matter is in our hands. The sword is within our grasp. We need only to reach out, and seize it.

Apocalypse never. Kokura forever. Let us, too, hold in our hearts the barest glimpse of a human destiny of infinite possibility.

ACKNOWLEDGMENTS

A GREAT MANY FAMILY MEMBERS, friends, and colleagues have aided and abetted my efforts to launch this project, think it through, and bring it to completion. Some are political professionals or nuclear policy specialists, but a great many more are simply people who care about me and the human race—and want us both to live long and thrive.

My mother, Diana Jankey Daley, who died terribly young in 1979, might have looked like an average suburban housewife transplanted from Brooklyn to the northwest suburbs of Chicago in the 1960s and 1970s— except for that subscription to the science fiction magazine *Galaxy*. She devoured each issue, passed them on to me, and then encouraged me to let my imagination soar. After she died I came across a letter she had apparently started writing to someone but never sent, confessing that she hoped her fifth-grade son would grow up to become "another George Bernard Shaw." I'm giving it my best shot, Mom—just sixty-six more literary works, one Nobel Prize, and one Academy Award to go.

My father, Claude Daley, Jr., also died too young in 1997. He was a conservative Georgia Republican, and after I grew up we spent much of our time together talking politics. I'm not sure if he ever read Plato, but he sure did have the Socratic method down—always interrogating me, always inviting me to defend my often-muddled liberal positions, always forcing me to answer hard and penetrating questions. Many of my arguments herein were crafted in response to challenges that I know, Dad, you would have insisted I confront. *Imparido Pectore*.

My brothers, Jeff Daley and Buzz Daley, have inherited both my dad's conservative politics and his determination to fire hard questions at me. But the two of them, along with their wives Audie and Terri as well as Jeff's son Carl (an Iraq war veteran), all love me and believe in me. That is also true of my father's sole surviving brother, Walter Randolph Daley, also a Pacific World War II airman, who told me he supports nuclear weapons abolition but doesn't believe it can ever happen. I intend for this book to change his mind.

My wife Kitty Felde's brothers, Jerry, Dominick, Danny, Alex, Matt, and Mitch, encouraged by their father, Tom, and his wife, Cindy, took me out into the garage to beat me up before letting me into the family. I'm glad they did. Bill and Julie Case; their children, Lili, Tim, James, and Andrew; and Julie's parents, Kendall and Wilda Schlenker, have often shared their sublime and serene New Mexico refuge with Kitty and me. Barry Wolf, my best friend from RAND and member of my kitchen cabinet, insisted that I keep plugging away at my writing while reminding me never to take things too seriously. Steve Gamber, my best friend from St. Monica's Catholic Church, shows up at almost every one of my speaking appearances, then insists on beer and karaoke afterward. Christina Linhardt, who sang exquisitely before I delivered an "alternative presidential inaugural address" (available at www.common-dreams.org) on January 20, 2005, reads all my articles and tells me both what's good about them and what can be better.

Progressive videographer David Lionel has always pressed me to make my proposals bigger and bolder, and directed me away from intellectual timidity. Witney Schneidman and Steve Goodman in Washington, D.C., have insisted that my writings pass their inside-the-beltway credibility tests, and motivated me to catch up to their own books (*Engaging Africa* and *College Admissions Together*, respectively). Rachel Landis Heslin has generously managed www.daleyplanet.org pro bono for many years because she believes in the message and believes in me. Greg Wright, my fellow board member at Southern California Americans for Democratic Action who performed several crucial research tasks for this book, pumps out new ideas every day for revitalizing the Democratic party. Jane Shevtsov was sort of a protégé of mine when I served as a visiting scholar at UCLA. Now a Ph.D. candidate in ecology at the University of Georgia, she has a remarkable mind, an extraordinary imagination, and an uncanny ability to move me to take my arguments one step further. And my monthly visits to Staples Center to watch the Los Angeles Clippers with my devout friend Joe Sterbinsky reminded me of the importance of sticking with a cause, however long shot, for the long haul.

Many good friends provided not so much substantive advice, but simple encouragement, friendship, and an indefatigable conviction that

I should see this project through. They include Sandy and Bob Hobbs, Bernie Altman, Becky and Jack Doody, Renee Sands, Coco Saavedra, Kristine Aronsohn, Joyce Alexson, Jeff Trosper, Irene and Rob, Celeste Adams, Valerie Stansfield, Bibi Caspari, Bruce Ablin, Kathleen Gildred, Steve and Elaine, Andy Papp, Margie and Antony, Steve and Joyce Chelski, Kathleen Rosenblatt, Orrin and Shahla, Kathleen Gildred, Mary Howard, Dave Blackburn, Leanna Wolf, Aunt Maryjane and Uncle George, Tracy Pennington, Melly McQueen and John Leslie, Rosalie Fox and Dan Huntington, Jana and Dana Jankey, Ed Elkin, Phil Laier, Billy Coyne, Sheryl Shultz, Diane Bulgatz, Joe and Allison Grover Khoury, Gordon Brooks, Valya Walker, Jean Wilson, Lauren Gentry, Cheryl Murray, Molly O'Brien, Sue Hausmann, Courtney and Maurice Young, James Cremin, Diane Peaches Gilbert, Janet Shicaina Allen, Robb Curtis, John Silva, Kermit Ganier, Rhonda Bogante, Craig Butler, Reggie Thornton, Jennifer Hartman, Noore Ali, Norman Toy, Carla Calmenson, Debra Mayes, Iyob Tessema, Sally Aristei, Andrea Orr, Deepa Shinde, Denise Baldonado, Lisa Hauck, Mary Dirstine Bock, Anne Cherian and Lon Kurashige and their boys Cole and Reed, and Pola Churchill.

Several good friends who are decidedly not nuclear policy wonks nevertheless engaged me in many conversations about the substance of the book. They helped me immeasurably to write a book that, I hope, engages a broad audience. They include Ara Easley, Emily Condit, Mitch Gunzler, Brian Gould, Bob Eklund, Ron Glossop, Lucy Webster, Thesil Morlan, Troy Davis, Barry Cutler, Susie Nowak, Benton Musslewhite, Julia Prange, Aliza Weidenbaum, Curt Steindler, Nick Dragon, Justeen Ward, Tova Fuller, Maria Armoudian, Bill and Dee Dee Chappelle, Nima Dilmaghani, Kelly Green, David Moore, Dick Nordrum, Konrad Wilk, Mark Gallagher, Andrew Connally, Chicago alderman Joe Moore, Angela Boerger, John Sutter, Joe Schwartzberg, Mariel Leonard, Scott Hoffman, Don Kraus, Steve Damours, Stan Lankowitz, Myron Kronisch, Thesil Morlan, Larry David, Bob Enholm, Jim Ranney, Tom Camarella, Ted Leutzinger, Wendell Harter, Marcy Winograd, John Glass, Brian Gould, Mimi Kennedy, Jodie Evans, Dave Kelley, Tim Carpenter, Mary Jack, Dave Dayen, Marc Saltzberg, Cara Robin, Jim Kennedy, Kelley Willis, Doctor Dave, Norman Solomon, Jeff Cohen, Joel Bellman, Harold Meyerson, Rick Ponzio, Rob Lempert,

Tom Hayden, Don Bustany, John Seeley, Aris Anagnos, Bill McCarthy, Norma Foster, and the late David Tait.

I engaged on the content of the book, and shared several draft chapters, with nuclear policy professionals who identified many sins of commission and omission. They helped me eliminate my errors, sharpen and refine my arguments, and more thoroughly forge the path to a nuclear weapon–free world. They include John Burroughs, Jackie Cabasso, Richard Falk, Saul Mendlovitz, Richard Ponzio, Bob Musil, Michael Intriligator, John Loretz, General Robert Gard, Joe Cirincione, Jonathan Schell, Dave Schramm, Bill Potter, John Simpson, Stephen Schwartz, Phil Coyle, Bennett Ramberg, Alice Slater, Paul Kawika Martin, Kevin Martin, Doug Roche, David Krieger, Jonathan Granoff, and the late Joseph Rotblat. Daniel Ellsberg went a step further, demanded to read every word, and improved the book immeasurably as a result of his vast experience and expertise.

I spent the better part of four years conceptualizing, researching, and writing this book. During the first two I was writing fellow in the Los Angeles office of Physicians for Social Responsibility under the leadership of Jonathan Parfrey. During the second two I was writing fellow with its international umbrella organization, International Physicians for the Prevention of Nuclear War, the 1985 Nobel peace laureate group led by Michael Christ and John Loretz. They struggled mightily to secure funding to support my work, because they believed the book might play an enormous role in reawakening the movement for abolition.

I served as chief policy wonk for the first presidential campaign of Congressman Dennis Kucinich. Both the congressman and his campaign manager, Dot Maver, actually apologized for making me spend so much time on issues in which I was far from expert. After that stint ended, both have consistently encouraged me to focus my fire on the pursuit of universal nuclear disarmament.

I met Congresswoman Diane Watson and her former chief of staff, Jim Clarke, when she and I both ran for an open congressional seat to represent mid-city Los Angeles. After Watson and I debated each other (and fourteen other candidates) many times, she told me she liked what she had heard and—after she won—hired me as a foreign policy consultant. She and Clarke both agree with Dick Gregory's long-ago sentiment: the greatest problem facing inner-city Americans, still, is global thermonuclear war.

I served for two years as a visiting scholar at the UCLA Burkle Center for International Relations under the leadership of Professor Mike Intriligator. Mike strongly encouraged me to spend my time writing and publishing because I had spent several previous years focusing on grassroots organizing at the expense of my writing. He has continued to deliver the same message ever since. My work for former U.S. senator Alan Cranston (described in Chapter 1) was one of the main vehicles for that grassroots organizing. Alan, too, believed I had a book or three in me, and reminded me that abolishing nuclear weapons was a step on the road to abolishing war itself.

The chair of my Ph.D. dissertation committee, Jeremy Azrael, of the RAND Corporation and formerly of the University of Chicago, died a few weeks before I completed this work. He, along with committee members Graham Fuller and John Van Oudenaren and RAND mentors Larry Caldwell, Frank Fukuyama, Harry Gelman, Arnold Horelick, Warren Walker, J. F. Brown, Zalmay Khalilzad, Robert Nurick, David Ochmanek, Charlie Wolf, and Jim Steinberg, shepherded me through the RAND Graduate School of Policy Studies Ph.D. program, the specialty training at the RAND/UCLA Center for Soviet Studies, and my dissertation on "The Lessons of Afghanistan." My Ph.D. program was commencing as the cold war was concluding; and these mentors led me directly to this book on one of the cold war's most enduring legacies.

I wrote the book while living in Los Angeles—great chunks of it at the Vineyard Café, where Christina, Lindsay, Zack, and Tony always welcomed me with great joie de vivre. Other chunks were written at the Holy Spirit Retreat Center in the San Fernando Valley. The Catholic sisters welcomed me with blessings and prayers, partly because nuclear weapons abolition is a longtime Catholic social justice teaching, partly because they are themselves filled with the spirit of the divine. Other chunks were written at the Denny's in Culver City. Managers Katherine Fitkin and Debra McKinney, along with their intrepid crew including Christine, Amber, Monique, Josh, Denise, Mike, Norma, Matthew, Maria, Leo, Derrick, Chris, Richard, and Kelly, not only put up with me but cheered for me as I camped out for hours in a remote back booth. And after a move across the country from Los Angeles to

Washington, D.C., the staff of the Capitol Skyline hotel, led by David Trezevant, Dixie Eng, and Mera Rubell, convinced me that the only possible place to polish it to completion was within view of the Capitol dome.

I managed to get away from the apocalypse occasionally with Friday night bicycle rides with the South Bay Cruisers, Saturday morning runs with ClubRunLadera, Sunday morning bicycle rides with the Los Angeles Wheelmen, Thursday night geek gatherings with the Los Angeles Science Fantasy Society, and Sunday afternoon brainiac sessions with the Philosophy in LA Café. My greatest refuge, however, was the Baldwin Hills Branch Library Chess Club, which I founded along with my aquabrothers Bob Lloyd, Edwin Cruz, and Berhane Azage in January 2003. The head librarian, Laura Dwan, and her successor, Selena Terrazas, believed strongly in the value of getting inner-city kids to sit down and concentrate—on anything. So every Monday night, I spent time over the chessboard with Clarence Griffin, Jeffrey Hirsch, Izzy Wood, Jorge and Julio and Perla, Keith Killough, Austin and Gianni and Lorraine and Maxwell Sampson, Dorian and Johanna, Brandon Morrison, George from Argentina ("the deep south"), Mike and Sean and Dominic Perry, Rhiannon Sayce, Achille, David and Carmen, Marvin, Diana, Karely, Queen Victoria and Queen Sophia, Kelson Haas, and Morgan and Jihad McDougal, reminding me that there are many things, in inner-city Los Angeles at least, worth saving from the apocalypse.

When I was a couple of months away from my deadline my wife, Kitty Felde, playwright and longtime public radio journalist with KPCC-FM 89.3 (National Public Radio for southern California), was asked to open a bureau in Washington, D.C.—to report on how Washington affects California and on the shenanigans of the California congressional delegation. Kitty went, along with our cat Cricket and all our stuff. I stayed behind for several weeks to finish *Apocalypse Never*. Fortunately, our friend Doctor Ildiko Tabori and her adorable baby daughter Mari offered me a place to do so, and many of the finishing touches were performed on their dining room table. Ildi said she considered me her "artist in residence"; and while I don't know about that, I do know that she should be considered a patron of the arts.

My literary agent, Paul Levine, worked long and hard to find just the right publisher for *Apocalypse Never*. He has a 100-percent success rate with his clients because, like Churchill, he never gives up. He did so with exceptional effort and determination in this case, he says, because he believes it will make him some money, and believes it may save the world. Marlie Wasserman of Rutgers University Press, along with her staffers Christina Brianik, Suzanne Kellam, Elizabeth Scarpelli, Lisa Fortunato, Allyson Fields, Michael Tomolonis, Karen Baliff Ornstein, and freelance copyeditor Dawn Potter, believe much the same thing. They have expended enormous efforts both to get this book out the door and to amplify its message.

Dora Anne Mills and Michael J. Fiori, and their enthusiastic children, Julia and Anthony, have repeatedly welcomed Kitty, me, and Cricket to their lakeside camp on Tallwood Peninsula in Maine. They always provide me with an opportunity for both deep thinking and deep escape.

John Shaw of Washington, D.C., my best friend on the east coast, was my roommate at Knox College and the best man in my wedding. No friend has bugged, cajoled, or annoyed me more to write and write. Jack is a couple of books ahead of me with *Washington Diplomacy* and *The Ambassador*, and *The Senator* in the works. I expect that no matter how many more books I manage to pump out, the dude will always stay a couple of literary works ahead.

Doctor Susan Beryl Arjmand of Chicago, my best friend on the midwest coast, is a family practice physician who sings glorious opera on the side (she is widely known as "the diva doc"). No one does a better job of helping me to let go of the little stuff—and reminding me that it's all little stuff.

Dana Bigman of Los Angeles, my best friend on the west coast, called me one day while she was listening to *Fresh Air with Terri Gross* on KPCC. "Tad," she said breathlessly, "there's some dull political guy on with Terri Gross right now and he is so boring and you are so charismatic and you are going to be so much better when you get on with her." I do not know if they'll actually invite me on *Fresh Air* to talk about *Apocalypse Never*, but I do know that Dana will be first in line to complain if they don't.

No one has stepped up to the plate for me more often, or more thoroughly, than Andy Okun. When, rather abruptly, I decided to make that long-shot bid for U.S. Congress, Andy volunteered, rather abruptly, to serve as my campaign manager. His wife, Julia, and his children, Will and Emily, proved to be amazingly tolerant when the campaign took over both of our lives. Now, for *Apocalypse Never*, Andy has repeatedly served at short notice as my de facto research assistant on matters great and small, helped me wrestle with maddening computer formatting issues, and always been ready to step up to the plate. Although neither one of us is of Italian origin, Andy, surely, is my *paisano*.

But the person I acknowledge last, and most, is my wife, Kitty Felde, who became my one true love shortly after I asked for her number in 1987 . . . five times. Kitty was convinced long before I was that writing this book should become my primary calling, here and now. Her energies were boundless and her faith unflagging as she endeavored to dispatch with countless details of our lives, including many genuine struggles, to make it possible to bring it to fruition.

But you are mistaken about one thing, sweetheart. This book, and any subsequent books, and all other challenges great and small, can never be more than my secondary calling. My primary calling is you.

NOTES

CHAPTER I APOCALYPSE SOON?

1. In Joseph Gerson, *Empire and the Bomb: How the U.S. Uses Nuclear Weapons to Dominate the World* (Ann Arbor, Mich.: Pluto, 2007), 57.
2. See http://www.commondreams.org, posted May 2, 2005. Jennet Conant's *109 East Palace* (New York: Simon and Schuster, 2005) tells the story of Robert Oppenheimer and the Manhattan Project through the eyes of Dorothy McKibbin, the woman who processed scientists as they arrived to work on the project.
3. U.S. Postal Service, ceremony honoring the issuance of a stamp bearing John Hersey's likeness, National Press Club, Washington, D.C, April 22, 2008.
4. Much of the literature about nuclear weapons uses the term *Nuclear Weapon State* to refer to the five states recognized as such in the Nuclear Nonproliferation Treaty: the United States, Russia, China, Great Britain, and France. Unless otherwise noted, I use the uncapitalized version *nuclear weapon state* in its more commonsense meaning: "to designate a country that wields a nuclear arsenal." As of today, those states also include Israel, India, Pakistan, and North Korea. So far.
5. George F. Kennan, *At a Century's Ending: Reflections, 1982–1995* (New York: Norton, 1996), 143.
6. Quoted at Lawyers' Committee on Nuclear Policy (http://www.lcnp.org/disarmament/Commentary/commentary4.htm).
7. Wells wrote about all three of these works in his *Experiment in Autobiography: Discoveries and Conclusions of a Very Ordinary Brain (Since 1866)* (New York: Macmillan, 1934), 569–84. It is perhaps not surprising that Wells played such a seminal role in envisioning the military and political consequences of the unraveling of the mysteries of the atom. Futurist and science fiction giant Robert A. Heinlein spoke about the breadth and depth of Wells's genius in 1941, when Wells was seventy-five years old and reaching the end of his writing life: "H. G. Wells, in his trilogy, *The Outline of History, The Science of Life* and *The Work, Wealth, and Happiness of Mankind,* is, so far as I know, the only writer who has ever lived who has tried to draw for the rest of us a full picture of the whole world, past and future, everything about us, so we can stand off and get a look at ourselves" ("Guest of Honor Speech at the Third World Science Fiction Convention" [Denver, 1941], reprinted in *Requiem,* ed. Yoji Kondo [New York: TOR, 1992], 218).
8. See the Radiation Effects Research Foundation (http://www.rerf.org.jp).
9. "Prescription for Action," *Physicians for Social Responsibility Newsletter* (fall 2007).

10. Most of these details are from Sarah J. Diehl and James Clay Moltz, *Nuclear Weapons and Nonproliferation: A Reference Handbook* (Santa Barbara, Calif.: ABC-CLIO, 2002), 181–82.
11. Martin Rees, *Our Final Hour, A Scientist's Warning: How Terror, Error, and Environmental Disaster Threaten Humankind's Future in This Century—On Earth and* Beyond (New York: Basic Books, 2003), 25.
12. William J. Perry, keynote address, Committee on International Security and Arms Control, National Academy of Sciences, Washington, D.C., August 11, 2004 (available at http://www7.nationalacademies.org).
13. *San Francisco Examiner,* November 19, 2000, p. C1.
14. Jonathan Schell, "The Gift of Time," *Nation,* February 2–9, 1998, p. 29. This special issue features Schell's interviews with several nuclear policy professionals and scholars.
15. Reed Johnson, "The Bomb Is Back," *Los Angeles Times,* June 18, 2002, p. E1.
16. Daniel Ellsberg, personal communication, February 5, 2009.
17. Quoted at http://www. globaldialoguecenter.com/events/mandela.
18. Robert A. Heinlein, "The Last Days of the United States," in *Expanded Universe* (New York: Ace Books, 1980), 145–47.
19. Quoted at History News Service (http://hnn.us/articles/1212.html).
20. Henry A. Kissinger, Sam Nunn, Willam J. Perry, and George P. Shultz, "A World Free of Nuclear Weapons," *Wall Street Journal,* January 4, 2007; George P. Shultz, William J. Perry, Henry A. Kissinger, and Sam Nunn, "Toward a Nuclear Free World," *Wall Street Journal,* January 15, 2008.
21. The full text of the Prague speech appears at http://www.huffingtonpost .com/2009/04/05obama-prague-speech-on-nu_n_183219.html.
22. Theodore Sturgeon, *More Than Human* (New York: Farrar, Straus, and Young, 1953).

CHAPTER 2   THE ESSENCE OF THE PROBLEM

1. Ashton B. Carter and William J. Perry, "If Necessary, Strike and Destroy: North Korea Cannot Be Allowed to Test This Missile," *Washington Post,* June 22, 2006.
2. *Los Angeles Times,* July 5, 2006; Paul Richter and Barbara Demick, "A Level Reply to N. Korea Missiles," *Los Angeles Times,* July 6, 2006; Barbara Demick, "With Few N. Korea Facts, a Rumor Got Launched," *Los Angeles Times,* July 7, 2006.
3. "Kwajelein Test Range," *Associated Press,* June 14, 2006.
4. Robert S. Norris and Hans M. Kristensen, "U.S. Nuclear Forces, 2008," *Bulletin of the Atomic Scientists* (March–April 2008): 50–51.
5. *Pretoria News,* June 30, 2006.
6. *BBC News,* July 9, 2006.
7. See, for example, Maggie Farley, "Iran's President Refuses to Forgo Atomic Activities," *Los Angeles Times,* September 18, 2005, p. A3.
8. *Los Angeles Times,* July 12, 2005.
9. *Global Security Newswire,* September 14, 2005.
10. Quoted at http://www.middlepowers.org.
11. Quoted at http://www.fcnl.org.
12. Alan Cranston, "Nukes Beget Nukes: Away With Bombs," *San Francisco Examiner,* November 16, 1999, p. A19.

13. *Nation,* February 2/9, 1998.
14. William Sloane Coffin, *Credo* (Louisville, Ky.: Westminster John Knox Press, 2004), 101.
15. Bryan Bender, "World's Nuclear Powers Decried As Hypocrites," *Boston Globe,* June 22, 2004.
16. Gorbachev was interviewed by Cal Fussman in *Esquire* (September 2008): 204.
17. In *Securing Our Survival: The Case for a Nuclear Weapons Convention,* ed. Tilman Ruff and John Loretz (Boston: IPPNW, 2007), i.
18. "Iran Hasn't Answered Questions on Nuclear Program, Arms-Control Chief Says," *Los Angeles Times,* September 23, 2008, p. A19.
19. In *Nuclear Disorder or Cooperative Security: U.S. Weapons of Terror, the Global Proliferation Crisis, and Paths to Peace,* ed. Michael Spies and John Burroughs (New York: Lawyers' Committee on Nuclear Policy, 2007), 4.
20. Hans Blix, *Why Nuclear Disarmament Matters* (Cambridge, Mass.: MIT Press, 2008), 54.
21. See the documents appendix of *Securing Our Survival* for copies of several such resolutions.
22. In William Langewiesche, *The Atomic Bazaar: The Rise of the Nuclear Poor* (New York: Farrar, Strausm and Giroux, 2007), 104.
23. The Archive of Nuclear Data (www.nrdc.org) is a well-detailed compilation of these figures.
24. Douglas Frantz, "Israel's Arsenal Is a Point of Contention," *Los Angeles Times,* October 12, 2003, p. A14.
25. In Peter Valenti, "The Nuclear Wave: Arab World Caught between Israeli Hammer, Iranian Anvil," *Washington Report on Middle East Affairs* (May–June 2007): 41.
26. Ibid.
27. Ibid., 40.
28. Maggie Farley, "UN Still Probing Iran Nuclear Case," *Los Angeles Times,* October 30, 2007.
29. The account of Gates's trip to Bahrain is from *Washington Post,* December 9, 2007.
30. All Soltanieh statements are from "Iran Rejects Tougher Atom Checks, Citing Hypocrisy," *Reuters,* May 5, 2008; and Alexander G. Higgins, "Iran Rejects Nuclear Inspections Unless Israel Allows Them," *Associated Press,* May 5, 2008.
31. Higgins, "Iran Rejects Nuclear Inspections."
32. In Langewiesche, *The Atomic Bazaar,* 178.
33. See http://www.globalsecurity.org or http://www.sipri.org for excellent and elaborate calculations of these figures.
34. In Friends Committee on National Legislation, "Still in the Shadow of Nuclear Weapons," March 2006, p. 11 (available at http://www.fcnl.org).
35. William D. Hartung, "Avoiding the Toughness Trap," *Nation,* November 19, 2007, p. 22.
36. Rebecca Johnson, interview with Ambassador Dhanapala, New York, May 13, 1995, quoted in Robert D. Green, *Fast Track to Zero Nuclear Weapons* (Cambridge, Mass.: Middle Powers Initiative, 1998), 37.
37. Robert Holloway, "Gap over Nuclear Disarmament Seems Unbridgeable, but NPT is Not at Risk," *Agence France-Presse,* May 9, 2000.

38. In Jonathan Granoff, "Power over the Ultimate Evil," *Tikkun* (November–December 2003), 49.
39. Robert S. Norris and Hans M. Kristensen, "Indian Nuclear Forces," *Bulletin of the Atomic Scientists* (November–December 2008): 38–40.
40. Douglas Roche, "An Unequivocal Landmark: Report on the 2000 NPT Review Conference," working paper no. 00-2, *Ploughshares* [Canada] (June 2000).
41. In Joseph Cirincione, *Bomb Scare: The History and Future of Nuclear Weapons* (New York: Columbia University Press, 2007), 67.
42. See http://www.counterpunch.org, posted May 17, 2003.
43. In Walter Pincus, "UN Hopes to Ban New Fissionable Material, Space-Based Weapons," *Washington Post,* June 2, 2009, p. A13.
44. Harris Interactive poll, August 2008 (available at http://blog.nuclearweapons free.org/index.cfm/2008/9/8/New-poll-indicates-Americans-get-it).
45. The full report is available at the Australian government website (http://www.dfat.gov.au/cc/cc_report_mnu.html).
46. The Canberra Commission on the Elimination of Nuclear Weapons, executive summary, August 1997, in Diehl and Moltz, *Nuclear Weapons and Nonproliferation,* 247.
47. *Los Angeles Times,* November 29, 2007.
48. See http://www.haaretz.com/hasen/spages/995511.html.
49. "World Recalls Hiroshima Anniversary," *Sydney Morning Herald,* Aug 6, 2005.
50. Joseph Cirincione writes about all three episodes in *Bomb Scare,* 56–58, relying heavily on Jonathan D. Pollack and Mitchell B. Reiss, *Without the Bomb: The Politics of Nuclear Nonproliferation* (New York: Columbia University Press, 1988).
51. Ariel Levite, "Never Say Never Again," *International Security* (winter 2002–2003): 59–88.
52. Conrad Brunk, "Realism, Deterrence, and the Arms Race," in *Nuclear War: Philosophical Perspectives,* ed. Michael Allen Fox and Leo Groarke (New York: Lang, 1985), 238.
53. Heinlein, "Guest of Honor Speech," 256.
54. In Graham T. Allison, *Nuclear Terrorism, The Ultimate Preventable Catastrophe* (New York: Times Books/Holt, 2004), 142–43.
55. In Jonathan Schell, *The Seventh Decade: The New Shape of Nuclear Danger* (New York: Holt, 2007), 100.
56. *Los Angeles Times,* March 12, 2002, p. A1.
57. Edwin Chen, "Bush Insists He Has 'No Timetable' for War on Terrorism in Iraq," *Los Angeles Times,* August 11, 2002.
58. In Granoff, "Power over the Ultimate Evil," 48.
59. "All Things Considered," *National Public Radio,* April 13, 2004.
60. "Morning Edition," *National Public Radio,* December 14, 2005.

CHAPTER 3   THE NIGHTMARE OF NUCLEAR TERROR

1. *Sydney Morning Herald,* January 21, 2006.
2. Ibid.
3. All Bin Laden quotations in this section are from "People Realize That Bush Does Not Have a Plan," *Los Angeles Times,* January 20, 2006.

4. Paul Joseph, "From MAD to NUTS: The Growing Danger of Nuclear War," *Socialist Review* 61 (1982): 13–56.

5. This is the framework adopted by Charles D. Ferguson and William C. Potter in their excellent book *The Four Faces of Nuclear Terrorism* (New York: Routledge, 2005).

6. Pervez Hoodbhoy, "A Victory without Spoils," *Bulletin of the Atomic Scientists* (July–August 2005): 54.

7. See, for example, Steve Coll, *The Bin Ladens: An Arabian Family in the American Century* (New York: Penguin, 2008); Lawrence Wright, *The Looming Tower: Al Qaeda and the Road to 9/11* (New York: Vintage, 2007); Peter Bergen, *The Osama bin Laden I Know: An Oral History of Al Qaeda's Leader* (New York: Free Press, 2006); Ferguson and Potter, *The Four Faces of Nuclear Terrorism;* and Allison, *Nuclear Terrorism.*

8. David Albright, *Al Qaeda's Nuclear Program: Through the Window of Seized Documents,* Nautilus Institute special forum no. 47, November 6, 2002 (available at http://www.nautilus.org).

9. In Graham T. Allison, "The Ongoing Failure of Imagination," *Bulletin of the Atomic Scientists* (September–October 2006): 37.

10. In Julian E. Barnes, "Al Qaeda's Primary Threat Is Nuclear, Book Says," *Los Angeles Times,* April 28, 2007.

11. Middle East Media Research Institute, report, June 12, 2002, in Allison, *Nuclear Terrorism,* 12, 14.

12. Noah Feldman, "Islam, Terror, and the Second Nuclear Age," *New York Times Magazine,* October 29, 2006, p. 57.

13. Ibid., 56.

14. Brian Michael Jenkins, personal communication, RAND Corporation, 1995.

15. "The Terrorism Index," *Foreign Policy* (July–August 2006).

16. "The Terrorism Index 2008," *Foreign Policy* (September–October 2008): 80.

17. The entire text of the Russell-Einstein Manifesto appears at http://www.nuclearfiles.org.

18. Sebastian Rotella, "Obama to Face a Third War—Against Stateless Extremists," *Los Angeles Times,* November 9, 2008, p. A13.

19. See the first report of Al-Zawahiri's statement at http://www.thesun.co.uk/sol/homepage/news/article1948196.ece.

20. Lawrence Wright, "The Rebellion Within," *New Yorker,* June 2, 2008 (available at http://www.newyorker.com).

21. Peter Bergen and Paul Cruickshank, "The Unraveling," *New Republic,* June 11, 2008 (available at http://www.tnr.com).

22. Noah Feldman, "The End of the War on Terror," *Esquire* (October 2008): 263–65, 312.

23. This analysis probably applies less to Hezbollah, one of today's major terrorist actors, which is centered primarily in Lebanon, wields significant power within that state, and to some extent acts as the agent of Syria and Iran.

24. Kim Murphy, "UN Nuclear Watchdog Warns of Extremist Threat," *Los Angeles Times,* February 10, 2008.

25. *Nation,* April 1, 2002; *Bulletin of Atomic Scientists* (December 1947), in P.M.S. Blackett, *Fear, War, and the Bomb* (New York: McGraw-Hill, 1949), 89.

26. Anecdote told by Kai Bird and Martin J. Sherwin, "Bin Laden's Nuclear Connection," *Nation,* April 25, 2005, p. 22, adapted from their biography of Oppenheimer, *American Prometheus* (New York: Knopf, 2005).

27. Richard L. Garwin, "The Technology of Megaterror," *Technology Review,* September 1, 2002.
28. In Blackett, *Fear, War, and the Bomb,* 141.
29. Eugene J. Carroll, Jr., "We Are Taking a Detour from Deterrence," *Los Angeles Times,* July 14, 2000.
30. *Securing Our Survival,* 118.
31. Ibid.
32. Murphy, "UN Nuclear Watchdog Warns of Extremist Threat."
33. Peter D. Zimmerman and Jeffrey G. Lewis, "The Bomb in the Backyard," *Foreign Policy* (November–December 2006).
34. Langewiesche, *The Atomic Bazaar,* 2007.
35. William Langewiesche, "How to Get a Nuclear Bomb," *Atlantic Monthly* (December 2006): 98.
36. See, for example, the Provisional IRA statement to British prime minister Thatcher after the 1984 Brighton bombing: http://www.news.bbs.co.uk/2/hi/uk_news/1201738.stm.
37. Mark Straus, "Five Years Later," *Bulletin of the Atomic Scientists* (September–October 2006).
38. John Mueller, *Overblown: How Politicians and the Terrorism Industry Inflate National Security Threats, and Why We Believe Them* (New York: Free Press, 2006).
39. Brian Michael Jenkins, *Will Terrorists Go Nuclear?* (New York: Prometheus, 2008).
40. Luis W. Alvarez, *Adventures of a Physicist* (New York: Basic Books, 1988), 125.
41. Other than the Alvarez quotation, all the information on this scenario is from Nick Schwellenbach and Peter D. H. Stockton, "Nuclear Lockdown," *Bulletin of the Atomic Scientists* (November–December 2006).
42. Ibid.
43. Physicians for Social Responsibility, Los Angeles (www.psrla.org).
44. *Los Angeles Times,* August 16, 2006.
45. O. B. Toon et al., "Atmospheric Effects and Societal Consequences of Regional Scale Nuclear Conflicts and Acts of Individual Nuclear Terrorism," *Atmospheric Chemistry and Physics Discussions* (November 2006).
46. In David Shorr, "UN Reform in Context," policy analysis brief (Muscatine, Iowa: Stanley Foundation, February 2006), 4.
47. In James Fallows, "Declaring Victory," *Atlantic Monthly* (September 2006): 70.
48. *Newsweek,* July 7–14, 2008.
49. Marvin R. Shanken, "General Tommy Franks: An Exclusive Interview," *Cigar Aficionado,* December 2003.
50. Hoodbhoy, "A Victory without Spoils," 54.
51. B. H. Liddell Hart, *The Revolution in Warfare* (1947), in Blackett, *Fear, War, and the Bomb,* 6–7.
52. Michael Finnegan and Mark Barabak, "Lively Exchanges Fill Second GOP Debate," *Los Angeles Times,* May 16, 2007.
53. See http://www.whitehouse.gov, posted January 20, 2009.
54. Michael Levi, *On Nuclear Terrorism* (Cambridge, Mass.: Harvard University Press, November 2007).

55. Ibid., 5.
56. David E. Sanger and William J. Broad, "US Secretly Aids Pakistan in Guarding Nuclear Arms," *New York Times,* November 18, 2007.
57. Cirincione, *Bomb Scare,* 92.
58. *Los Angeles Times,* September 27, 2007, p. A10.
59. Robert Gard, personal communication, February 28, 2009.
60. See http://www.cnn.com, posted October 1, 1997.
61. See http://www.armscontrol.org.
62. See http://www.whitehouse.gov, posted January 20, 2009; also Levi, *On Nuclear Terrorism;* Ferguson and Potter, *The Four Faces of Nuclear Terrorism;* and George Perkovich, Jessica T. Mathews, Joseph Cirincione, Rose Gottemoeller, and Jon Wolfsthal, *Universal Compliance: A Strategy for Nuclear Security* (Washington, D.C.: Carnegie Endowment, 2005).
63. Ralph Vartabedian, "US to Install New Nuclear Detectors at Ports," *Los Angeles Times,* July 15, 2006.
64. "Preventing the Importation of Illicit Nuclear Materials in Shipping Containers," *Risk Analysis* (October 2006).
65. *Florida Today,* February 26, 2009.
66. *Week,* February 3, 2006.
67. Kai Bird and Martin J. Sherwin, "The Myths of Hiroshima," *Los Angeles Times,* August 5, 2005.
68. "The 9/11 Commission Report," *Playboy* (June 2005): 162.
69. Thom Shanker, "170,000 Troops Likely to Stay in Iraq," *New York Times,* December 10, 2006.
70. See http://www.dictionary-quotes.com/i-destory-my-enemy-when-i-make-him-my-friend-abraham-lincoln.
71. Max Frankel, "Shell Game," *Los Angeles Times Book Review,* March 12, 2006.

CHAPTER 4   ACCIDENTAL ATOMIC APOCALYPSE

1. Lloyd J. Dumas, *Lethal Arrogance: Human Fallibility and Dangerous Technologies* (New York: St. Martin's, 1999).
2. Lloyd J. Dumas, "The Nuclear Graveyard Below," *Los Angeles Times,* September 3, 2000, p. M2.
3. In Schell, "The Gift of Time," 50–51.
4. Shultz et al., "Toward a Nuclear-Free World."
5. The Petrov incident has been reported by the BBC, the television programs *Nova* and *NBC Dateline,* and London's *Daily Mail.* The information and quotations here are from Douglas Mattern's excellent "Ending the Fool's Game; Saving Civilization," *Humanist* (March–April 2004): 16–19.
6. See, for example, Lachlan Forrow, Bruce G. Blair, Ira Helfand, George Lewis, Theodore Postel, Victor Sidel, Barry Levy, Herbert Abrams, and Christine Cassel, "Accidental Nuclear War—A Post-Cold War Assessment," *New England Journal of Medicine,* April 30, 1998, pp. 1326–32; Bruce G. Blair, Harold Feiveson, and Frank von Hippel, "Taking Nuclear Weapons off Hair-Trigger Alert," *Scientific American* (November 1997); Dumas, *Lethal Arrogance;* and Lloyd J. Dumas, "Selected Accidents Involving Nuclear Weapons, 1950–1993," March 1996 (available at http://www.greenpeace.org).

7. See http://www.globalsecurityinstitute.org.
8. See www.globalsecuritynewswire.org, posted February 17, 2009.
9. Norris and Kristensen, "U.S. Nuclear Forces, 2008," 51.
10. Peter Spiegel, "Chain of Errors Blamed for Nuclear Arms Going Undetected," *Los Angeles Times,* October 20, 2007.
11. Ibid.
12. Robert Windrem, "U.S. Warhead Error Adds to Troubled History," *Deep Background: The MSNBC Investigative Blog* (www.msnbc.com), posted March 25, 2008.
13. Except for the material in note 12, all information in this paragraph is from Julian E. Barnes, "U.S. Says Missile Parts Mistakenly Sent to Taiwan," *Los Angeles Times,* March 26, 2008.
14. "Defense Secretary Robert Gates Fires Air Force's Top 2 Officials," *Los Angeles Times,* June 6, 2008.
15. Lisa Burgess, "Are Air Force Firings about More Than Nuclear Weapons?" *Stars and Stripes,* June 8, 2008.
16. Spiegel, "Chain of Errors Blamed."
17. Ibid.
18. Rajon Menon, "Shakier Fingers on the Nuclear Buttons," *Los Angeles Times,* June 15, 2003.
19. Gary Chapman, "Do Computers Pose a Nuclear Threat?" *Los Angeles Times,* May 4, 1998, p. D3.
20. See http://www.cdi.org/blair/hair-trigger-dangers.cfm.
21. "Cyber Attacks Are Costly for Pentagon," *Associated Press,* April 8, 2009.
22. Diehl and Moltz, *Nuclear Weapons and Nonproliferation,* 32.
23. Ibid., 33; *Los Angeles Times,* September 3, 2000, p. M2.
24. *Los Angeles Times,* November 9, 2008, p. A14, and November 10, 2008, p. A3; http://www.russiatoday.com/Top_News/2008–11–13/Nuclear_sub _doubts_remain_despite_sailors_confession.html.
25. http://www.globalsecuritynewswire.org, posted February 17, 2009.
26. Raissa Kosolowsky, "US Nuclear Submarine Collides in Strait near Iran," *Reuters,* March 20, 2009.
27. In Ron Rosenbaum, "The Return of the Doomsday Machine?" posted August 31, 2007 (http://www.slate.com).
28. *Los Angeles Times,* October 4, 2002, p. A37; Francie Grace, "A Different Kind of Asteroid Risk: Asteroid Explosions Could Be Mistaken for a Nuclear Attack," posted October 4, 2002 (http://www.cbsnews.com/stories/ 2002/10/04/tech/main524332.shtml).
29. Bennett Ramberg, "Outside View: World Free of Nukes," *United Press International,* January 24, 2008.
30. See www.whitehouse.gov, posted January 20, 2009.
31. Daniel Lang, *An Inquiry into Enoughness: Of Bombs and Men and Staying Alive* (New York: McGraw-Hill, 1965), 191.
32. John F. Kennedy, letter to Albert Schweitzer, June 6, 1962, in Albert Schweitzer, *On Nuclear War and Peace,* ed. Homer A. Jack (Elgin, Ill.: Brethren, 1988), 152.
33. Schweitzer, *On Nuclear War and Peace,* 69.
34. Ibid., 81–82.
35. Eugene Burdick and Harvey Wheeler, *Fail-Safe* (New York: Dell, 1962), 7–8.

36. John Steinbruner, "Consensual Security," *Bulletin of the Atomic Scientists* (March–April 2008): 24.

CHAPTER 5 NUCLEAR CRISIS MISMANAGEMENT

1. The incident was reported in Laura King and Henry Chu, "Hoax Call during Mumbai Siege Threatened War on Pakistan," *Los Angeles Times,* December 7, 2008, p. A10.
2. In Bruce G. Blair, "Primed and Ready," *Bulletin of the Atomic Scientists* (January–February 2007): 35.
3. Bertrand Russell, *Common Sense and Nuclear Warfare* (1959; reprint, London: Routledge, 2001), ix.
4. David Hochman, "Playboy Interview: George Carlin," *Playboy* (October 2005): 144.
5. Quoted at http://www.worldbeyondborders.org.
6. Nicholas Wade, *Before the Dawn: Recovering the Lost History of Our Ancestors* (New York: Penguin, 2006).
7. Two recent books about the Cuban missile crisis are among the best available. Theodore Sorensen, probably JFK's closest advisor and confidant during the last eleven years of the president's life, has finally released his long-awaited memoir *Counselor: A Life at the Edge of History* (New York: HarperCollins, 2008). He offers new details about the crisis (for example, apparently Sorensen himself wrote the decisive letter to Premier Khrushchev) and underscores how close the human race came to committing collective suicide. Simultaneously, *Washington Post* reporter Michael Dobbs has published *One Minute to Midnight: Kennedy, Khrushchev, and Castro on the Brink of Nuclear War* (New York: Knopf, 2008), an hour-by-hour account of how officials on both sides desperately tried to defuse the nuclear time bomb. Dobbs's account, which reads like a thriller, emphasizes how easily things could have turned out otherwise.
8. In Nuclear Age Peace Foundation, "Cuban Missile Crisis Closer to Nuclear War Than Previously Believed," *Sunflower,* November 2002 (available at http://www.nuclearfiles.org/menu/key-issues/nuclear-weapons/history/cold-war/cuban-missile-crisis/article-sunflower.htm).
9. In Robert S. McNamara and James G. Blight, "Reducing the Risk of Conflict, Killing, and Catastrophe in the 21st Century," *Commonwealth,* November 15, 2001, p. 7.
10. John Somerville, "Nuclear War Is Omnicide," in *Nuclear War: Philosophical Perspectives,* 6–7.
11. Both this quotation and the information that follows are from John Lewis Gaddis, *The Cold War: A New History* (New York: Penguin, 2005), 227–28.
12. Windrem, "U.S. Warhead Error Adds to Troubled History."
13. Barnes, "U.S. Says Missile Parts Mistakenly Sent to Taiwan."
14. *The Onion Presents Our Dumb Century,* ed. Scott Dikkers (New York: Three Rivers, 1999), 98.
15. Jane Shevtsov, email to the author, spring 2007.
16. In Schell, "The Gift of Time," 25–26.
17. In *Securing Our Survival,* 17.
18. Jarosław Anders, "Amid Turmoil, Optimism for an Era of Peace," *Los Angeles Times,* June 1, 2003, p. R7.

CHAPTER 6   INTENTIONAL USE

1. James Wirtz, *Nuclear Transformation: The New U.S. Nuclear Doctrine* (New York: Palgrave Macmillan, 2005); Amy Woolf, *U.S. Nuclear Weapons: Changes in Policy and Force Structure* (Hauppauge, N.Y.: Novinka, 2005); Steven Weinberg, *Glory and Terror: The Growing Nuclear Danger* (New York: New York Review of Books, 2004).
2. Schell, *The Seventh Decade.*
3. Jeffrey Sachs, *The End of Poverty* (New York: Penguin, 2005).
4. Ghida Fakhry, James Bone, and Richard Roth, "World Leaders Examine Nuclear Non-Proliferation at the UN," *CNN International: Diplomatic License,* April 29, 2000.
5. "US Plans to Resume Making Plutonium Triggers for Nuclear Bombs," *Associated Press,* June 1, 2002; *Nation,* June 24, 2002.
6. Schell, *The Seventh Decade,* 123.
7. See, for example, U.S. Joint Chiefs of Staff, "Doctrine for Joint Theater Nuclear Operations," no. 30-12.1, Washington, D.C., February 9, 1996. For more about the nuclear policy of this period, see Janne E. Nolan, *An Elusive Consensus: Nuclear Weapons and American Security after the Cold War* (Washington, D.C.: Brookings Institution, 1999).
8. Most of the NPR text appears at http://www.globalsecurity.org/wmd/library/policy/dod/npr.htm.
9. Mike Allen and Barton Gellman, "Preemptive Strikes Part of Strategy, Officials Say," *Washington Post,* December 11, 2002, p. A1.
10. Matthew Rothschild, "The Human Costs of Bombing Iran," *Progressive,* April 12, 2006.
11. In Ralph Dannheisser, *Washington File,* March 12, 2002 (available at http://usembassy-israel.org.il/publish/peace/archives/2002/march/031306.html).
12. Transcript of press conference available at http://www.whitehouse.gov/news/releases/2006/04/20060418-1.html.
13. Rothschild, "The Human Costs of Bombing Iran."
14. Ibid.
15. Transcript of press conference available at http://www.state.gov/secretary/rm/2006/67103.htm.
16. Norris and Kristensen, "U.S. Nuclear Forces, 2008," 50; Seymour Hersh, "Annals of National Security: Last Stand," *New Yorker,* July 10, 2006; "Revealed: Israel Plans Strike on Iran," *Sunday Times of London,* January 7, 2009.
17. See http://www.cnn.com, posted June 5, 2007.
18. The full report is available at http://www.psr.org.
19. Quoted at http://www.un.org/Pubs/chronicle/2003/issue3/0303p31.asp.
20. Arthur Schlesinger, Jr., "Good Foreign Policy a Casualty of War," *Los Angeles Times,* March 23, 2003.
21. In Alexander Cockburn, "Will the US Really Bomb Iran?" *Nation,* September 24, 2007, p. 9.
22. Richard Falk, "The New Bush Doctrine," *Nation,* July 15, 2002, p. 11.
23. In William Safire, "Gore Versus Blair," *New York Times,* September 26, 2002.
24. Brian Urquhart, "The Outlaw World," *New York Review of Books,* May 11, 2006, pp. 25, 28.

25. Friends Committee on National Legislation, "Still in the Shadow of Nuclear Weapons," 12.
26. "U.S. Nuclear Forces, 2007," *Bulletin of the Atomic Scientists* (January–February 2007): 81.
27. Jonathan Schell, "A Revolution in American Nuclear Policy," *Nation,* June 13, 2005, p. 12.
28. In Schell, *The Seventh Decade,* 125–26.
29. Jennifer Nordstrom and Felicity Hill, "A Gender Perspective," in *Nuclear Disorder or Cooperative Security,* 167.
30. Kennan, *At a Century's Ending,* 116.
31. J. Peter Scoblic, "Disarmament Redux," *Bulletin of the Atomic Scientists* (March–April 2008): 37.
32. Colin S. Gray and Keith Payne, "Victory Is Possible," *Foreign Policy* (summer 1980): 14–27.
33. In Schell, *The Seventh Decade,* 186.

CHAPTER 7   THE GRAND BARGAIN

1. Robert Holloway, "Fifty-Fifty Chance of Success Seen for NPT Conference," *Agence France-Presse,* May 14, 2000.
2. See http://www.usnewswire.org, www.armscontrol.org.
3. See http://www.middlepowers.org.
4. Robert Holloway, "Reassurances on Disarmament by Nuclear-Weapons States Backfire," *Agence France-Presse,* May 3, 2000.
5. For a complete text of both the NPT and the official review documents at the 1995 and 2000 review conferences, see the U.N. Department of Disarmament Affairs website (http://disarmament2.un.org). The politics behind those conference agreements are well discussed in John Burroughs, "The Nuclear Non-Proliferation Treaty," in *Nuclear Disorder or Cooperative Security,* 29–32.
6. International Court of Justice, "Legality of the Threat or Use of Nuclear Weapons," advisory opinion, July 8 1996 (available at http://www.icj-cij.org/docket/files/95/7495.pdf).
7. In *Securing Our Survival,* 179.
8. In Burroughs, "The Nuclear Non-Proliferation Treaty," 31–32.
9. Robert S. McNamara and Thomas Graham, Jr., "New Bush Policy Will Cause Spread of Nuclear Weapons Globally," *New Perspectives Quarterly* (spring 2002).
10. British American Security Council/Oxford Research Group, "Turning Security Assurances into a Legally Binding Instrument," briefing no. 3, 2005 (London, n.d.).
11. See the excellent discussion in Michael Spies, "Iran and the Nuclear Fuel Cycle," in *Nuclear Disorder or Cooperative Security,* 138–42.

CHAPTER 8   NUCLEAR WEAPONS ARE MILITARILY UNNECESSARY

1. Ivo Daalder and Jan Lodal, "The Logic of Zero: Toward a World without Nuclear Weapons," *Foreign Affairs* (November–December 2008): 80–95.
2. Ibid., 81.
3. Ibid., 80, 84–85.

4. See http://www.huffingtonpost.com/2009/04/05/obama-prague-speech
   -on-_n_183219.html.
5. See http://www.globalsecurity.org/military/world/spending.htm.
6. Paul Nitze, "A Threat Mostly to Ourselves," *New York Times,* October 28,
   1999.
7. In Andrew Lichterman, "Delivery Systems," in *Nuclear Disorder or Cooperative
   Security,* 111.
8. "U.S. Nuclear Forces, 2007," 81.
9. In Lichterman, "Delivery Systems," 112.
10. Wade Boese, "Panel Endorses U.S. Global Strike Initiative," *Arms Control
    Today* (June 2007): 34–35.
11. Ibid.
12. Lichterman, "Delivery Systems," 110.
13. Michael Klare, "Endless Military Superiority," *Nation,* July 15, 2002, p. 15.
14. Julian E. Barnes, "Taking Spying to New Heights," *Los Angeles Times,* March
    13, 2009, p. A18.
15. Nitze, "A Threat Mostly to Ourselves."
16. I have a treasured tiny photograph of the entire ten-man crew standing out-
    side the *Jus' One Mo' Time.* On the back they are identified as "Airplane
    Commd: Frank J. Kawalec, 1st Lt.; Pilot: William C. Sliger, 1st Lt.; Bomb:
    William A. (Yogi) Tilford, F/O; Navigator: Carl G. Strickland, 1st Lt.; Radar
    Obs: Claude Daley, Jr., 2nd Lt.; Radio Oper: Robert D. Clark, Cpl.; Right
    Scanner: Robert R. Gosselin, Sgt.; Engineer: John C. Bilsky [or possibly
    Belsky], T/Sgt.; Left Scanner: Carrol V. Shelly, Sgt.; Tail Gunner: Floyd A.
    Pelky, Sgt." I have never met any of these gentlemen, nor do I remember my
    father being in touch with them during my childhood. Needless to say, I
    would dearly like to meet any of them if any of them are still alive.
17. In Blackett, *Fear, War, and the Bomb,* 134.
18. Cirincione, *Bomb Scare,* 69.
19. Colin L. Powell, *My American Journey* (New York: Random House, 1995),
    540.
20. In Schell, "The Gift of Time," 43.
21. Thomas C. Reed and Michael O. Wheeler, "The Role of Nuclear Weapons
    in the New World Order," statement before the Senate Armed Services
    Committee, January 23, 1993, p. 7.
22. *Los Angeles Times,* April 10, 1973, pp. 1, 4; Daniel Ellsberg, eulogy for
    Anthony Russo, Crescent Heights United Methodist Church, Los Angeles,
    November 15, 2008.
23. Gerard Prunier, *Africa's World War* (New York: Oxford University Press,
    2008).
24. Robert M. Gates, "A Balanced Strategy," *Foreign Affairs* (January–February
    2009).
25. Interview with Mahmoud Ahmadinejad, *60 Minutes,* September 23, 2007.
26. In Lang, *An Inquiry into Enoughness,* 167.
27. In Arjun Makhijani, "Nuclear Targeting: The First 60 Years," *Bulletin of the
    Atomic Scientists* (May–June 2003): 65.
28. Arthur M. Schlesinger, Jr., *A Thousand Days: John F. Kennedy in the White
    House* (1965; reprint, Boston: Houghton Mifflin, 2002), 349–58.
29. In Steven C. Patten, "Commentary: Does Nuclear Deterrence Theory Rest
    on a Mistake?" in *Nuclear War: Philosophical Perspectives,* 219.

30. Jeffrey Lewis, "Minimum Deterrence," *Bulletin of the Atomic Scientists* (July–August 2008): 38–41.
31. Jeffrey Lewis, *The Minimum Means of Reprisal* (Cambridge, Mass.: MIT Press, 2007).
32. In Lewis, "Minimum Deterrence,"38.
33. Bernard Brodie, *Strategy in the Missile Age* (1965; reprint, Princeton, N.J.: Princeton University Press, 1971), 274.
34. Schell, "The Gift of Time," 40.
35. Patten, "Commentary: Does Nuclear Deterrence Theory Rest on a Mistake?" 221.
36. Glenn Kessler, "Hussein Pointed to Iranian Threat," *Washington Post,* July 2, 2009, p. A1.
37. In *Securing Our Survival,* 37.
38. In Schell, *The Seventh Decade,* 141.
39. Borzou Daragahi, "Obama's Gambit Could Work, Iran Observer Says," *Los Angeles Times,* April 7, 2009.
40. Robert Levine, "Reality Fights: The Future of War," *Playboy* (June 2007): 53.
41. The likely security calculations of nuclear weapon states (other than the United States) as they contemplate nuclear disarmament are well examined in George Perkovich and James Acton, "Abolishing Nuclear Weapons," Adelphi paper (London: International Institute for Strategic Studies, September 2008).
42. Charles J. Hanley, "Gorbachev: US Military Power Blocks 'No Nukes,'" *Associated Press,* April 17, 2009.
43. Corky Siemaszko, "Russia's Medvedev Halts Military Action, Rips into Georgian President," *New York Daily News,* August 13, 2008.
44. In Guy T. Saperstein, "Democrats Need an Iran Strategy ASAP," *Tikkun* (March–April 2008): 39.
45. Conn Hallinan, "An Uncomfortable Conversation About Nukes," July 17, 2008 (available at http://www.commondreams.org).

CHAPTER 9   THE ARCHITECTURE OF A NUCLEAR
WEAPON–FREE WORLD

1. Barbara Demick, "N. Korea Makes Plutonium Claim," *Los Angeles Times,* January 18, 2009, p. A3.
2. In *Securing Our Survival,* 175.
3. Robert Wright, "America's Sovereignty in a New World," *New York Times,* September 24, 2001.
4. In Blackett, *Fear, War, and the Bomb,* 144–45.
5. Ibid., 117.
6. Ibid., 221–25.
7. *Securing Our Survival.*
8. See http://www.irena.org; also, the excellent analysis in Alice Slater, "Sustainable Energy: Shifting the Paradigm," International Network of Engineers and Scientists (available at http://www.inesglobal.com/_News/Alice.pdf).
9. In Cirincione, *Bomb Scare,* 146.
10. Schell, *The Seventh Decade,* 140.
11. Ibid.
12. See http://www.whitehouse.gov, posted January 20, 2009.

13. "The Bulletin Interview: Thomas R. Pickering," *Bulletin of the Atomic Scientists* (November–December 2008): 11.

14. *Securing Our Survival.*

15. In Michael Spies, "Climate Change and Nuclear Power," in *Nuclear Disorder or Cooperative Security,* 132.

16. Spies, "Iran and the Nuclear Fuel Cycle," 138.

17. Kennan, *At a Century's Ending,* 9.

18. *Securing Our Survival,* 130.

19. In Spies, "Climate Change and Nuclear Power," 133.

20. In *Securing Our Survival,* 132.

21. Ibid.

22. In Langewiesche, *The Atomic Bazaar,* 144.

23. This history is discussed in depth in the excellent policy analysis brief by David Cortright, "Overcoming Nuclear Dangers" (Muscatine, Iowa: Stanley Foundation, November 2007); and in Diehl and Moltz, *Nuclear Weapons and Nonproliferation,* 18–19.

24. In George A. Lopez and David Cortright, "Containing Iraq: Sanctions Worked," *Foreign Affairs* (July–August, 2004).

25. In Gaddis, *The Cold War,* 232.

26. See http://www.vertic.org.

27. In Schell, "The Gift of Time," 28–29.

28. Paul Richter, "U.S. Drops North Korea from Terrorism List after New Deal," *Los Angeles Times,* October 12, 2008, p. A3.

29. *Securing Our Survival,* 162.

30. Ibid., 63–64.

31. My discussion about the Security Council's contemporary enforcement difficulties derives from John Burroughs, "The Role of the UN Security Council," in *Nuclear Disorder or Cooperative Security,* 35–43, but application of his analysis to a hypothetical NWEC is my own.

32. Ibid., 37.

33. Ibid.

34. Ibid.

35. John H. Fenton, "Dulles Suggests That U.N. Overhaul 'Obsolete' Charter," *New York Times,* August 27, 1953, p. 1.

36. Russell, *Common Sense and Nuclear Warfare,* 55–56.

37. Mark Gallagher, personal communication, September 2003.

38. Thomas Hobbes, *Leviathan, The Matter, Forme and Power of a Common Wealth Ecclesiasticall and Civil* (1651; reprint, New York: Penguin, 1982).

39. H. G. Wells, *The Outline of History* (Garden City, N.Y.: Garden City Books, 1920), 2:938.

CHAPTER 10   BREAKOUT

1. Schell, "The Gift of Time," 29.

2. See, for example, Alan Cranston, "Nuclear Abolition Statement by International Civilian Leaders: An Assessment and an Appeal," *Disarmament Diplomacy* (February 1998).

3. Sir Arthur Conan Doyle, "The Adventure of the Beryl Coronet" (1892), in *The Penguin Complete Sherlock Holmes* (London: Penguin, 1981), 315.

4. Peter Beinart wrote well about these commentators in "World War What," *Los Angeles Times*, December 9, 2007, pp. M1, M5.
5. David Morgan, "Clinton Says U.S. Could 'Totally Obliterate' Iran," *Reuters*, April 22, 2008.
6. Alissa J. Rubin, "Iranian Leader Reaffirms Offer of Talks," *Los Angeles Times*, March 22, 2006, p. A3.
7. Mark Gaffney, *Dimona, The Third Temple: The Story Behind the Vanunu Revelation* (Brattleboro, Vt.: Amana, 1989), 131.
8. In Schell, "A Gift of Time," 56.
9. Jerry Pournelle, personal communication, August 2007.

CHAPTER 11   HOW IT MIGHT HAPPEN

1. In *Organizing for Social Change: A Mandate for Activity in the 1990s,* ed. K. Bobo, J. Kendall, and S. Max (Washington, D.C.: Seven Locks, 1991).
2. Michael Allen Fox, "The Nuclear Mindset," in *Nuclear War: Philosophical Perspectives,* 113.
3. Geoffrey Blainey, *A Short History of the World* (Chicago: Dee, 2002).
4. In Eric Vollmer, *Forgotten Horizons,* an unpublished 2008 play based on the works of George Bernard Shaw, Albert Einstein, and Sigmund Freud.
5. In Fox, "The Nuclear Mindset," 123.
6. Kennan, *At a Century's Ending,* 75.
7. The entire text of Yeats's masterpiece poem "The Second Coming" is available at http://www.potw.org/archive/potw351.html.
8. I owe much in this list to the thoughtful January 2005 monograph by Alyn Ware, Kate Dewes, and Michael Powles, "Snaring the Sun," New Zealand Public Advisory Committee on Disarmament and Arms Control (available at http://www.disarmsecure.org).
9. See http://www.planetafilia.org, http://www.dwfed.org, http://www.wfm .org, http://www.globalsolutions.org, http://www.transformUN.org, and http://www.worldbeyondborders.org for more information about this and other U.N. restructuring ideas and initiatives.
10. Letter to Samuel Kercheval, July 12, 1816, inscribed on the walls of the Jefferson Memorial, Washington, D.C. (available at http://www.nps.gov/ thje).
11. Winston Churchill, *A History of the English Speaking Peoples* (New York: Dodd, Mead).
12. No scholar has done more to chronicle the history of antinuclear activism since the dawn of the nuclear age than Lawrence Wittner in his masterful *The Struggle against the Bomb,* 3 vols. (Stanford, Calif.: Stanford University Press, 1993, 1997, 2003). A one-volume compilation was recently released: *Confronting the Bomb* (Stanford, Calif.: Stanford University Press, 2009).
13. In *Securing Our Survival,* 123.
14. Scoblic, "Disarmament Redux," 35.
15. The information about the Aldermaston March is from Lang, *An Inquiry into Enoughness,* 17–25.
16. Ibid., 63.
17. Schweitzer, *On Nuclear War and Peace,* 121–22, 135.
18. In *Securing Our Survival,* 124.

19. Ibid., 122–23.
20. In Schlesinger, *A Thousand Days,* 901, 112.
21. Diehl and Moltz, *Nuclear Weapons and Nonproliferation,*187–89.
22. Dennis Hevesi, "Randall Forsberg, 64, Nuclear Freeze Advocate, Dies," *New York Times,* October 26, 2007.
23. In Schell, *The Seventh Decade,* 191.
24. Ibid., 186.
25. The politics and lost opportunity of Reykjavik are exquisitely dissected by Richard Rhodes, *Arsenals of Folly: The Making of the Nuclear Arms Race* (New York: Knopf, 2007).
26. Quoted at http://www.worldbeyondborders.org.
27. Friends Committee on National Legislation, "Still in the Shadow of Nuclear Weapons," 12.
28. See ibid. for more about citizen advocacy efforts to stop the RNEP.
29. Julian E. Barnes, "Better Oversight of Nuclear Arms Urged," *Los Angeles Times,* November 26, 2008, p. A8.
30. Pew Research Center for the People and the Press, report, September 4, 2003.
31. Quoted at http://www.wagingpeace.org.
32. Quoted at http://www.worldbeyondborders.org.
33. *Securing Our Survival,* 27.
34. The entire text of Kennedy's speech is available at http://www.nasm.si.edu/exhibitions/attm/md.3.html.
35. Nathan Pyles, "Building Political Will: Branding the Nuclear-Free-World Movement," *Nonproliferation Review* (November 2008).
36. Zahn's story is exquisitely told by Michael W. Hovey, "Gordon Zahn, 1918–2007," *Catholic Worker* (January–February 2008).
37. Gordon Zahn, "Memories of Camp Warner," *Catholic Worker* (October–November 1977).
38. Quoted at http://www.worldbeyondborders.org.

CHAPTER 12   APOCALYPSE NEVER

1. In Schell, *The Seventh Decade,* 197.
2. Arundhati Roy, "The End of Imagination," *Guardian,* August 1, 1998, p. 37.
3. Jonathan Schell, *The Unfinished Twentieth Century* (New York: Verso, 2001).
4. The entire text of the Einstein-Russell Manifesto appears at http://www.pugwash.org.
5. Howard Benedict, "The Eagle Landed Ten Years Ago Friday," *Associated Press,* July 15, 1979.
6. In Martin Redfern, "Science: A New View of Home," *Independent,* April 21, 1996.
7. Quoted at http://www.spacequotations.com/earth.html.
8. Carl Sagan, *Contact* (New York: Simon and Schuster, 1997), 279.
9. John Kenneth Galbraith, "The New Internationalism: The Fact and the Response," *United Nations Chronicle* 3 (1997).
10. Robert C. Tucker, *Politics As Leadership,* rev. ed. (Columbia: University of Missouri Press, 1995).
11. This central statement from the tenets of the Bahai faith can be found at http://www.bahai.org.

12. Spider Robinson, speech at the Robert A. Heinlein centennial celebration, Kansas City, Missouri, July 7, 2007.
13. Schlesinger, *A Thousand Days,* 819.
14. In William C. Gay, "Nuclear War: Public and Governmental Misconceptions," in *Nuclear War: Philosophical Perspectives,* 15.
15. The full text of H. G. Wells's "Discovery of the Future" lecture appears at http://www.archive.org/stream/discoveryoffutur00well/discoveryoffutur00well_djvu.txt.
16. In *Theodore Roosevelt Association Journal* 27, no. 2 (2006): 30.
17. Rees, *Our Final Hour,* 8.
18. See, for example, Jonathan Schell, "Genesis in Reverse," *Bulletin of the Atomic Scientists* (January–February 2007): 27–29.
19. Somerville, "Nuclear War Is Omnicide," 4–5.
20. Rees, *Our Final Hour,* 170.
21. In Steve Connor, "The Big Question: Do We Need to Send People into Space, or Could Robots Do It Better?" *Independent,* May 8, 2007.
22. Robert A. Heinlein, "Guest of Honor Speech," 257–58.
23. Robert A. Heinlein, "The Pragmatics of Patriotism," in *Expanded Universe,* 462–65.
24. Quoted at http://www.worldbeyondborders.org.
25. Rees, *Our Final Hour,* 157, 168.
26. Ibid., 181, 7–8, 188.

Glossary of Acronyms

AEC U.N. Atomic Energy Commission, an international body created in 1946, the first act of the new United Nations, as a way to tackle the problems of the nuclear age. Confusingly, Congress created a U.S. government body called the Atomic Energy Commission that same year. (It became the Nuclear Regulatory Commission in 1975.)

BWC Biological Weapons Convention, which outlaws the development, production, possession, and use of biological weapons.

CD U.N. Conference on Disarmament, created as a forum for multilateral arms control negotiations.

CND Campaign for Nuclear Disarmament, a British advocacy organization.

CTBT Comprehensive Test Ban Treaty, which would outlaw all nuclear test explosions but which has not yet come into force.

CWC Chemical Weapons Convention, which outlaws the development, production, possession, and use of chemical weapons.

DPRK Democratic People's Republic of Korea (North Korea).

HEU Highly enriched uranium—that is, uranium in which the proportion of the isotope U-235 has, through enrichment, reached a high-enough level (roughly 20 percent or more) for use in atomic bombs.

IAEA International Atomic Energy Agency, the body charged with encouraging the peaceful use of nuclear energy and discouraging its military use.

IALANA International Association of Lawyers against Nuclear Arms, a nuclear disarmament advocacy organization.

ICBM Intercontinental ballistic missile. These missiles, based on land (most in the American Great Plains or Russian central Asian steppes), can deliver nuclear warheads to virtually any point in the world.

ICC International Criminal Court, created in 1998 to adjudicate charges against individuals of genocide, war crimes, and crimes against humanity when national courts are unwilling or unable to do so.

ICJ International Court of Justice, known informally as the World Court, which adjudicates disputes between states.

IJU Islamic Jihad Union, a splinter branch of Al Qaeda.

INESAP International Network of Scientists and Engineers against Proliferation, a nuclear disarmament advocacy organization.

INF Intermediate range nuclear forces. These missiles are limited in range to a few thousand miles. They were deployed in Western Europe to strike targets in the USSR, and vice versa. (The 1987 INF Treaty between the Soviet Union and the United States eliminated these weapons in the arsenals of these countries.)

IPPNW International Physicians for the Prevention of Nuclear War, a nuclear disarmament advocacy organization that won the 1985 Nobel Peace Prize.

LCNP Lawyers' Committee on Nuclear Policy, a nuclear disarmament advocacy organization.

LTBT Limited Test Ban Treaty of 1963, which banned nuclear test explosions underwater, in the atmosphere, and in space but not underground.

MAD Mutually assured destruction.

MNWC Model Nuclear Weapons Convention, a draft of a treaty to abolish nuclear weapons, created in the 1990s by a large group of scholars, scientists, lawyers, and nuclear policy experts.

NGO Nongovernmental organization.

NATO North Atlantic Treaty Organization, an alliance created in 1949 to oppose and deter a hypothetical Soviet invasion of Western Europe.

NIE National intelligence estimate, a report on a particular topic that is usually a product of multiple U.S. intelligence agencies and officials.

NORAD The joint American and Canadian North American Aerospace Defense Command.

NPR The Bush administration's December 2001 "Nuclear Posture Review"; also, National Public Radio. Other administrations have also issued Nuclear Posture Reviews.

NPT Nuclear Nonproliferation Treaty of 1968, in which non-nuclear weapon states agreed never to acquire nuclear weapons, and nuclear weapon states agreed to get rid of theirs.

NUTS A term of endearment for professional nuclear policy specialists, or "nuclear use theorists."

NWEC A hypothetical Nuclear Weapon Elimination Convention.

PAL Permissive action links, complex security mechanisms to prevent unauthorized detonation of nuclear weapons.

PGM Precision-guided munitions.

PRC People's Republic of China (often referred to as "mainland China" in the west or, at one time, as "Red China").

PSR Physicians for Social Responsibility, the American branch of IPPNW.

RNEP Robust nuclear earth penetrator, a new nuclear bomb proposed by the Bush administration that would burrow underground before detonating.

ROC Republic of China (on Taiwan).

ROK Republic of Korea (South Korea).

SAC American Strategic Air Command (now known as Strategic Command, or STRATCOM), headquartered in Omaha, long the nerve center of American nuclear command and control.

SALT Strategic Arms Limitation Treaties, the first generation of nuclear arms control agreements between the United States and the Soviet Union.

SLBM Submarine-launched ballistic missile. These missiles, deployed from submarines, can deliver nuclear warheads to virtually any point in the world.

SORT The 2002 Strategic Offensive Reductions Treaty between the U.S. and Russia.

START Strategic Arms Reduction Treaties, the second generation of nuclear arms control agreements between the United States and the Soviet Union.

UD Unacceptable damage, the alternative model of nuclear deterrence described in Chapter 8.

UNGA U.N. General Assembly, the body in the United Nations where every single member state, no matter how large or small, holds a single seat and wields a single vote.

UNMOVIC U.N. Monitoring, Verification, and Inspection Commission (formerly known as UNSCOM), established by the U.N. Security Council to monitor Iraqi compliance with the disarmament obligations imposed after the first Gulf War and to dismantle discovered unconventional Iraqi weapons.

USAAF U.S. Army Air Forces, the World War II predecessor of the U.S. Air Force.

VERTIC Verification Research, Training and Information Centre, a British organization that pioneers new techniques for verifying arms control agreements and other international treaties.

WMD Weapons of mass destruction, usually taken to mean nuclear, chemical, or biological weapons.

Organizations Working to Abolish Nuclear Weapons Forever

Each of these organizations is plugging away at one or another aspect of the nuclear disarmament agenda. Join, participate, and donate the money they so desperately need, and I have no doubt that, together, we can make nuclear weapons abolition happen.

- Abolition 2000 Global Network to Eliminate Nuclear Weapons, http://www.abolition2000.org
- Acronym Institute for Disarmament Diplomacy, http://www.acronym.org.uk
- Alliance for Nuclear Accountability, http://www.ananuclear.org
- American Friends Service Committee, http://www.afsc.org
- Arms Control Association, http://www.armscontrol.org
- Atomic Mirror, http://www.atomicmirror.org
- Beyond Nuclear, http://www.beyondnuclear.org
- British American Security Information Council, http://www.basicint.org
- Campaign for America's Future, http://www.ourfuture.org
- Campaign for Nuclear Disarmament, http://www.cnduk.org
- Campaign for a Nuclear Weapons Free World, http://www.nuclearweaponsfree.org
- Carnegie Endowment for International Peace, http://www.carnegieendowment.org
- Center for Arms Control and Non-Proliferation, http://www.armscontrolcenter.org
- Center for Defense Information, http://www.cdi.org
- Churches' Center for Theology and Public Policy, http://www.cctpp.org, http://www.mci-nwd.org

- Coalition for World Peace, http://www.coalitionforworld peace.org
- Council for a Livable World, http://www.clw.org
- Economists Allied for Arms Reductions, http://www .epsusa.org
- Faithful Security, http://www.faithfulsecurity.org
- Federation of American Scientists, http://www.fas.org
- Fellowship of Reconciliation, http://www.forusa.org
- Fourth Freedom Forum, http://www.fourthfreedom.org
- Friends Committee on National Legislation, http://www .fcnl.org
- Friends of the Earth Australia, http://www.foe.org.au
- Global Green USA, http://www.globalgreen.org
- Global Network against Nuclear Weapons and Power in Space, http://www.space4peace.org
- Global Security Institute, http://www.gsinstitute.org
- Global Zero, http://www.globalzero.org
- Henry L. Stimson Center, http://stimson.org
- Institute for Energy and Environmental Research, http://www .ieer.org
- Interfaith Committee for Nuclear Disarmament, http://www .zero-nukes.org
- Interfaith Communities United for Justice and Peace, http:// www.icujp.org
- International Association of Lawyers Allied against Nuclear Arms, http://www.ialana.net
- International Association of Peace Messenger Cities, http:// www.iapmc.org
- International Campaign to Abolish Nuclear Weapons, http:// www.icanw.org
- International Institute for Strategic Studies, http://www .iiss.org
- International Network of Engineers and Scientists against Pro-liferation, http://inesap.org
- International Panel on Fissile Materials, http://www.fissile materials.org
- International Peace Bureau, http://ipb.org

- International Philosophers for Peace, http://www.philosophers forpeace.org
- International Physicians for the Prevention of Nuclear War, http://www.ippnw.org
- Lawyers' Alliance for World Security, http://www.cdi.org/laws/index.html
- Lawyers' Committee on Nuclear Policy, http://www.lcnp.org
- Los Alamos Study Group, http://www.lasg.org
- Los Angeles Area Nuclear Disarmament Coalition, http://www.udcworld.org/laandc; http://www.globalassembly.net
- Mayors for Peace, http://www.mayorsforpeace.org
- Middle Powers Initiative, http://www.middlepowers.org
- Monterey Institute for International Studies/Center for Non-Proliferation Studies, http://www.cns.miis.edu
- Mountbatten Centre for International Studies, University of Southampton, http://www.mcis.soton.ac.uk
- Natural Resources Defense Council, http://www.nrdc.org
- Nautilus Institute, http://www.nautilus.org
- Nevada Desert Experience, http://www.nevadadesertexperience.org
- No Bases Network, http://www.nobasesnetwork.org
- Nonproliferation Policy Education Center, http://www.npec-web.org
- Nuclear Age Peace Foundation, http://www.wagingpeace.org, http://www.nuclearfiles.org
- Nuclear Darkness and Global Climate Change: The Deadly Consequences of Nuclear War, http://www.nucleardarkness.org
- Nuclear Free Future Campaign, http://www.nuclearfreefuture.org
- Nuclear Policy Research Institute, http://www.beyondnuclear.org
- Nuclear Threat Initiative, http://www.nti.org
- Oxford Research Group, http://www.Oxfordresearchgroup.org.uk
- Partnership for Global Security, http://www.ransac.org
- Pax Christi USA, http://www.Paxchristiusa.org

- Peace Action, http://www.peace-action.org
- Physicians for Social Responsibility, http://www.psr.org
- Physicians for Social Responsibility, Los Angeles, http://www.psrla.org
- Ploughshares Fund, http://www.ploughshares.org
- Progressive Democrats of America, http://www.pdamerica.org
- Pugwash, http://www.pugwash.org
- Reaching Critical Will, http://www.reachingcriticalwill.org
- Simons Centre for Disarmament and Nonproliferation Research, http://www.lige.ubc.ca
- Stanley Foundation, http://www.stanleyfoundation.org
- Stockholm International Peace Research Institute, http://www.sipri.se
- Tri-Valley Communities against a Radioactive Environment, http://trivalleycares.org
- Two Futures Project, http://www.twofuturesproject.org
- Union of Concerned Scientists, http://www.ucsusa.org
- United for Peace and Justice, http://www.unitedforpeace.org
- VERTIC, http://www.vertic.org
- War Resisters League, http://www.warresisters.org
- Western States Legal Foundation, http://www.wslfweb.org
- Women's Action for New Directions, http://www.wand.org
- Women's International League for Peace and Freedom, http://www.wilpf.org
- World Peace Council, http://www.wpc-in.org

INDEX

About the Author

Tad Daley, J. D., Ph.D., is the writing fellow with International Physicians for the Prevention of Nuclear War, the 1985 Nobel peace laureate. He has held many professional positions in the progressive peace advocacy arena. He has served as a speechwriter and policy advisor to Congressman Dennis Kucinich, Congresswoman Diane Watson, and the late U.S. Senator Alan Cranston. He also ran for U.S. Congress himself to represent mid-city Los Angeles. The *LA Weekly* wrote, "Tad Daley . . . boasts the most impressive credentials and much the most thoughtful platform of all the 16 candidates in the race . . . . (His vision) is as sensible as it is unconventional." Tad spent several years at the RAND Corporation in Santa Monica, California, where many of the nuclear theories of the cold war era were originally forged. He has written articles on abolishing nuclear weapons, reinventing the United Nations, ending genocide, and the progressive U.S. foreign policy agenda for the *Baltimore Sun*, the *Bulletin of the Atomic Scientists*, the *Christian Science Monitor*, the *Foreign Service Journal*, the *Forward*, the *Futurist*, the *Humanist*, the *International Herald Tribune*, the *LA City Beat*, the *LA Jewish Journal*, the *Los Angeles Times*, the *Miami Herald*, the *Philadelphia Inquirer*, *Sojourners*, the *Tidings*, *Tikkun*, the *United Nations Chronicle*, *USA TODAY*, and frequently in the blogosphere at AlterNet.org, CommonDreams.org., HuffingtonPost.com, TruthDig.com, and TruthOut.org. He lives in Washington, D.C. with his wife, public radio journalist and playwright Kitty Felde.

The words of the late Joseph Rotblat, the 1995 Nobel peace laureate, best capture Tad's vision for the world: "My short-term ambition is to abolish nuclear weapons. My long-term ambition is to abolish war itself."